The Right Touch: Understanding and Using the Language of Physical Contact

D1598226

SCA Applied Communication Publication Program

Gary L. Kreps, Editor
Northern Illinois University

The SCA Program in Applied Communication supports the Speech Communication Association mission of promoting the study, criticism, research, teaching, and application of artistic, humanistic, and scientific principles of communication. Specifically, the goal of this publication program is to develop an innovative, theoretically informed, and socially relevant body of scholarly works that examine a wide range of applied communication topics. Each publication clearly demonstrates the value of human communication in addressing serious social issues and challenges.

Editorial Board

Mara Adelman
Northwestern University

Charles Bantz
Arizona State University

Eileen Berlin Ray
Cleveland State University

Ellen Bonaguro
Northern Illinois University

Mary Helen Brown
Auburn University

Ken Cissna
University of South Florida

Larry Frey
Loyola University of Chicago

Paul Friedman
University of Kansas

Susan Glaser
University of Oregon

Dan O'Hair
Texas Tech University

Gerald M. Phillips
Penn State University

Linda Putnam
Purdue University

Barbara Sharf
University of Illinois, Chicago

Stella Ting-Toomey
Calif. St. University-Fullerton

Lynne Webb
Memphis State University

All SCA Publication Program materials are reviewed within the spirit of academic freedom, promoting the free exchange of ideas. The contents of this publication are the responsibility of its authors and do not necessarily reflect the official policies or positions of the Speech Communication Association, its members, its officers, or its staff.

The Right Touch: Understanding and Using the Language of Physical Contact

Stanley E. Jones
University of Colorado

Hampton Press, Inc.
Cresskill, New Jersey

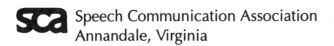

Speech Communication Association
Annandale, Virginia

Copyright © 1994 by Hampton Press, Inc.

All rights reserved. No part of this publication may be reproduced, stored in a retrieval system, or transmitted in any form or by any means, electronic, mechanical, photocopying, microfilming, recording, or otherwise, without permission of the publisher.

Printed in the United States of America

Library of Congress Cataloging-in-Publication Data

Jones, Stanley E., 1935-
    The right touch : understanding and using the language of physical contact / Stanley E. Jones.
        p. cm. -- (The Speech Communication Association/Hampton Press applied communication program)
    Includes bibliographical references and indexes.
    ISBN 1-881303-41-1. (cloth) -- ISBN 1-881303-42-X (pbk.)
    1. Touch. 2. Nonverbal communication (Psychology) 3. Touch-
-Social aspects--United States. 4. Nonverbal communication
(Psychology)--United States. I. Title. II. Series.
BF275.J66 1993
153.6'9--dc20   93-5499
                                                                                           CIP

Hampton Press, Inc.
23 Broadway
Cresskill, NJ 07626

This book is dedicated

to Susan, who supported me all along the way;
to Christopher and Trevor, who inspired my interest in touch
and gave me ample opportunity to practice what I preach;
and to the memory of Albert Scheflen, teacher and friend.

Acknowledgments

I have many people to thank for their help and encouragement in my work on this book. I am especially indebted to Albert Scheflen for his mentoring early in my career; his "contextual analysis" approach provides the conceptual framework for much of my research on touch and for *The Right Touch*. The title of the book itself was given to me by my once-upon-a-time student, Eva Margolis, now a successful author and sex therapist, who also critiqued Chapter 5 on "Touch and Sexuality." Communication consultant Susan Baile gave me considerable help on the writing throughout the book. Gary Kreps, editor of SCA series of which this volume is a part, read the entire manuscript and made many useful suggestions. From sociologist George Rivera, with whom I co-taught a course in Interracial Communication for a number of years at Colorado University, I gained insights into ethnic relations which I hope are accurately reflected in Chapter 12. Brenda Allen, my colleague in Communication at C.U., also gave me useful ideas for that chapter. Numerous other colleagues at C.U., including Professors Sally Planalp, George Cheney, and Phil Tompkins and Administrative Assistant Jan Cresap, provided encouragement in various forms such as reviewing my ideas for the cover design. I am also indebted to my interviewees from many fields who are too numerous to name here—the doctors, nurses, therapists, teachers, business people, and other professionals who freely shared their experiences with me. Finally, I would like to thank "the group," my friends who urged me along by repeatedly asking "Is your book out, Stan?" and "When are we going to have a book-signing party?"

Contents

Introduction: Why the Right Touch Matters

O N NOVEMBER 20, 1985, negotiations between Ronald Reagan and Soviet Premier Mikhail Gorbachev at Geneva seemed to be going nowhere. According to an account reported by *Washington Post* correspondents, the right touch got them back on the track:

> Secretary of State George Shultz turned to Georgi Korniekno, the Soviet first deputy foreign minister, and accused him of trying to stall negotiations on several issues.
>
> "You, Mr. Minister, are responsible for this," Shultz declared. Then, turning to Gorbachev, Shultz added forcefully: "This man is not doing what you want him to do. He is not getting done what you want done."
>
> The outburst prompted an appeal from Reagan to Gorbachev. "To hell with what they're doing," the President said. "You and I will say, 'We will work together to make it come about.'" Reagan and Gorbachev then shook hands. White House officials said Friday the handshake . . . marked a turning point in the summit and set in motion an agreement early the next morning on a joint statement on arms control and other issues. ("Handshake," 1985, p. 1-A)

1

What is "the right touch"? This question can be answered on several levels. At the most basic level, the right touch is a matter of appropriateness. Because touch is such a powerful form of communication, inappropriate touch behavior can easily jeopardize the rapport and trust that are essential for healthy, satisfying relationships.

At another level, the right touch suggests the special sensitivities to the moment that distinguish the exceptional communicator from the merely competent one. When we hear that someone has "just the right touch," we usually imagine a person who brings a certain finesse to behavior that is otherwise simply adequate. Although the phrase "just the right touch" may often refer to behaviors other than touching, it is frequently a person's facility with tactile communication that earns him or her this reputation.

Finally, the right touch can refer to a situation such as the one at the Geneva summit described above in which a touch marks a dramatic shift in a relationship. In these cases, the touch results in more than simple appreciation for the toucher's obvious communication skill; it also causes a change in our perceptions of ourselves, the other person, or the relationship between us. This was the case with the handshake between Reagan and Gorbachev. What made this simple touch so powerful was that it happened at an unusual point, not at the beginning or end of the meeting, when it might have been only a formal gesture, but at a time when conflict might otherwise have blocked further negotiations. In this context, the handshake, a traditional sign of trust, took on special significance.

Examples of the right touch are plentiful if you look for them. Do you remember the televised debates between Walter Mondale and Ronald Reagan? Mondale discovered that he had a formidable opponent in "the great communicator" when it came to conveying a personable image in general and using touch in particular. Many people were surprised at how well Mondale argued in the first televised debate with Reagan, who often seemed at a loss for words. Yet Reagan pulled off one especially adroit move. At the end of the debate, Reagan walked over to a surprised Mondale and offered his hand, a gesture which said, in effect, "Nice going—we're in this together," thus emphasizing Reagan's statesman-like attitude. As one debate coach told me, "Mondale technically won the debate, but Reagan won the image battle."

As another example, take the situation a nurse described to me about her first meeting with a suicidal female patient who had recently tried to slash her wrists. The nurse took one look at the sad expression on the woman's face and immediately embraced her. No one had come near the woman since her suicide attempt, and the uncalculated and spontaneous touch was exactly what was needed. It said not only "I care," but also, "You are touchable, someone I want to reach out to." It provided the first step in establishing a relationship in which the nurse could guide the woman back to physical and psychological health.

Opportunities for the right touch need not be as dramatic as those cited above, however. In fact, there are countless daily moments for people in all professions and walks of life to use the right touch. For instance, an attorney may want to communicate a personal as well as professional commitment to a client, a teacher may want to gently redirect a student's attention, a manager may want to recognize an employee for a job well done, or a parent may want to reassure a crying child. The question is, if so many opportunities for the right touch exist, why do we hold back? Professional public speaker Greg Risberg, who gives talks to groups around the country about the power of touch, found in surveys of his audience members that nearly 90% reported resisting their inclination to touch others. The answer, I believe, is that many of us worry that our touches will be rejected or misunderstood, and there is good reason to be worried. Just as there can be the right touch for a given situation, there is also the possibility of "the wrong touch."

The purpose of this book is to describe how people communicate effectively with touch and what has gone wrong when their touches are rejected. The guidelines I suggest are based mainly on the research I have been conducting over the past decade. My primary method of study has been to train hundreds of persons to record their touches immediately after they occur. By analyzing literally thousands of these events, I believe I have been able to crack "the touch code," a language which is "secret" in the sense that people are usually unaware of how they communicate with touch, even when they do it successfully.

Some of the specific findings that I discuss in the chapters that follow are:

- The 18 different meanings that can be conveyed by touch in this culture, and how each is communicated in its own distinctive way;
- The 7 American "taboos" of touch, the most commonly violated principles of tactile communiation;
- The 10 rules of touch in the workplace;
- The various differences between men and women in the ways they use touch; and
- The numerous ways people use touch to influence others, including tactile "power plays."

These and other topics are used to give practical advice about touching and comprise the bulk of the book. They are covered primarily in Section II, "The Many Meanings of Touch (and How to Communicate Them);" Section III, "Touch Gone Astray;" and Section IV, "Touch in the

Workplace." I also draw on the knowledge of others who have made a close examination of touch. If you are not yet convinced that touch is as powerful as I claim, or you would like to review the evidence in order to persuade others who are not convinced, you may want to begin with Section I, "Touch: Our Most Basic Form of Communication." In this section, I summarize the findings of experts in child development, animal behavior, medical research, psychology, and other fields—discoveries that show why touch is so fundamental to being human. In Section V, the final portion of the book on "Special Applications," I discuss the insights of successful practitioners and research scholars about touch in cross-cultural situations and the helping professions. In this section, I also show how you can diagnose and change your own touching patterns.

My objective throughout this book is to encourage you to act on your inclinations to touch so that you can use this extremely powerful form of communication with greater confidence and enjoyment.

Section I
Touch:
Our Most
Basic Form of
Communication

1

Skin Hunger and the Power of Touch

M Y SECOND child, Trevor, had a very traumatic birth. Because of a placental abruption during labor, he was severely asphyxiated. He arrived blue, only minutes away from death. I was attending the birth and could only stand by helplessly while I watched the doctors work on him. They were soon able to establish breathing, but 24 hours later Trevor began to have seizures, a result of the oxygen deprivation he had experienced in birth. He was put on medications which dulled his responses at the same time that they prevented the life-threatening episodes.

Five days later the period of danger was over, and he was taken off the medicine. He gradually began to move and to open his eyes for the first time since he was born, but he did not seem to look at anything, and his eyes rolled back in his head. This condition worried me and my wife and also concerned the nurse in his intensive care unit at Children's Hospital in Denver. We were fearful that he had experienced brain damage during the seizures and would not be able to respond normally.

I had just read Tiffany Field's research showing the dramatic effects of massage on premature infants (Field et al., 1986; see also Field, 1990). Newborns who received this treatment were more responsive, gained weight faster, and were discharged from the hospital sooner than those who were not massaged. While Trevor was not technically "premature," since he was born only three weeks early, he nevertheless shared with these babies the experience of a distressed beginning.

I began to massage Trevor gently, following the instructions of the nurse. Almost immediately, he began to appear less drowsy, and at the end of a 15-minute period of massage, the eye-rolling behavior stopped, and he began to look around him. Our anxiety was relieved considerably. In addition, I was surprised to discover that I suddenly felt much closer to my newborn son. I had thought a lot about his arrival previously, but until this moment, it had not been real for me that he was a permanent part of my life.

Later that day, my wife and I received the news that Trevor's EEG test, taken earlier, was within normal ranges. Undoubtedly, he was already on the road to recovery. This act of touch and the gentle massages which the nurses and I administered at regular intervals for the next few days did not cure him, but they did apparently speed up the process of bringing him out of the stupor caused by the medicine and in helping to establish normal functioning. We were soon able to take him home.

Not long after this event, I found myself thinking repeatedly about a related experience. My mother, now deceased, was a victim of Alzheimer's disease and was cared for in a nursing home in the city where I live. She had lost the ability to speak and didn't seem to know who I was when I would first see her. On each visit, I began by gently stroking her hair, face, shoulders, arms, and hands. In time, on each occasion, she raised her eyebrows and smiled at me in recognition.

At about the same time, I read a story in an article about police chaplains which struck a similar chord in me. A distraught mother reached out to a chaplain at the scene of her son's suicide and said, "You look just like my son. Can I hold you and say good-bye to my son?" They stood in the front yard and hugged (Pierce, 1986, p. 1B).

Despite the differences in these incidents, they stayed in my mind. They seemed to have something in common which was more important than the simple fact that touch was involved, although at first I couldn't "put my finger on it." Then, it struck me. In each case, touch was a more powerful way of relating than any other behavior could have been. Since talk was omitted because it would have been meaningless, the link between touch and our basic need to feel attached to and emotionally involved with others is more obvious than usual in these instances. The potential of touch as a significant way of affecting others is also present in most everyday circumstances, but it is often overlooked.

WHY TOUCH IS POWERFUL

Touch is our most fundamental form of communication. Evidence for this can be seen in the very language we use everyday. We are constantly describing our experiences in terms of touch, although so habitually that we don't think about it. In particular, it is almost impossible to talk about establishing or maintaining communication with someone without saying something like "I'll contact you" or "Let's stay in touch." In addition, when an event has a strong emotional impact on us, we describe it tactilely. We may be "touched" by what someone said or did. Something interesting "tickles my fancy," but when I'm really involved, it's a "gripping experience." It means something to get "strokes" or "a pat on the back," and when we need help, we seek "support."

Our language also suggests that touch is our most trusted way of knowing and thus is associated with personal competence. We "grasp" an idea or "come to grips" with a problem. We "touch off" a campaign and later add in the "finishing touches." A person who "handles" things well has the "Midas touch" or, of course, "the right touch." People who no longer understand a situation must get "back in touch," and those who have lost emotional control must "get a grip on themselves."

This last point, that touch is associated in our minds with a sense of reality, is exemplified by a scene from the movie *Oh God, You Devil*. Toward the end of the film, "God" (played by George Burns) has saved the hero, a rock musician named Bobby Shelton, from a contract with the "devil." After a long conversation, Shelton is almost convinced that this really is God, but as he is about to leave, he stops and reaches out hesitantly. God says, "Go ahead, touch me. . . , Now, go back to your family." In other words, seeing is not believing, touching is.

Most touch expressions have positive connotations, but our language also reflects the fact that touch can be misused. A person who is anxiety-prone or highly dependent on someone is described as "clutching" or "a clinging vine." Overly aggressive people are "pushy" or "heavy-handed." Some individuals attempt to "poke around" in other's private affairs, and others "rub people the wrong way."

Thus, our spontaneous speech reflects what we know intuitively. For several decades, scientists have been documenting a number of reasons why this is true.

Touch Gets Attention

Every tactile contact sends a split-second message to the brain. In general, we have to be selective in screening the sensory data, which compete for our attention, or else we would be overwhelmed with information. When we are driving on a city street, for example, our visual sense is especially important, but we focus only on the input that seems especially relevant. If we look in the rear-view mirror and spot a structure on the roof of a vehicle which looks like the emergency lights of a police car, we may automatically ease up on the accelerator and check the speedometer, although a second visual screening may reveal that it is only a car with a ski rack.

It's much the same with touch, except that we are less selective than we are with our other senses. Even though a person may ignore how the seat feels beneath him for a while, any sudden change in tactile sensations will bring an immediate reaction, followed by an assessment of its source. This is especially true of a touch from another person. Research shows that when we are touched unexpectedly, or even when another person comes surprisingly close so that touching can easily occur, our first reaction is arousal— our heart rate goes up. Immediately after this, our thoughts take over—we quickly decide whether we feel positively or negatively about the touch (Patterson, 1976). It is almost impossible not to respond to a touch.

Scientists have speculated about why we have such an immediate response to variations in tactile stimulation. Cofer and Appley (1964, p. 186) have theorized that the ability to detect whether contact is pleasurable or painful had a survival value for our prehistoric ancestors. Those humans who were able to respond quickly to the heat of a fire or the violence of an attack were more likely than others to live to have offspring and to pass on their natural tendencies to succeeding generations.

So initially, the touch message almost always gets through. From then on, it may have a number of important effects which depend on the nature of the contact, the situation, and the person touched.

Touch Stimulates Emotions

The skin is our largest sense organ and the one with the most nerve-ending receptors (Frank, 1957). This makes the skin our major source of sensory stimulation. While it acts as as antenna for danger, the skin is also a primary means of experiencing pleasure. This includes not just sexual arousal, but the joy of a firm embrace and the contentment of being caressed or massaged.

Gentle Touch Can Be Therapeutic

The "laying on of hands" as a means of curing illness has been known for centuries. Many people are familiar with the idea of "faith healing" through stories in the New Testament, although the tradition is actually more ancient. Some people believe that almost anything can be cured with touch, although traditionally it is commonly assumed that only certain healers have the "gift." While there are many stories about the miraculous effects of touching, there is little solid scientific evidence to support the claim. Nevertheless, there is scientific evidence to support the idea that touch can contribute to the healing process in subtle ways.

Even casual forms of touching can have therapeutic effects. In *The*

Broken Heart, physician James Lynch (1977, pp. 125-139) reports evidence that the simple act of a nurse taking the pulse of hospitalized patients recovering from a heart attacks lowered their heart rate, an important exception to the principle that touch usually produces initial arousal. The heart rate of these patients also stabilized for a period of time after the nurse had left the room. Even more remarkable is a study conducted a number of years ago which found that persons who had suffered a cardiac arrest were less likely to have a second attack if they had pets in their homes (interview with A. Katcher, reported in Cohen, 1987, pp. 167-168). Apparently, the opportunity for otherwise unavailable physical contact afforded by stroking an animal has a calming effect. On the basis of this and other similar research, pets have been introduced in such diverse settings as nursing homes and prisons with positive effects (Toufexis, 1987).

A number of explanations have been offered as to why touch has a curative influence. One is simply that touch, and especially prolonged touching, provides undivided attention to a person and raises his or her spirits. Another closely related explanation, which applies to especially "authorized" forms of touch such as faith healing, refers to the "placebo" effect—that is, people are more likely to be cured if they believe in it. Another notion, that electrical impulses are transferred from one person's body to another under certain circumstances, applies especially to methods like the "therapeutic touch" developed by nurse Dolores Krieger (1979), since her approach does not involve actual contact, but rather the placing of hands just over the patient's body. In one study, Krieger (1973) was able to provide evidence that therapeutic touch can have a direct effect on the physiology of the body by increasing the production of white corpuscles, blood cells that contribute to healing.

It has also been suggested that active stroking, as in the "pet therapy" research mentioned earlier, may act directly on the brain by releasing endorphins, the "pleasure chemical" (interview with A. Katcher, cited in Toufexis, 1987). Pleasurable responses counteract pain and thus speed medical recovery. The implication is that touch not only facilitates the healing process, but also that it can work as a preventive measure by reducing stress and contributing to our sense of well-being in everyday life.

Touch Appeals to Basic Physiological and Psychological Needs

There is one other especially important reason why touch is significant. It is our first, most comforting, experience of the world. In reviewing the discoveries of physiologists who have studied the developmental processes in the human nervous system, psychologist Lawrence Frank (1957) points out that touch is the very first sense to emerge in the growing human fetus. It is not surprising that we speak of communication as "contact" because it is through tactile responses that the infant first comes to know the mother and vice versa. Floating in the warmth of the womb, the yet-to-be born child's every need is met. The birth itself is a terrible shock, a painful expulsion from the Garden of Eden; little wonder that the newborn infant has a powerful and immediate need to be held and nursed.

Over four decades ago, child development expert Rene Spitz (1946) became aware of a disturbing phenomenon. He reviewed statistical records that showed orphans and abandoned children are much more likely to die in the first years of life than other children. In addition, he found that even the survivors of such experiences were most likely to suffer from psychological and physical problems than children brought up in family settings. He called this condition "marasmus," from a Greek word which means "a withering away." In his further studies, he discovered that touch was a critical factor. For example, in one European village where women came regularly to a foundling home to hold and caress infants and young children, Spitz observed that the withering away did not occur.

About a decade after Spitz made his observations, psychologist Harry Harlow (1958) began a series of scientific experiments that documented a similar phenomenon among monkeys. Harlow isolated newborn monkeys from their mothers and found that they exhibited a variety of neurotic behaviors. The instinctual drives in these animals for contact were clear: Given a choice between food and clinging to a wire or terrycloth figure remotely resembling their mothers, hungry monkeys would pick the fake "surrogate" mother.

Thus, we know that young primates, and other mammals as well, must have touch. By implication, human infants, who are much less fully developed at birth than the animals Harlow studied, are especially vulnerable to this need.

While scientists continue to study this connection between touch and infant health and survival through animal studies, an especially intriguing (and more humane) line of research in recent years concerns the most vulnerable of newborn infants—those born prematurely and under conditions of traumatic birth. One of the first and most remarkable discoveries was that premature infants did better in the hospital if they were simply placed on a sheepskin rug, thus replacing, to some degree, the human touch which could not be provided within the incubator. Earlier, I mentioned the work of Tiffany Field who has shown positive effects of 15-minute massages applied 3 times a day with premature infants. Other investigators have demonstrated similar results with infant waterbeds, which also provide tactile stimulation (see Korner, 1990).

The effects of touch on institutionalized infants (who would ordinarily not get the touch they need) and premature babies (who left the mother's womb before they were ready) are especially dramatic. However, this should not obscure the fact that all newborns need touch for normal development. One reason is that these infants must have the stimulation that only touch can provide. Ashley Montagu (1971) has pointed out that it is widely believed that animals like cats and dogs lick their newborns simply in order to clean them, whereas, in fact, this act of contact is necessary to help their offspring develop certain normal functions like digestion. Among humans, tactile stimulation is necessary for the development of such vital reflexes as the sucking response needed for nursing. In addition, behaviors needed for further development in human infants require touch; as research by White and Castle (1964) demonstrates, handling enhances the visual alertness of babies.

A second reason why children must have touch in early infancy is that it provides them with the security necessary for normal psychological development. Studies by psychiatrist and medical researcher Martin Reite (1984) have shown that young monkeys who are separated from their mothers at first become agitated, searching frantically for the parent and making sounds of distress. In a day or two, they exhibit a slouched posture and sad face, and they stop play activity altogether. This is very much like the behavior of a human infant who cries to be picked up. The cries may become more and more frantic for a while, but if no one comes, eventually the child stops making sounds and sinks into a listless, depressed state.

There was a time when parents were urged by some "experts" to allow this to happen so as not to "spoil" the child. Fortunately, modern child authorities generally advise the opposite, since repeated experiences of neglect such as this are profoundly damaging to the infant's sense of well-being and ultimately his or her self-concept. The happy, secure infant is one whose needs for touch are met.

What happens after the first few months of life? Not surprisingly, touch continues to play a significant part in the child's development. Gradually, however, the role of touch shifts somewhat from providing only stimulation and security to helping the child to explore his or her environment. That is, touch becomes essential to learning. Child development experts L. Alan Stroufe and Everett Waters (1977) explain that, at first, the infant clings to the mother or other caretakers for simple protection. However, as the child begins to examine new objects and eventually strangers, in time crawling away to do this, he or she rushes back to the caretaker repeatedly when frightened, and after being reassured, sets out again. Touch provides the security needed for exploration.

The basis of this process is a remarkable phenomenon called "attachment," which involves the child and the mother (or other principle caretaker) growing closer and closer emotionally. This begins with touch and later includes other communication acts such as eye contact and exchanges of smiles. Contrary to some popularized notions, in which the term "bonding" is often used as a synonym for "attachment," it is not essential, but only desirable, that the mother be able to hold the infant immediately after the birth for attachment to occur. While it is true that there are some accounts of mothers rejecting a baby when they have been separated for some time after the birth because of prematurity or some other problem (Klaus & Kennell, 1976, pp. 1-15), this is rare, especially if the parents are prepared emotionally and intellectually for this eventuality.

Even in cases in which the parents are able to hold the newborn immediately, the process occurs gradually. It is the mother who first becomes attached to the infant. Even if she has had only one hour with her baby, research shows that she can identify her own child from others by simply touching the back of the baby's hand when her eyes and nose are covered, and the baby is asleep. That is, she "knows" her child from tactile cues alone, not from the baby's smell, cry, or any other cues (Kaitz, Lapidot, Bonner, & Eidelman, 1992). The mother's attachment (and potentially, that of the father as well) continues to grow with contact and interaction, but the baby becomes attached to the mother (crying when she leaves) much later, during the second half of the first year of life (Ainsworth, 1972). Thereafter, the baby may become attached to the father and other members of the family. Infant attachment, achieved initially through touch and later thorough touch in combination with other emotionally connecting interactions, grows with time and is the earliest form of love experienced by humans.

The role of touching in satisfying our deepest psychological needs is rooted firmly in these fundamental experiences. It follows that we will still need touch as adults. This can be seen in responses to interviews conducted with women by psychiatrist Marc Hollender (1970). For example, one said, "I would sooner have him (her husband) hold me every day . . . than a Cadillac convertible" (p. 446). Some said they especially needed to be held when they were depressed or anxious; others said it gave them a feeling of being needed. Some women described it simply as a physical need. As another woman put it, "It's kind of an ache" (pp. 447-448). Most indicated at least a moderate desire to be held, and only a few were indifferent. In a follow-up study, Hollender (1976) also found that men were nearly as high as women in their ratings of the desire to hold or be held.

A married couple shared this experience with me: Shortly after they had met, the man convinced the woman, by a series of lengthy long-distance phone calls, to join him in another part of the country. The move required her to break off a romantic relationship with another man, a person she described as rather cold who did not touch much, and to find a new job. The series of events was very unsettling for the woman, and one afternoon when the couple was together, she talked about the emotional strain she was experiencing and began to cry hysterically. The man took her in his arms and rocked her on his lap, much as one would a child. After a time, her feelings of panic subsided. On the basis of Hollander's research, as well as various experiences reported to me by others, I conclude that this is not a rare incident. The need for touch and holding has profound significance throughout life.

WHY ADULTS DON'T GET THE TOUCHES THEY NEED

Our "skin hunger," as Ashley Montagu (1971) called it, does not go away, but it does become less crucial to our survival and, therefore, may be neglected as we grow into adulthood. At the same time, touch becomes more difficult to obtain. It has often been pointed out that Americans are cautious tactilely, a fact documented some years ago in a study by the psychologist Sidney Jourard (1966, pp. 221-222). He went to cities in various countries and observed how often couples in cafés touched on the average per hour. The score: San Juan, Puerto Rico, 180; Paris, 110; Gainesville, FL, 2; London, 0.

It has also been frequently suggested that Americans are "touch deprived." Kathleen Mosby (1978) investigated this issue by asking people to tell how often they thought various parts of their body came into contact with their fathers, mothers, and best same-sex and best opposite-sex friend. She also asked them to describe their "ideal" about touching with these persons—how much touch they would like. The results showed they wanted more intimate and more frequent contacts than they believed they actually had. In a study which I conducted (Jones, 1991), I asked people to tell what body parts would come into contact with those same four people on a typical day. I then compared these expected touches with actual touching based on recordings the participants made immediately after each touch with these persons. Consistently, people expected to experience more intimate touching (more body parts involved) than had actually happened. This suggests that not only do most people want more touching than they expect to get, but also that the touches they expect to get may be based on wishful thinking.

A number of explanations have been offered as to why people in this culture are reluctant to touch. The two most popular notions, as presented by James Hardison (1980) in his book *Let's Touch*, are that (a) Americans believe touching is inherently sexual in nature; and (b) they are concerned that their touches will be perceived by others as attempts to control. Each of these explanations can be related to certain aspects of the American culture.

In a society in which freedom of choice is emphasized, including choice about sexual relations, and in which sexual promiscuity is common, it follows that touches may be used as a way of testing the other person's availability. Thus, people may resist touching the opposite sex for fear it will be seen as an overture or "come-on." What has sometimes been called "homophobia" makes it even more obvious why people might be reluctant to touch others of the same sex. While fears about touching may be greater when we are alone with someone we do not regard as a potential sexual intimate, married couples and other romantic pairs may also be anxious that their touching will be read as a sexual advance when they are not interested.

Concerns about control issues may be related to the fact that Americans value individualism, the right of each person to decide for him- or herself. Thus, touch may be perceived as a threat to a person's independence. This argument has been used to explain why children may resist kissing and other forms of intimate touching associated with their "baby" years and why some adolescents stop touching their parents altogether. Similarly, some people may be suspicious of business or professional associates who touch a lot on the assumption that these persons have "something up their sleeve."

Both of these explanations are plausible in some ways, but I don't find either of them very convincing. My research suggests that very few touches are sexual in nature. Also, my findings show that while touches are occasionally used to influence others, this is generally acceptable. Usually, it simply makes a request more personal. We need not be concerned that our touches will be seen as reflecting a desire to control unless touching is used aggressively or in order to manipulate—that is, to get someone to do something they don't want to do. Even with adolescents, a touch from a parent will not necessarily be seen as threatening their independence, although rejection may occur if the teenager perceives that he or she is being treated as a child.

Anthropologist Edward Hall's (1981) concept of "high-context" and "low-context" cultures provides a more satisfying explanation for American touch reluctance. In high-context cultures, people tend to interpret the actions of others in terms of total situation or context—what happened just before the act, what is known about the other person, the social occasion, and so forth. Members of high-context cultures rely strongly on nonverbal messages and their intuitive readings of others; they do not require that meanings be "spelled out" with words. On the other hand, Americans and members of other low-context cultures tend to be unsure and uneasy about their abilities to communicate effectively with subtle, contextual nuances of meaning. They feel more comfortable when messages are verbalized specifically. This orientation has distinct advantages in certain situations in which planning, organization, and intellectual exchange are especially important. Yet, for everyday interpersonal relations, there is no way to escape the need to use contextual cues in communication, even in a low-context culture.

Touch is a perfect example of a form of communication which requires contextual interpretation. Take, for example, the most common touch of all, a simple contact of a person's hand resting briefly on another's shoulder. It can convey "I want to comfort you," "Thanks for what you did," "I like you," "I was only kidding," "I want you to do something for me," or several other messages. The exact meaning, and often there is a rather precise meaning, has to do with the situation, the timing and manner in which the touch is delivered, what is said, and/or other nonverbal messages which accompany the touch.

I believe the difficulty touch presents to Americans is that it requires a certain degree of mastery of a complex code of a type which many people in this culture do not feel confident in using. It is true that people are sometimes worried that their touches will be seen as sexual or controlling, but the more basic reason for these concerns is an underlying uncertainty about how to touch in such a way that intentions are conveyed accurately and appropriately. In the early years of life, touch is largely a response to or an expression of biological needs. As we grow older, however, in order to satisfy our impulses for tactile experiences, we must learn the language of touch.

Research has shown that members of "high-touch" families are more likely to be "touchers" as adults (Gladney & Barker, 1979). However, we can learn to touch later in life. I was brought up in the Midwest in a family in which touching was not the norm. Later, I moved to New York City and taught at a college where 80% of the students were Jewish (a high-touch subculture). I participated in "sensitivity training" groups (where touch is encouraged) and thus became more of a toucher. Fascinated with the changes in myself, I began to study touch and became even more tactilely oriented. I have found that understanding touch makes me value and practice it more.

WHY TOUCH IS A UNIQUE FORM OF COMMUNICATION

In part, the rarity of touch is a source of its power. If we all touched constantly, it would have less effect. However, most people could touch much more than they do without it losing its impact. The power of touch as a means of communication comes primarily from the fact that it has certain unique characteristics.

Touch is Our Most Intimate Way of Communicating

The association between touch and intimate relationships is so strong that it has been capitalized on in the familiar AT&T commercial asking us to "Reach out and touch someone," a phrase that suggests making a long-distance telephone call to a loved one is almost like the ultimate intimacy of touching. We touch those most with whom we are most involved. However, studies have shown that it also works the other way—we become more involved when we touch.

For example, John Bardeen (1971) conducted an experiment in which people got to know others in three different ways. In one situation, both persons looked at each other without talking; in another, they were blindfolded, but could talk with one another; in a third, they were blindfolded, but were instructed to communicate only by touching. Actually, it was the same person in each case, but the participants didn't know this, and it seemed to them as though there were three very different people. The communication was described by the participants as cold and unsatisfying when they could only see or talk to the other person, but as warm, serious, mature, and trustful in the touching situation.

In another investigation, Cary Cooper and David Bowles (1973) studied the effects of participating in touching exercises on members of "encounter groups" (a type of therapy group in which people learn about expressing emotions and interpersonal communication). People who experienced the touching activities with one another at the beginning of the groups were more open in talking about themselves and revealing their feelings later in the sessions than those who had not had the introductory touch exercises.

Although the circumstances in these experiments are unusual, the results match up in basic ways with everyday experiences. For example, physicians have reported the discovery that touching their patients creates more trust and better communication about physical ailments (Lewis, 1982). Similarly, most people have had the experience of feeling freer about talking with someone who has touched them in a warm and appropriate way. As we grow closer to another person emotionally, just sitting and holding them can be the most intimate communication of all—it requires no talk.

A Touch is an Undeniable Message

Another unique characteristic of touch is that it is almost impossible to touch someone and claim we didn't "mean" anything by it. For example, a person can engage in flirtatious looks and gestures, and even make joking comments about wanting sexual involvement with the other person, and then, if challenged, deny that any such meaning was intended. It is much more difficult to deny the implications of a sexually suggestive touch.

Perhaps the only exceptions to the principle that touches are undeniable messages are cases in which the contact is part of performing a task or when we brush against someone "accidentally." Even in those situations, however, the person who receives the touch may feel that the toucher is trying to "say" something to him or her.

Touch Almost Always Gets Feedback

"Feedback" is a term that refers to a response which tells a communicator how his or her message was received. Whenever we touch, we immediately find out whether the touch was accepted or rejected. If the other person smiles and looks at us, returns the touch, moves toward us, cuddles into our embrace, or reacts in some other positive way, it's an acceptance. On the other hand, if the other person looks at our hand, grimaces, scowls, or in extreme cases, says, "What are you doing?"—it's a rejection. Even if the person simply "freezes up" physically or does not respond to touch in an expected way, it's still a rejection.

If we ask someone a question or make a request and get an ambiguous verbal response, we may not be sure how they have reacted. Not so when we receive a reaction to our touch. This is the unique feature that makes touch especially risky. At the same time, it is also what makes touch so appealing and personal; the person who initiates touch puts him- or herself in a vulnerable position.

Touch Communicates Many Meanings with a Few Types of Contact

This is the feature of touch which is most difficult to "grasp," both intellectually and in practice. It is a common belief, even among persons who do research on touch, that "ambiguity of meaning is an inherent element in tactile communication" (Johnson & Edwards, 1991, p. 43). Not so, since the meaning of a touch does not come from the type of touch alone, but from a subtle combination of touch and the surrounding context (accompanying behaviors and the situation in which the touch occurs). It is true that we can hold, hug, kiss, caress, massage, pat, pinch, punch, push, pull, squeeze, tap, tickle, shake hands, and simply "spot touch" (make contact without exerting pressure or moving skin on skin). However, these variations do not have specific meanings.

Rather, *different touches can have the same meaning, depending on the context.* For example, when a male and a female who are close but not sexually intimate see one another after a period of absence, they are likely to kiss one another briefly (on the cheek or the mouth) or hug (usually from the front rather than the side). These two kinds of touches are very different in the way they are done, but they have essentially the same meaning: "I missed you, our relationship is close." (Only rarely would both behaviors be done together, especially if the embrace and kiss were prolonged, since this would imply a romantic relationship.)

On the other hand, *the same touch can have different meanings, depending on the context.* For example, if a man sees a male friend on the street or at a party and comes up and touches him on the shoulder while saying "How are you doing?", the meaning is something like, "I'm glad to see you, let's talk." But suppose the friend has a father who has just been hospitalized with a serious illness, and the other man comes to the hospital to be with his friend. The same touch and comment means, "I am here to support and comfort you."

By means of various touches, conveyed within the context of a social situation and accompanying behaviors, touching can convey virtually all of the fundamental relational messages we would want to communicate—liking, attraction, thanks, control, and so forth. In addition, different kinds of touches allow us to purposely communicate with varying degrees of clarity or ambiguity. My research shows there are at least 18 different meanings which can be communicated. Here are the possibilities:

1. Four meanings involve the expression of positive emotions toward the other person and are rather unambiguous (*support, appreciation, togetherness*, and *affection*).
2. One type of touch, an expression of *sexual* involvement, is also usually clear in meaning, although flirtatious touches, which imply but do not communicate sexual interest directly, are deliberately ambiguous.
3. Also generally clear are three types of power touches. The meanings are *attention getting* ("Direct your focus here"), *compliance* ("Do what I ask"), and *announcing-a-response* ("Notice my feeling and share it").
4. *Greeting* and *departure* touches are similarly straightforward in meaning because they are simply parts of daily rituals. Examples are a handshake between business associates when they meet, or a touch on the arm to an acquaintance when one person is leaving. They do not express strong feelings, but might be noticed if they were left out.
5. Touches of *playful affection* and *playful aggression* are slightly

more ambiguous than the meanings described above. The underlying meaning is made unclear by the suggestion that the person is only kidding (for example, when a person initiates an exaggerated, comic kiss or participates in mock wrestling).

6. "Hybrid" touches are somewhat more complex, since two meanings are communicated at the same time, often making it unclear which meaning is more important. The two most common ones are *greeting/affection* and *departure/affection*, in which the intent of an affectionate touch such as a hug is obscured by the fact that it is also part of the expected ritual of saying hello or good-bye.

7. Even more potentially ambiguous are three kinds of "task-related" touches that appear to simply accomplish some job. Ambiguity is common because a secondary implied meaning, such as attraction or liking, is frequently conveyed. The types are *incidental* contacts (as when a clerk touches a person's hand when giving change), *instrumental* touching (as when we help someone put on a coat), and *reference-to-appearance* (when clothing, jewelry, hair, etc., are touched as part of complimenting a person on how they look).

8. Finally, the *accidental* touch appears to have no intended purpose, yet it can carry ambiguous meanings, as when a slight brush suggests flirtatiousness, hints at a desire for attention, or implies that the other person should move out of the way.

This list provides only sketches of the various touch meanings, but gives some idea of the complexity and richness of the code. I go into more detail on each type of touch elsewhere in this book, giving examples, showing how each meaning is communicated, and suggesting when and how these messages can be used most effectively.

WHY LEARNING ABOUT TOUCH IS WORTH THE EFFORT

There are some risks in learning about touch, just as there are risks anytime we become more aware of some subtle aspects of our body language, although the risks are often more imagined than real. One is that touch may seem to be even more intricate, and therefore more difficult, than we thought before. This can be discouraging, at least at first, for people who want to touch more. Another risk is that we may initially become self-conscious and more anxious about our touching. A third risk is that the way we touch might reveal something about us that we would prefer to keep private.

I was a guest in a studio for a radio talk show recently where I dis-

cussed my research on touch. When the host of the show was thanking me
after the program, he extended a handshake and entangled his fingers awk-
wardly with mine. He looked embarrassed and said, "It makes a person feel
uncomfortable since you know so much about this." I assured him that it
happens all the time and does not necessarily reflect any deep meaning.

Incidents like this one have taught me that it is important to stress
certain principles. The first is that even though touch communication is
complicated, the overriding factor in determining how people will respond
to our touches is the apparent intention. The most basic rule of touch is
that it should not be aggressive, manipulative, or designed to put the other
person down. Even an uncomfortable attempt to make contact, like that of
the talk show host in my example, will usually be appreciated if this rule is
followed. Exceptional effectiveness can come later with experience. A second point is that self-consciousness is a natural reaction to trying something new, and the awkwardness soon goes away with practice.

The third principle is that it is not very useful to look at touch as a
way of psychoanalyzing people. I do not think that touch or other kinds of
body language tell much about the deep secrets of people, although they
do provide clues as to what the person may be feeling at the moment.
There are too many possible explanations for why a person touches a lot
or a little, aggressively or subtly, warmly or coldly, to make simple gener-
alizations about personality. Essentially, when I observe people's touches,
I mainly discover what they are trying to communicate and how well they
have learned to touch from their past experiences.

Touch is a communication skill. It's much like riding a bicycle or
fixing a car in the sense that it involves certain knowledge and practice.
The difference is that touch is more personal and involves sensitivity to
people and social situations. Like other skills, it can be learned.

Obviously, I think the risks are well worth taking. While there is
always a risk in learning to communicate powerfully and intimately, the benefit is greater effectiveness in personal and professional relationships. Touch
is not the only way of accomplishing this, but it frequently opens the door.

We begin life inside our mothers in a sea of warm and comforting
tactility. We are born into a world where we are surrounded by nourish-
ing, supportive, and stimulating touches. Somewhere in the process of
growing up, we lose much of this experience of being connected with others. Regaining our sense of touch is a way of reasserting our right to the
satisfaction of one of our basic needs, and a way of helping others satisfy
this need as well.

2

Touch and Self-Concept

A UTHOR EVA LeShan tells the following story:

> I recently visited a friend who had been widowed about two years. (She lives in Chicago and I live in New York, so we don't see each other very often.) When she opened her door, I gave her a good solid bear hug—and was shocked when she responded with tears. She explained by saying, "you can't imagine how good that felt. Aside from my grandchildren, whom I see only about twice a year, nobody has given me a really good hug like that since Al died." (LeShan, 1981, p. 42)

Touch is more than a physiological need and an aid to communication; it is also intimately related to our self-identity. This becomes especially apparent when an important source of touch is suddenly removed, as in the case of the woman in LeShan's story whose husband had died. Apparently, her friend's hug meant more to this woman than "I'm glad to see you;" it also said, "You are loveable."

Many commentators on the human condition have called attention to the connection between touch and self-concept. For example, the philosopher Jean-Paul Sartre wrote that loving touch "incarnates the flesh" of the toucher and the person touched; that is, it makes us more alive and aware of our physical existence (Sartre, 1956, pp. 389-397). The connection is anchored to the fact that our skin is the boundary between ourselves and the rest of the world. Ashley Montagu put it this way:

> Awareness of self is largely a matter of tactile experience. Whether we are walking, standing, sitting, lying, running, or jumping, whatever the other messages we receive from muscle, joint, and other tissue, the first and most extensive of these messages are received from the skin. Long before body temperature either falls or rises from external causes, it is the skin that will register the change and communicate to the cortex the necessary messages designed to initiate those behaviors which will lead to the appropriate response. (Montagu, 1971, p. 286)

At about six months of age, the child comes to distinguish him- or herself from surrounding objects and persons. This is literally the birth of self-concept, and especially at this time, sensations from the skin are a constant reminder of one's separateness and individuality. Later, the concept of self becomes more elaborate as the child grows into adulthood, guided largely by the ways others react to him or her. Yet, touches from others remain a significant part of this self-learning.

The psychologist Michael Argyle developed a model of the self-concept (Argyle, 1967, 1969) which draws attention to the centrality of touch. According to his model, each of us has a picture of ourselves in our minds, a self-image. The "core" of the self-image consists of the self-perceptions we carry with us into all situations, while a less central aspect of the self-image consists of our "sub-identities," the various roles we see ourselves taking in different situations. Another aspect of the self-concept is the way we evaluate our self-image—how likeable or praiseworthy we feel we are in general—our self-esteem.

Obviously, the core self-image is especially important. It develops earlier, stays with us, and largely determines self-esteem. As it happens, the core includes those elements that are most influenced by touch experiences with others: our body image and our perceptions of our personality traits, sex role, and age.

In the pages that follow, I discuss what is known about the relationship of touch to each of these parts of the core self-concept. I begin with body image, since it develops first and also tends to influence all the other self-perceptions.

BODY IMAGE AND BODY SELF-CONFIDENCE

Body image is our impression of what our body looks like and, more significantly, our subjective feeling of being comfortable with that image.

While physical activities of various kinds, athletic exercise, and even self-touching can help to create body self-awareness, acceptance of one's own body comes largely from the reactions of other people, especially those who are close to us. This process of learning begins when we are children and continues into adulthood. The psychologist Sidney Jourard (1966, p. 228) has suggested "that parents convey their acceptance of their children's bodies through physical contact, and the children come to experience themselves as acceptable in appearance in this way." In one study, Jourard and Secord (1955) found that college-age people were more likely to approve of their own bodily appearances if they thought their parents did, showing that parents play an important role.

In another study, Jourard (1966) asked college students to estimate the number of their body parts that were touched by significant others (mother, father, best same-sex friend, and best opposite-sex friend). He discovered that persons whose bodies were generally more accessible to touch also rated themselves as more attractive. It may be that attractive people just get touched more, but it seems just as likely that it works the other way. People who have been touched more in the past may *feel* more attractive, communicate this to others, and promote touching with more confidence.

More direct evidence of the contribution of touching to body image, at least among 8-10-year-olds, is found in a study by Sandra Weiss (1975). She assessed body image in children by asking them to draw a picture of a person and sort a puzzle of the human body into parts the child liked and disliked. The idea is that the more accurate and detailed the picture, and the more body parts that are liked, the better the body image. She also observed the touching of both the mother and the father with the child by having the parents lead the child, who was blind-folded, through a series of activities. The results showed that the more vigorous the contact when the parents touched, the more positive was the child's body image. (As I discuss in Chapter 4 on "bonding," this result applies especially to this preadolescent age group; gentler touches are more appropriate for younger children.)

Among studies of adults, Stembridge (1973) found that people who were more actively involved with touching significant people in their lives also felt better about their bodies. Walker (1970) found that even in situations in which people participated in touching exercises with complete strangers, those who were observed to be more accepting of touch also had a more positive body image. Clearly, in both children and adults, touching is related to good feelings about one's own body.

LEARNING ABOUT OURSELVES THROUGH TOUCH: PERSONALITY TRAITS AND SELF-ESTEEM

In general, what kinds of people are favorably or unfavorably disposed toward touch? To explore this question, Peter Andersen and Kenneth Leibowitz (1978) developed a "touch avoidance" questionnaire that measures people's attitudes toward touch with members of the same and opposite sex. It asks people to agree or disagree with statements such as "I enjoy getting a back rub from a member of the opposite sex" or "A hug from a same-sex friend is a true sign of friendship." The questionnaire does not directly predict how people will initiate touch, but it does show how they are likely to *react* to an unexpected touch (Sorensen & Beatty, 1988).

Recently, Janis and Peter Andersen and Myron Lustig of San Diego State University administered the opposite-sex part of this questionnaire (presumed to be especially important because same-sex touching among Americans is less common), along with a set of personality tests, to nearly 4,000 university students from all sections of the country (Andersen, Andersen, & Lustig, 1987). Their results show that, regardless of the region people come from, those who have positive feelings about touching also tend to talk more, to be less anxious about talking to others, and to disclose more personal information about themselves. That is, people who are more receptive toward touch are also more inclined toward communicating in a personal way than are touch avoiders. In fact, in another study, Andersen and Sull (1985) found that touch avoiders have a tendency to literally "keep others at arm's length" by staying farther away during conversations.

Not surprisingly, people who like touch from others are not only more communicative, but they also tend to be more self-confident in general. In the national survey described above, the authors found that people with positive attitudes toward touching rated themselves somewhat higher in self-esteem. Furthermore, other research shows that having good feelings about one's self in general is even more strongly related to the *initiation* of warm touches to others. In one study (Fromme et al., 1989), the authors were able to demonstrate that their "touch test" not only measured *attitudes* toward touch, but also that it was predictive of actual touch *behaviors* because persons with scores indicating favorable inclinations toward touch were also more likely to volunteer to participate in a study in which they would hug strangers of both sexes. The link to self-confidence was even clearer than in the previous study of "touch avoidance": People who scored high on the touch test tended to have high self-ratings on satisfaction with life, oneself, and one's childhood, and they generally regarded themselves as assertive, socially acceptable in self-presentation, and likely to use active rather than passive modes of coping with problems.

In still another study, Alan Silverman, Mark Pressman, and

Helmut Bartel (1973) asked people to touch another person in such a way as to communicate "love, as to a friend." The participants also rated their own self-esteem on a questionnaire. Those who rated higher in self-esteem were more likely to hug, rather than touching in a cautious way, such as shaking hands or patting the other person on the back. Compared with less self-confident people, they also rated the task of communicating with touch to be easier and felt that they had communicated the emotion more clearly. Knowing how to touch makes us feel better about touching, and, by enhancing our ability to develop relationships, touching helps us to feel better about ourselves.

Children: How the Link Between Touch and Personality Gets Started

For some time, scholars in the field of child development have been in agreement that a definite relationship between touch and personality exists very early in life. However, there has been some controversy over two points: (a) whether reactions to touch among young children are inborn or whether they are learned from experiences with parents; and (b) the degree to which early orientations toward touch are related to healthy personality development. Recent research has begun to resolve these disagreements, but it has taken some time to put the pieces of the puzzle together.

Cuddlers and non-cuddlers.

About three decades ago, two Scottish investigators, H.R. Schaffer and Peggy Emerson (1964), challenged the accepted idea that a large amount of intimate touching was essential for all infants. Basing their claim on interviews with mothers conducted periodically in their childrens' first 1 1/2 years, Schaffer and Emerson found that the children could be divided into three groups:

1. The majority, one-half of the children, were described as "cuddlers." These children sought out and reacted positively to holding and extensive affectionate contact of all kinds.
2. Another group, about one-fourth of the children, could be described as "sometimes-cuddlers." They wanted to be held, especially when they were tired or ill or had experienced something frightening.
3. The remaining one-fourth were described as "non-cuddlers," children who consistently resisted holding and generally tolerated only brief touches, although they liked vigorous play—being swung, danced, or bounced.

Schaffer and Emerson were particularly interested in the non-cuddlers because they were unusual. The investigators noted that in some ways these children were more advanced than others of their age because they related more freely to persons other than their mother and walked at earlier ages. Based largely on the fact that the mothers of these children said they made frequent attempts to hold the child, Schaffer and Emerson concluded that these tendencies in the children were most likely inborn and that the non-cuddlers apparently had less need for touching.

The flaw in Schaffer and Emerson's research is that they relied on the mothers' reports of their own behaviors. Self-reports are notoriously inaccurate when they involve recollections of behaviors like touching since people are often unaware of how they touch. In addition, people remember selectively, favoring the recall of socially approved behaviors on their own part. Recent research using the more valid method of direct observation suggests that it is largely the way a mother touches her infant that determines the child's responses to touch and ultimately affects personality development. The work of child development expert Mary Salter Ainsworth is especially extensive and revealing (Ainsworth, 1979; Bell & Ainsworth, 1972).

The mother's touch and the infant's response.

Ainsworth employed a team of trained observers who went directly into homes to watch mothers and their infants. The observations were made during four evenly spaced periods in the child's first year. Ainsworth found that there were three styles of touching by the mothers, which accounted for four kinds of reactions on the part of the children:

1. *Nurturing mothers/secure babies:* These mothers provided a great deal of body contact by responding consistently and quickly to messages from the infant that he or she wanted to be held, especially when the child was crying. These babies, about one-half of the total, readily accepted contact.
2. *Inconsistent mothers/passive or anxious babies:* These mothers, over one-fourth of the cases, sometimes cuddled their children, but oftentimes did not. They also responded promptly to crying by holding the child on some occasions, but not at other times. The reactions of the babies to this inconsistent behavior actually fell into two categories. Some became passive in apparent response to the uncertainty of the mother's provision of comfort, seldom responding to touch when they were held and appearing listless much of the time. The other children were anxious, crying frequently and oftentimes not being comforted by being held.
3. *Rejecting mothers/rejecting babies:* These mothers comprised the smallest group. They seldom held their babies, although

they did touch them in more limited ways such as kissing, They often let the child "cry it out" and showed apparent anger or annoyance at those times when they did come in response to crying. Eventually, the babies tended to resist being held by their mothers. It would appear that these infants closely match the non-cuddlers described by Schaffer and Emerson.

Although these patterns were largely set in the first three months, longer-term results were evident by the end of the first year. Ainsworth found that the secure infants cried less at the year's end than the other children and were more cooperative in response to corrective instructions from the mother. The rejecting babies tended to avoid the mother when she returned from outside the room and continued to resist being held by her, although they sometimes responded affectionately to others.

M. Louise Bigger (1984) videotaped the interactions of mothers and their 1-year-olds, including the same mother-infant pairs studied by Ainsworth. In close inspection of the videotapes, Bigger found evidence of subtle forms of aversion to touch in some mothers, such as welcoming the approach of the child with open arms, but wearing facial expressions of distaste or wincing. Bigger also observed that those children from Ainsworth's study whose mothers had avoided contact in the first three months often exhibited "odd" behaviors suggesting internal confusion, such as flapping the hands, echoing the speech of the mother, and laughing in a way that sounded false. These children were also more likely to strike or angrily threaten to strike the mother. These findings strongly suggest that early personality development is influenced by parental touching.

There is evidence that these kinds of patterns may endure well beyond the first year of life. Bigger extended her research to include observations of 6-year-olds with parents who had been especially avoidant of touching when the child was an infant. While these children as infants may still have made some attempts at contact, by this age there was evidence of mutual and broader avoidance of intimate nonverbal involvement. The parents and children Bigger observed rarely faced one another directly. Further, Bigger comments, "Returning to a room in which the 6-year-old has been examined, these parents approach the child from behind, speak to the child from behind, and touch the child only gingerly" (Bigger, 1984, p. 67). It seems likely that the stabilization of avoidance patterns of communication between child and parent would also have long-range effects on the child's personality formation.

The research I have cited here does not prove that touching by the principal caretaker or caretakers is the only influence on infant touch responsiveness. Some infants may be more difficult to comfort than others because of illness, traumatic birth experiences, or some unknown factor, including inherited tendencies. For the great majority of children, touch is the primary causal factor affecting responsiveness to touch. However, two main exceptions to this rule deserve comment: the touch-defensive child and the autistic child.

Tactile defensiveness.

Children with this condition may respond negatively to normal contact, especially very light touch, and exhibit behaviors such as arching the back and stiffening when held (Wilbarger, 1984). Many are hyperactive in general and respond to various forms of stimulation besides touch, such as noises or jostling, in extreme ways. There are therapeutic methods involving touch (swaddling, rocking on a large therapy ball, heavy massage, etc.) which can be used by trained professionals (pediatric occupational and physical therapists) to help alleviate this condition, but nonspecialists should not attempt these methods. Later, when defensiveness has been reduced, normal touch from parents may be accepted and beneficial. These cases are rare; however, they do not account for non-cuddlers or aversion to touch in other normal infants.

Autism.

Although some autistic children exhibit tactilely defensive behaviors, autism is even rarer and more problematic. These children not only fail to respond positively to touch, but they are profoundly withdrawn, engage in repetitive movements which are meaningless to others, and appear not to be able to use any communicative signals such as eye contact, smiles, or language (Gartner & Schultz, 1990, p. 162). Even in the most severe cases, however, there is sometimes hope. One of the most inspiring examples is documented in Barry Neil Kaufman's book, *Son-Rise* (1976). Suzi and Barry Kaufman sought help from various institutions when they discovered their son Raun was autistic at age 1. Having received no encouragement from professionals that anything could be done, they decided to invent their own therapeutic program for establishing communication with their child. For months on end, they imitated whatever behaviors he exhibited—for example, rocking for hours in rhythm to his rocking. Eventually, he began to respond by smiling, reaching out to be touched, and so forth. Then, when it appeared that Raun had come completely out of his shell and was behaving normally, he had a relapse back into autistic patterns. The parents, with help from other family members, reinstituted the original procedures. When he "came out" again, it was for good. Today, he is a healthy, intelligent, normally functioning adult.

Similarly, although with somewhat less severe cases of autism in children as old as 5 years, therapists in New York City have been employing tactile stimulation and other attachment behaviors to establish communication with these children (Gartner & Schultz, 1990). The theory on which they are operating is that the child and mother somehow missed the essential early attachment exchanges necessary for normal development and that the mother undoubtedly became discouraged at some point, withdrawing from further efforts to establish communication. The idea of the therapy is to reestablish contact by instigating attachment behaviors anew and training the mother to respond when the child begins to show a readiness to interact. At first, the therapist treats the child as a very young baby by holding him or her, playing with the child's feet, and so on. When the child exhibits "weak cues," such as looking at or reaching out slightly toward the therapist, the mother takes over, looking into the child's eyes, cooing, touching extensively, and so forth. Progressively, if the therapy is successful, the mother learns to respond to any encouraging sign, and she and the child develops more normal patterns of communication.

Adults: Relationships Between Touch and Personality Types

We do not know how closely early touch experiences are related to personality development in the long run. There has not been enough time for investigators such as Ainsworth to follow individuals from infancy all the way into adulthood. However, a study by communication professor John Deethardt and his associate Debbie Hines (1983) is provocative in suggesting that adult touch inclinations are closely associated with certain personality characteristics; they call these clusters of traits "tactile-personalities" or "tactypes."

Deethardt and Hines divided people into four groups according to how much they were inclined to touch and accept touches, using a questionnaire that measured attitudes toward touching, similar to the "touch-test" measure mentioned earlier. These groups, from the "highest" touchers to the "lowest" touchers, were found to have certain personality characteristics:

1. *Tactype-1: Nonconformist High Touchers.* These highly tactile individuals are independent and innovative, dominant and assertive, and enthusiastic and energetic people. They also tend to reject traditional standards of morality and etiquette and are somewhat insecure about their social acceptability. They tend to match the stereotype of the radical student or perhaps that of creative people such as writers and artists.
2. *Tactype-2: Confident High Touchers.* This group, comprised of the second highest touchers, is similar to the first group in personality characteristics, except that they have a normal concern for traditional moral standards and social etiquette and are not

socially insecure. The image of an outgoing and successful business executive is illustrative.

3. *Tactype-3: Conservative Low Touchers.* These less tactile people are less independent than the first two groups. Social reputation and proper social behavior are extremely important to them. Again, stereotypically, a government bureaucrat in Washington, D.C. comes to mind as an example of this type.

4. *Tactype-4: Sober Low Touchers.* This group is lowest in touch orientation and also enthusiasm and emotional stability. The highly cautious, unexpressive personal style of this type seems to be a way of coping with strong feelings of anxiety. Since individuals of this type often go unnoticed, it is difficult to specify a stereotypic image, but a low-level office worker who occasionally displays fits of temperament or signs of depression might serve as an example.

There appear to be certain parallels between Ainsworth's infant touch types and Deehardt and Hines's tactypes, suggesting the possibility that the adult patterns were set at an early age. For example, the secure, tactilely oriented children who were touched responsively as infants logically match up with the confident, high-touch adults. Similarly, anxious infants, who were touched inconsistently, might find touching (and most personal relationships) risky and unreliable and become conservative low touchers in adulthood. Passive children, who responded to inconsistency with an absence of response, could become sober low touchers as adults.

The fourth possible parallel, between Ainsworth's rejecting infants and Deehardt and Hines's nonconformist high touchers, may seem improbable. That is, we might expect those with unrewarding early tactile experiences to be low rather than high touchers as adults. However, it does make sense that children who felt rejected and angry would later become independent and rebellious with authority figures and that early experiences of rejection would make them fearful of rejection and therefore socially insecure as adults. It would also make sense that they would be high touchers if they continued beyond childhood to seek contact with others which they did not get from their parents.

Although high touchers are generally more communicative and self-confident than others, Deethardt and Hines's research suggests there is not a one-to-one correspondence between the amount of touching an adult does and his or her self-esteem. This is especially evident in the nonconformist high touchers, who are more assertive communicators than the low touchers, but who also seem to have lower self-esteem than the confident high touchers. The apparent reason is that the total amount of touching is not the only factor to consider. A person can touch frequently out of anxiety as well as self-assurance. Skill in touching is probably also related to personality and self-esteem. As Deethardt and Hines suggest, the non-conformist high touchers may touch inappropriately at times. It seems likely that the confident high touchers use the right touch more often.

SEX ROLES AND TOUCH

I have said that the infant begins to develop a concept of self at about the half-way mark in their first year. By this point, tactile patterns with parents have been established. These patterns may have long-range effects on self-esteem because they influence how lovable or worthy of attention the child will feel. What is perhaps even more remarkable, however, is the fact that the sex role of the child has also begun to take form. He or she has begun to learn what it means to be male or female in this culture. Here again, touch plays a critical part.

How Male and Female Children Are Touched

Like Ainsworth, child development investigator Michael Lewis and his associates observed mother-infant communication from the earliest months. However, he was interested primarily in the differences in the ways male and female children are handled physically. Lewis (1972) found that baby boys receive more touch from their mothers than do girls in the first few months. Perhaps male infants are more highly valued by mothers, or perhaps boys simply need more holding than girls at this age. Whatever the reason, this pattern is soon reversed. By 6 months of age, girls are touched more and also talked to more than boys (Kagan & Lewis, 1965).

Susan Goldberg and Lewis (1969) observed children with their mothers at 13 months of age in a nursery play room. At this age, the boys show signs of greater independence and adventurous qualities. Girls touch their mothers more, stray away from their mothers for shorter distances, and are more distressed when a barrier is placed between themselves and their mother. Boys, on the other hand, explore the room more freely, and they play more vigorously with toys.

It seems clear that the mother's touch influenced these patterns in important ways. Those children who were touched most at an early age touched their mother more later. Generally these are girls, but the boys who were touched most at 6 months also touched their mothers more than other boys at 13 months. Eventually, touch must be replaced, in part, with eye contact and verbal communication, but this happens sooner with boys. Apparently, girls also "cling" more because they are picked up sooner when they stray away than are little boys.

While Lewis's research has been limited to mother-child communication, other investigators have also examined the role of the father. Michael Lamb (1977) observed infants of 7 to 13 months of age at home with both parents. He found that the children showed signs of being attached to both parents at these ages; that is, they sought contact with both the mother and father and could be comforted by touching from either parent. However, the mothers specialized more in meeting the child's basic needs (feeding, bathing, changing, etc.). The fathers, on the other hand, engaged in more playful touching, including games such as "peek-a-boo" and rough-housing. The effect is that the father's touch is enjoyed somewhat more, but the mother is involved in more physical contact overall.

By the time the child is 3 and up until the age of 5, the touches of the parents become even more clearly differentiated. Patricia Noller (1978) observed mothers and fathers separately when they were leaving their children at child-care centers. She found that mothers touched more affectionately with both boys and girls than did the fathers. Both parents paid more attention to girls and what affectionate touching the fathers did perform was directed primarily to girls, not boys. Although Noller's study was conducted in Australia, it is apparent that these observations apply to Americans as well. In fact, the same patterns of touching between parents and children can be found when the children have grown up. Jourard's study (1966), as well as another study conducted a decade later by Lawrence Rosenfeld and his associates (Rosenfeld, Kartus, & Ray, 1976), shows that college-age adults have more intimate touching with mothers than fathers, and that daughters are favored regarding touch by both parents at this age.

In general, the research shows that by the time children enter school, touch has been used to teach them significant lessons about their sex roles, probably in combination with other verbal and nonverbal messages. Boys are expected to be more independent and girls to be more oriented toward personal relations. The price that boys pay is that they receive less affection. Children have also learned something about how males and females are expected to touch. By watching their parents, they discover that males do not touch as much or as affectionately as women, especially with one another.

Adult Sex Differences in Touch

It is not surprising that these patterns carry over into adulthood. Studies reveal that women generally touch more than men. What is surprising, however, is that most people believe it is the other way, especially when it comes to who initiates touch between men and women.

The myth of male touch dominance.

When people are asked on questionnaires to guess about male-female touching, or to recall their own experiences as adults, they usually say it is men who touch more. For example, Nancy Henley (1977) found that most people say it is the supervisor who touches the subordinate, the adult who touches the child, and the man who touches the woman. Similarly, in another study, both male and female employees at a university recalled more male-to-female touches than vice versa (Radecki & Jennings, 1980). Henley interpreted such findings as evidence that men, being in higher power positions in society, use touches as "status-reminders" to women.

It is important to keep in mind that what people think or recall about touching may be inaccurate. Guesses are often colored by stereotypes (in this case, that men are more aggressive and power-oriented), and remembrances are often limited to events that stand out, such as a particularly embarrassing or demeaning touch. When direct records of touching have been employed in studies (by observers or people keeping diary accounts of their own touches), the results generally show, contrary to popular belief, that women are the greater touch initiators in male-female communication (Stier & Hall, 1984).

The exceptions, in which men were observed to touch women more often than women touched men, are found in studies by Henley (1973) and by Major, Schmidlin, and Williams (1990). However, there is an explanation for these results. Each of these studies were conducted in public situations in which strangers were present and only touches from hand to body were recorded. In public, men may feel protective of or possessive toward women, and these motivations are likely to be expressed in touch by reaching out with the hand alone or with the hand and an encircling arm. In fact, one study by Richard Borden and Gordon Homleid (1976) shows that when couples are in public, the man will often position the woman by his "strong hand" (on the right for right-handers and the left for left-handers). From this position, the man can comfortably touch the woman, as if to say to others, "This one is with me." In another observation study of interactions in public, Hall and Veccia (1990) found that men specialized in initiating hand or "arm around" touches, but women were more likely than men to instigate other touches, such as linking arms (again, perhaps giving the man the protective role). Furthermore, according to Hall and Veccia's study, it appears that only young men express possessiveness with touch in public; among older couples, women initiated more touch than men. Even among young couples, in investigations in which college-age men and women used a personal log to record *all* of their touches on one or more days (Jones, 1986; Willis & Rinck, 1983), it is clear that women initiate more touches to men than men do to women. One possible explanation is that most touching occurs in private, and women touch more in private than in public (Willis & Rinck, 1983).

How and why men and women touch.

Some studies show that women also touch members of the same sex more than men do, but the major difference between men and women is not found in their amounts of touching so much as how and why they touch. Generally, women are more affectionate and intimate in their touching. Evidence of this comes from a study by Paul Greenbaum and Howard Rosenfeld (1980) who observed touches occurring at airports when travelers disembarked from their flights. They found that whenever women were involved, whether it was two women or a man and a woman who were touching, there were more hugs and kisses. When two men touched, it was usually a brief handshake. This is to be expected when we remember that people first learn to touch through experiences with their parents, and most of them remember their mothers as more affectionate touchers than their fathers, and their fathers as affectionate mainly with female members of the family.

Furthermore, women tend to use touch to convey different meanings and a wider variety of meanings than do men. While any of the 18 touch meanings uncovered in my research (Jones & Yarbrough, 1985) can be communicated by either sex, compared to men, women are especially likely to employ touch to express "pure" affection (no greeting or departure being involved) or to give a compliment. Even in simple acts such as handing an object to someone, women are more likely than men to allow their hand to make contact with the other person's hand. They are also more likely to assist others with a touch, such as helping them to put on an item of clothing. Women tend to specialize in warm or helpful touches.

TOUCH AND SELF-PERCEPTIONS OF MATURITY AND AGING

A person's age is objectively set by their birthdate, but subjectively, people of the same age may feel differently about how mature or old they are— that is, how well they are doing for their calendar years. Although there has been no research on how self-perceptions at different ages are affected by touch, it seems likely that there is a relationship. This is true even with young children. There is no greater compliment to a 5-year-old, in my experience, than for an adult to pick them up and exclaim, "You're getting so big I can hardly carry you anymore!"

There are two periods when touch is especially likely to affect self-concept about one's stage of life: adolescence and the senior years. At these times, when feelings about one's body may be in flux or declining, touch can be especially reassuring. Paradoxically, these are also the ages when we know people are touched the least.

As one book title says, teenagers are in a situation where they are *All Grown Up and No Place To Go* (Elkind, 1984). Mature sexually in biological terms, but emotionally immature and often physically awkward, adolescents need contact, yet they are not ready for sexually intimate relationships. They are also seeking independence from parents at this time and may be especially concerned about possible homosexual connotations of touches from same-sex friends. The result is that they are cut off from the sources of touch they have relied on for most of their lives. These factors may be major contributors to teenage promiscuity and pregnancies, as pediatrician Elizabeth McAnarney (1990) has suggested. (There are solutions to the problem of touching teenagers, and I have more to say about this in Chapter 4, on "Bonding.")

Initiating touch to senior citizens is usually less of a problem since it is likely to be warmly accepted, but it requires that others be available and motivated. That is, in the busy, youth-oriented culture of the United States, younger people often do not devote much of their time to being with older persons. What is more, in mobile America, nuclear families often move away from the neighborhoods or hometowns where grandparents and older relatives live. Also, some older people, perhaps feeling less attractive as they age, may stop initiating touch and isolate themselves from the reassuring touches they would receive in return.

PRACTICAL IMPLICATIONS: INFLUENCING SELF-CONCEPTS THROUGH TOUCH

We have said that touch is fundamental to the development of the core self-concept because it is the first way we learn about ourselves. The implications for parents are clear. The evidence shows that infant responses to touch are not primarily inborn and that consistently nurturing touch from the first months of the child's life contributes to the development of a healthy personality. The responsibility seems to fall mainly on mothers, and some may have more difficulty with this than others, especially mothers who are not touch-oriented themselves. However, even when mothers are not very responsive to the infant's needs for touch, a high degree of contact from the father, older siblings, or both can serve as a substitute, substantially contributing to the child's responsiveness and security. That is, the entire family can participate in providing a healthy tactile diet for the infant.

Research shows that well beyond the first year of life, parental touch continues to affect the child's self-concept, especially in terms of body image and sex roles. Parents need to be aware that they can contribute to the child's acceptance of his or her own body by frequent touching which involves many parts of the child's body. Some parents are overly concerned about the possible sexual implications of such touching. However, with the obvious exception that the child's sexual organs should not be stimulated by an adult, sensual touches such as a full body massage to a young child at bedtime will not constitute a problem as long as the parents are clear in their own minds that the touches are affectionate and not intended sexually.

Concern about the effects of touching on the child's development of an appropriate sex role can also cause parents to be overly cautious about certain kinds of contact. Some may be worried that too much rough-housing with a girl will tend to make her masculine in behavior. A more common worry, however, is that affectionate touching will make a boy effeminate. In particular, fathers may be unconsciously fearful that touching their sons lovingly will promote homosexual tendencies.

Such concerns are not well founded. The behaviors that we think of as masculine or feminine are not learned primarily by touching, but rather by imitation of the parent of the same sex. The technical term for these behaviors is "gender signals," and they consist mainly of the different ways that men and women typically hold their bodies and move (Birdwhistell, 1970, pp. 39- 46). For example, women tend to stand and sit with their knees close together and their arms held near the body. Men are more likely to spread their feet and legs apart and to hold their arms somewhat away from the body. Women also make more small movements, such as tilting the head to one side and gesturing quickly with the wrist bent. These behaviors are not ordinarily fully developed until adulthood, although children begin to learn them as early as age 2 as a way of differentiating themselves from the opposite sex. The more children feel comfortable with the parent of the same sex, including the way this parent relates to their opposite-sex partner, the more likely they are to copy the gender signals of that parent.

The way parents use touch with children does make a difference in sex roles in the development of independence and adventurous qualities, on the one hand, and sensitive, personal relating on the other. For example, if children are held when they want to get down, rather than being encouraged to explore, and if parents retrieve them quickly when they begin to venture a distance away, as is often the case with girls, the child will be discouraged from developing individualistic self-confidence. For parents who want to avoid rigidly traditional sex-role development, the ideal for both boys and girls is a fair amount of affectionate touch, comforting contacts when the child requests it, and a certain amount of age-appropriate physical play. In addition, parents should avoid the overly protective act of picking up children as soon as they stray away.

One of the things we learned from the popularity of encounter groups in the late 1960s and early 1970s was that touch can have profound effects on the self-concept of adults as well as children. Encounter groups were a form of short-term therapy in which individuals met with a "trainer" or "facilitator" in intensive sessions of several days or a week in order to learn how to become more aware and expressive of their emotions. Touch exercises were a primary method used in these groups. For example, people might be asked to mutually explore the face of another person to discover their own capacity for sensitive and loving feelings for others. Or they might be asked to allow themselves to fall backwards into the arms of another person to build trust. If two people in a group had trouble communicating their feelings toward one another in words, they might be asked to meet in the center of the group circle and to express their emotions with touch, excluding the use of violence. Hugging among members of groups was especially common toward the end of these sessions.

The result was that people often came to see themselves as more loving and lovable and more emotionally expressive and honest than they had before. When these people went back to their home and work environments, they wanted to express this "new self" with hugging and verbal directness. These behaviors often worried or annoyed family members and friends. Frequently, the changes in self-concept diminished or died out because they were not supported by others.

I believe that a major problem with these group experiences, in which I was involved as both a participant and a trainer, was that people did not know how to translate their newly discovered impulses into socially acceptable ways of touching and relating. In part, what they lacked was an understanding of the language of touch as it is practiced in everyday life.

The successors to the encounter group movement in terms of popularity have been certain kinds of "touch therapies," some of which were originated prior to encounter groups. These more current approaches to the use of touch for personal development are often directed to specific personal problems or concerns, but they may nevertheless have significant effects on self-concept. Probably the best known of these is the sex therapy method developed by William Masters and Virginia Johnson (1970). People learn techniques for rediscovering the pleasure of touch, without expectations or concern about whether touch will culminate in orgasm. They may acquire new perceptions of their sex roles as well. Men may learn that their masculine image can include sensitivity expressed through touching and that touching need not necessarily lead to sexual intercourse (although this makes sexual intimacy all the more enticing). Women may learn that they can be sexually assertive without losing their femininity and that they can use touch to make sex more enjoyable, rather than simply using sex to get the enjoyable touching that follows.

In other touch therapies, physical contact is used to accomplish different kinds of changes in self-image and self-esteem. For example, part of the rationale for the method known as "rolfing," which involves various forms of deep-tissue massage, is that certain types of long-held muscular tension are bodily defenses used to avoid experiencing uncomfortable feelings such as anger or sadness. Following treatment, some people report the surprising release of these emotions, accompanied by insights into the self-perceptions that allowed the suppression of feelings in the first place (Dychtwald, 1977, pp.11-15). Still another use of touch, specifically called "therapeutic touch," is employed by nurses and paramedical practitioners to identify and relieve disturbances in the bodies of physically ill patients, including those with psychosomatic illness (Krieger, 1975, 1979).

Finally, touching exercises similar to those used in encounter groups are employed by some family and couple therapists to improve communication, leading people to redefine their relationships and themselves within the relationships (Weiss, 1978). Even the simplest kinds of daily touches have been found in research to improve communication between medical professionals and physically or mentally ill patients (Aguilera, 1967; McCorkle, 1974). It seems likely that similar effects will be found with people who have closer relationships.

Can the normal, average person practice his or her own touch therapy to enhance self-concept without the help of professionals? For people who are committed to self-help and self-improvement, as many Americans are, the answer is obviously yes. We know that people who touch effectively tend to be effective in personal, face-to-face communication in general, and they also tend to be high in self-esteem. In part, this is because confident people reach out to others in various ways, including touch. But it also works in reverse. Touching opens channels of communication, and when we change one key behavior like touch, we tend to become more confident in ourselves in other ways as well.

We also know that people who touch more get touched more, and touches from others confirm positive perceptions of our body image. While exercise routines and diets are currently popular methods of improving body image and self-esteem, there is always a subjective element in self-concept. A direct method of enhancing body image, which will work regardless of one's state of health, age, or conditioning, is to initiate appropriately to others the kinds of touches we want to receive.

While we can sometimes improve communication and self-perceptions by actions based on intuition or by trial-and-error methods, the critical element in change is knowing the specific behaviors that lead to clear messages and better relations. The ways people use touch to build confidence in themselves and others are described in detail in the chapters that follow.

Section II
The Many Meanings
of Touch (and How to
Communicate Them)

3

Making Contact: How to Get Started in a Touching Relationship

THE FIRST touch in any relationship is usually the most difficult. This is especially true for people who are particularly cautious about touching, but nearly everyone experiences at least some discomfort on certain occasions. In my studies, in which people kept diaries of their daily touches, they often apologized for having so few touches to report when turning in their records, saying, "I thought I would touch more," or "I wish I touched more." Some added, as an explanation, that they were away from the people they usually touch, family and close friends. Away from their usual environment, many were unsure how to get started again.

When people feel cautious about touching someone for the first time, it is not due solely to timidity or lack of a strong self-concept. Rather, their hesitancy may be based on a realistic assessment of the significance of first touches. The initial act of physical contact announces an intention; frequently, it makes a request to change a relationship. It says, "I want to become more involved with you." Later, the use of a new form of touch in a relationship may carry the message, "I want to be even more involved—or involved in a new way—with you." Because of the potential for rejecting the touch and thus the request, initiating the first or a new kind of touch can make a person feel vulnerable.

Examples of the use of touch to define or redefine relationships are abundant. Even the most conventional touch—a handshake when people are introduced—signals a change in relationship from strangers to acquaintances. Figuratively, the people are "in contact" from that moment on. Similarly, when two people are moving from an acquaintanceship to a friendship, it will frequently be signaled by a friendly (and momentary) greeting touch to the elbow, arm, or shoulder.

Other cases of touch initiation may be even more ego involving. In his description of the steps in courtship "on the road to sexual intimacy," Desmond Morris lists touch as step number four. The first steps are eye-to-body, eye-to-eye, and voice-to-voice "contact," and only then does hand-to-hand contact occur (Morris, 1971). When a woman says that a man she knows has "made a move" on her, she may be referring to his first touch or, more likely, a contact that is more intimate in some way than his previous touches. One study shows that an unexpected touch (to the lower back, for example, rather than to the shoulder or elbow) will be more favorably evaluated if the touch initiator is perceived as "attractive" (Burgoon & Walther, 1990). Thus, the unexpected touch acts as a "litmus test"—if the person who is touched responds favorably, it suggests attraction, and further tactile overtures will follow.

Even when it is anticipated by both persons that a relationship will move to a new level eventually, a change in touch or the response to touch will often be used to announce the intention to progress to a new stage. The kiss is a good example. It is probably the first symbolic touch that a child learns. The reciprocal puckering and touching of the lips not only expresses affection, it also *stands* for an affectionate relationship. The child's awareness of this way of communicating alters his or her relationship with adults. Having been cuddled, petted, and kissed more or less at will by parents, relatives, and friends of the family, the child can now initiate—or refuse to return—this sign of affection. As children experiment with this newfound source of power, parents are forced to confront their child's transformation from being a "bundle of joy" to a person to be reckoned with.

The kiss also has special meaning among adolescents and adults in dating relationships. The first kiss is the cross-over point which signals the intention to go from an acquaintanceship or friendship to a romantic relationship. The anxiety usually experienced prior to this symbolic moment, and the potential humor in it (viewed from a distance), is nicely illustrated in a scene from Woody Allen's film *Annie Hall*. While walking toward a restaurant on their first date, the character played by Woody

Allen stops and says to his date, Annie (played by Diane Keaton), "We're probably both worrying about when we're going to kiss. Why don't we just get it over with now, and then we can enjoy the rest of the evening." Touches, whether they are kisses or other forms of contact, are often the benchmarks in developing relationships.

Given that the beginning of a touching relationship is a significant and potentially anxiety-arousing event, it is not surprising that people have experimented with different ways of establishing new forms of physical contact in an effective manner. One of the major reasons for the emergence of encounter groups in the late 1960s and early 1970s was that many of the people who participated were starved for touch. People went away for a weekend retreat where they learned to express their feelings more freely and came back home eager to hug family, friends, and acquaintances. In fact, the title of a popular book on this movement, *Please Touch*, by Jane Howard (1970), emphasizes the importance of physical contact in these experiences. However, as I mentioned in Chapter 2, many people found that the reawakened impulses for touch which they learned in these groups could not be transferred to back-home situations. Participants were often disappointed to discover that their uninhibited expressions of affection were rejected by others.

Fortunately, there are ways to get started in touching relationships that have stood the test of time. There are a few people whose touches seem to be warmly accepted almost every time, but most of them cannot say why. The rest of this chapter will attempt to unravel this mystery.

RITUALISTIC TOUCHES: THE FIRST AND LAST CHANCES FOR CONTACT

Recently, when I was a guest on a radio talk show in Denver, a woman called in to tell about her disappointing experiences with touching. She had been brought up in an Italian family and community where warm embraces and kisses among relatives, friends, and even acquaintances were an enjoyable part of everyday life. As an adult, married and away from home, she had tried to initiate touches with others many times and had been rejected. "I used to run up to people I knew and liked and hug them when I first saw them," she said, "but they froze up and looked embarrassed so often, I finally just gave up."

This woman's intuition that greeting another person is a good opportunity for touching was accurate. In my research, the most common occasion for touching was when people first saw one another. Second was when they said good-bye. In fact, about 20% of all touches occur during greetings and departures. The reason for this is that touching is an accepted—but not necessary—part of the *required* ritual of acknowledging people we know when we first see them and again when we leave them. Symbolically, the greeting touch says, "We're in contact again," while the departure touch says, "We will not lose contact." Why, then, did this woman get rejected? Not, chances are, because she touched, but rather because the way she touched was inappropriate in the developing relationships. I suggested to her that these new friends and acquaintances were not yet ready for warm embraces and that a subtler touch to the elbow, arm, or shoulder might work better.

My research suggests three basic guidelines for greeting and departure touches in developing relationships. First, acquaintances and friends who are not yet close generally limit their touches in terms of the body regions involved. That is, they almost always restrict their initiation of contact to what I call "nonvulnerable body parts"—the arm, elbow, or shoulder. The other areas of the body, which I call "vulnerable body parts," are touched almost exclusively by persons who are close—family members, romantic partners, and close friends—although many of the touches with these persons are also directed to nonvulnerable body zones.

What is more, persons who are not close seldom touch both sides of the body in greetings or departures. A two-handed touch to both arms or both shoulders is a much more intimate touch than a contact to only one arm or shoulder.

It might seem that the hand would be a safe place to touch, but actually, a casual touch on the hand of another often has intimate connotations and may be seen as flirtatious. The one exception, of course, is the formal handshake. This gesture is actually a very cautious symbol of trust. Some people have speculated that it originally represented an attempt to show that neither person held a weapon. (If this is accurate, it is not surprising that until very recently the handshake has been used predominantly among *men*.)

The second guideline of ritualistic greeting and departure touches is that they should be *brief*. Generally, people who have initiated a touch take their hand away as soon as they have said, "Hi, how are you?" or "Nice talking to you; see you later." When a touch lasts for even a few seconds beyond the initial greeting or the final departure phases, it will often be misinterpreted, unless the people are close.

This is true even for the handshake. Although some Latin Americans prolong handshaking for five or more seconds, persons from the United States are flustered by this gesture and wonder what the other person is trying to communicate. Similarly, a prolonged touch to the arm or shoulder during greetings or departures may suggest aggressiveness or excessive warmth, and a long touch to the hand is likely to have a sexual connotation, regardless of the sex of the persons involved. Hand holding is rather strictly limited to close relationships between the opposite sexes or between children and their parents or caretakers.

A third guideline is that it is usually best to start with greeting touches in these brief, nonintrusive contacts. Ritual departure touches are rarer among acquaintances than among friends (except for the obligatory handshake at the end of a business interaction) and suggest that the relationship has progressed to a level of somewhat greater involvement.

In calling these brief greeting and departure contacts "ritualistic," it may seem that I am labeling them as "cold." Yet, except for the most perfunctory of handshakes, in which a person presents a limp hand, maintains contact for only a second, or fails to smile, this interpretation is far from the truth. In fact, the function of the casual touch during hellos and good-byes, used mainly in relationships which are only moderately close, is to add extra warmth to the exchange. For example, a touch accompanying the verbal greeting, "Hi, how are you?" is translated, "I'm glad to see you." At the close of a conversation, a touch, along with the words, "Good talking with you," is translated, "I *really* mean it" or "Take care."

The opportunities for still warmer touches will come later as the relationship develops.

TOUCH UNDER COVER: HOW PEOPLE "SNEAK IN" THE TOUCHES THEY NEED

At times, people may not feel that another person is ready for even the brief greeting and departure touches I have described. Or, having made contact when they said hello, they may want to touch again, but in a way that does not seem "pushy." In my research, I found that people were able to do this by using several ingeniously subtle touches which *seem* to have a single, straightforward purpose, but which actually often have the secondary purpose of enhancing warm relations.

The "Reference-to-Appearance" Touch

In this kind of touch, the initiator makes a spoken comment—usually a compliment—about some aspect of the other person's appearance (clothing, jewelry, hair, etc.), while the touch casually "inspects" the object or body part. Most of these touches involve contact with vulnerable body parts (the head, face, neck, or chest of the recipient), so it is a subtly personal touch. Ordinarily, this touch would only be used between people who are at least acquaintances, although it is sometimes employed as a way of flirting in places like singles bars. Here are some examples from my research:

- A woman says, "What a pretty necklace!" while touching a pendant worn by another woman. (The touch recipient's translation: "I want to compliment you.")
- A mother touches the front of her daughter's hair and says, "It's so cute. Would you like me to curl it?" (Daughter's translation: "I want to touch you—I feel affectionate.")
- A young woman touches a man on the chest and says, "Nice tee-shirt." (Her translation: "Coy, I'm flirting.")
- A woman touches a man's hair and says, "I like your haircut." (Translation: "I like your hair, and I like you.")

As my examples indicate, this touch is used mainly by women, but I have talked to men who claim they use it, too. Men seem to use it more cautiously, however, especially with other men. For example, one man may say to another, "Nice sportcoat," while feeling the material at the lapel. (Translation: "I like your taste—let's be friends.")

The secondary meanings in the reference-to-appearance touch—"I like you" or "I'm attracted to you"—are rather transparent, since the toucher *creates* the "task" of inspection by his or her comment.

There are three other "task-related" kinds of touches which are even more "under cover" and therefore can be used, under certain circumstances, with almost anyone.

The "Attention-Getting" Touch

This contact involves a hand touch to an arm or perhaps a shoulder, followed immediately by an explanation: "Excuse me, do you have the time?" "Excuse me, could you tell me where to find . . . ?" "Could you hand me that . . . ?" It can be used in a variety of relationships, including strangers. (The touch is very brief. Holding on until you get your answer or the requested action is strictly taboo.)

This touch serves the purpose of directing attention, but it also says, "You look approachable." In fact, it can even be used as a cautious kind of greeting touch with a person you do not know very well. The other person doesn't see you, so you touch briefly to get their attention, then say, "Hi, how are you?"

The "Incidental" Touch

This touch involves a light contact which occurs during some mutual activity, but it is a touch that could have been avoided. The most common case is when a person gives an object to someone with momentary hand-to-hand contact. For example, clerks in stores have told me that they often just drop change into the customers' hands, but when they feel friendly toward the person, they will allow skin contact as well. Similarly, a person could sit down next to someone in a crowded car and neither would bother to shift around immediately to end the contact, or people reading a document together might permit occasional contact between their shoulders.

Although it might seem that such casual contact would be meaningless, a study by three researchers at Purdue University (Fisher, Rytting, & Heslin, 1976) indicates otherwise. Personnel at the university library were instructed to either touch or avoid touching students' hands when returning their library cards. The researchers then approached the students as they exited the library to ask them to fill out a questionnaire. Those who had been touched, especially the females, gave more favorable evaluations of the library clerk and were even in a better mood than the students who were not touched. Even though people may not be consciously aware that they received this simple, positive touch, the underlying meaning often gets across: "You are touchable. I feel comfortable touching you."

The "Instrumental" Touch

- A male hairdresser in a salon reports that some of his most frequent customers are older women whose hair actually looks rather good when they come in. "I think they enjoy having their hair 'fussed with' in an innocent way," he comments.
- A 16-year-old girl, who has an interest in athletic medicine, volunteers to tape the injuries of the boys on the wrestling team. She adds, "We have some really good conversations while I'm taping. It helps in getting to know boys."
- Workers who conduct the initial check-in procedure in a detoxification clinic, where people come to get treatment for alcoholism, are encouraged by their supervisors to ask questions and listen attentively to clients while performing preliminary blood pressure and other physical tests. "Frequently, the clients are in a state of intoxification when they enter, and you wouldn't ordinarily touch them," comments one of the workers, "but administering the tests provides a good reason for touching them and helps them to talk about their problem."
- A female clerk in a women's clothing store reports that she often holds jackets or coats for customers as they try them on. "It adds a personal touch, in both senses of the expression," she comments.

I refer to these kinds of touches as "instrumental"—that is, they accomplish a task in and of themselves and that is their apparent purpose.

Yet, while some of these touches are really necessary or expected—assisting an elderly person to get up from a chair, helping a person to regain a temporary loss of balance—most are simply a nice gesture. The primary meaning is "I want to help," and the secondary meaning is "I want to touch." Instrumental touches serve the purpose of permitting contact that might not otherwise occur, so that communication is improved. Interestingly, people usually say something that explains why they are performing the touch—"Here, let me help you"—even though what they are doing is clear. The words function to distract attention from the underlying meaning.

Instrumental touches occur between family members, friends, acquaintances, and even strangers, and can be initiated by males or females to either sex. In fact, this is one of the more common ways people touch (about 10% of all touches). Men receive these touches less often than women, but the main limitation on their use is that the body parts contacted should be justified by the task to be performed.

There was one especially intriguing finding in my research on the reference-to-appearance, incidental, and instrumental touches: They are very seldom used by people with their romantic intimates or spouses. (Intimates do use the attention-getting touch with one another; it's often a means of exercising subtle control with a distracted partner.) Although the absence of helping touches in these relationships may be a sign of the death of chivalry, it also points to what motivates many of these touches: Romantic intimates can readily get the touches they need with one another, whereas task activities provide opportunities for touch between people in other types of relationships.

"Accidental" Touches

Obviously, some touches are unintentional. These accidental contacts are generally "brushes" and light bumps that occur when people are passing one another in a tight place, sitting down next to someone, or getting up to leave. Because we know immediately when we are in physical contact with another person (the skin sends a split-second message to the brain), one characteristic of these touches is that they are *very* brief. Also, since people are *supposed* to "mean something" when they touch, at least one person almost always says "excuse me" or "sorry" when strangers brush. (Translation: "I didn't really mean to communicate with you.") When people know one another, the apology for an accidental touch is a nice gesture, but does not necessarily have to be offered.

One of the most intriguing results of my research involves accidental touches. In studying the diaries of peoples' touch behavior, I found many people who reported giving or receiving very few intentional touches, yet who had an inordinate number of accidental touches. I called them "bumpers." The existence of this pattern of touch behavior illustrates an important principle of tactile communication: People need touch. It may be that we all have a minimum "quota" of touches, and, one way or the other, we are going to get them.

Accidental touches, because they are so impersonal, are probably not the most desirable way of establishing warmer relationships. Yet, the beauty of the other kinds of "undercover" touches is that they *are* ambiguous to some extent. These touches are not fainthearted, but rather considerate, in that people express a wish for contact while acknowledging that they do not yet have a touching relationship which allows for warmer tactile involvement. These are the starting points for contact.

WHEN SPECIAL PERMISSION IS GIVEN

In certain situations, the usual rules about the touches which can be used in a given relationship are temporarily altered. These circumstances may provide a means of opening the door to greater warmth in touching at a later time.

"Greeting-with-Affection" and "Departure-with-Affection" Touches

These touches involve hugs, kisses, caresses, or a combination of such intimate touches. They are appropriate mainly in close relationships or relationships moving toward closeness. As with ritualistic touches, saying hello or good-bye provides a special reason for touching, but the difference is that (a) people are saying hello when they have not seen each other for a time, or (b) they are saying good-bye when they will not see each other again for some time.

Greeting and Departure "Rounds"

A special occasion for touching occurs when a group has gathered for the arrival or departure of one or more people. On such occasions, an informal rule specifies that if one person meeting or seeing someone off is touched, everyone should be touched. Even a person who is just "along for the ride" is likely to be touched. In my studies, I found that even a friend of the family who was not close to the arriving or departing person would sometimes be hugged.

There is a complex etiquette for this event. The nature of the touch with each person may differ, so that separate "touch statements" will be made with each person: mother may be hugged and kissed; father may just be hugged; brother may receive a side hug around the waist; and a distant relative may get a touch on the arm. There is usually even an order defining "who gets touched when" in this pleasant ritual. The first touches in a greeting and the last touches in a departure are reserved for the closest relationships; in a family, it is usually the mother who receives these touches.

Greeting and departure rounds give permission for touches that might not otherwise occur. Most of the rare cases in which men hug one another are during these kinds of events.

Emotional Occasions

People are especially open to warm touches when they have just expressed a strong feeling, or when others *know* that a person is affected emotionally. One such occasion is when a person has achieved something special. Anyone who watched the news on the day Pete Rose surpassed Ty Cobb's record for the most career base hits could not help but be moved. As soon as Rose reached first base, his teammates rushed to hug him. Tears of joy streamed down the faces of many of these "macho" ballplayers, as well as those of people who witnessed the event in the stadium.

An event need not be this dramatic to justify a touch, however. One of the rare occasions when hugging is appropriate in business organizations occurs when a person has received a long-deserved promotion. Just as in the baseball stadium, the members of the "team" may hug the person one by one in congratulations.

Similarly, but in very different circumstances, a person who has just experienced a great loss, such as the death of a loved one, will often receive hugs of condolence and support from family and friends. Ordinarily, it is only persons who are already close who offer warm touches of comfort. Yet, in unusual circumstances, anyone who is available may provide the needed touch. A policewoman described the difficulty of telling a woman that her husband had just been killed in an accident. "I stood at the door after breaking the news as gently as I could," she said, "and I saw that the woman was staggering and losing her balance. I took her in my arms and held her, standing there, for several minutes."

The timing of these types of touches is important. One woman described an occasion when she attended the funeral of a family member and received one hug after another from distant relatives whom she hardly knew. "I felt as though I had been crawled over," she said. After the initial impact of an emotion has passed, such touches may not be appreciated.

Touches from People with "Reward Power"

Finally, there is one other situation in which permission for an unexpected touch is given—when the potential recipient of the touch has especially positive feelings toward the other person. I mentioned earlier that we are more likely to react favorably to a touch of unanticipated warmth if the other person is seen as attractive. We are likely to have a similar response if the other person is someone we particularly like or respect (Burgoon & Walther, 1990). Such people have "reward power" for us; we see the touch as a compliment, not as a pushy gesture. I do not include here touches from persons we see as having power over us whom we do not especially respect or like, although we may tolerate such contacts reluctantly. Knowing whether we have this kind of "reward power" for someone else is not always easy to determine, of course. Yet, there are some clues which will help us to decide whether our touch will be welcomed, and that is the subject of the next section.

"TOUCH INVITATIONS": KNOWING WHEN ANOTHER PERSON WANTS TO BE TOUCHED

One of the best places to observe touch communication is on TV soap operas. This may be a surprising suggestion because the story lines are often exaggerated. But the actors must nevertheless improvise their parts to some degree, and intuitive actions such as touching are likely to be authentic.

While doing a close study of touching on episodes of the *Dallas* series, one of my students, Kathleen Campbell, noticed that most touches are preceded by some sort of subtle nonverbal behavior that indicates that a touch is wanted or expected. She calls these behaviors "touch invitations." They are the signals that tell whether a touch will be accepted.

Mutual Touches

The most familiar example of touch invitations are mutual touches in which both people reach out in advance of making contact. Like movements in a dance, these acts require split-second coordination between people. Most hugs, for example, are mutual. The two people first raise their arms slightly from their sides with the palms of their hands facing upwards while they move toward one another and then they encircle one another with their arms. If the two people always hug on certain occasions, their movements may be simultaneous.

If there is some uncertainty about whether a hug will occur, one person may begin the first movement tentatively, giving the other person an opportunity to follow the movement and complete the hug. If the second person were to hesitate, the initiator would probably stop reaching out.

The simple handshake is another example of a mutual touch. Rarely does one person reach out and seize the hand of another. Rather, as soon as one person begins to extend a hand, the other reciprocates, and the handclasp occurs. In contrast to a hug, handshake invitations are very seldom tentative because it is expected that the other person will reciprocate.

The handshake, as one person has put it, is the "distant cousin" of the mutual kiss. Both involve a rather clear touch invitation. The "kisser" is committed as soon as he or she presents the face and puckered lips (or a cheek); the other person had better respond!

Intention-displaying Movements

Sometimes when people are more cautious about initiating a hug, they display their intentions unconsciously. For example, at the end of a dinner party recently, I witnessed a departing conversation of two guests. As they were saying good-bye, the woman swayed slightly in the man's direction, as if to hug, and when the man offered his hand, she corrected herself, moved back slightly, and then shook hands. The man may not have anticipated or desired a hug, but the opportunity for a warmer contact was clearly signaled. Generally, when a person moves or leans toward another during a hello or good-bye without reaching out, it signals a wish for a hug.

Positioning for Touch

Another way that a desire to be touched can be projected to others is through physical positioning during conversation. Often, when a person would like to be touched, he or she will sit or stand slightly closer than usual, within the range where the other person could easily touch. Usually, this occurs between a man and a woman, and often it is the woman who moves closer, allowing the man to initiate the touch. If the other person moves back, however, the moment is lost. Assuming that it is the middle of a conversation, rather than at the beginning or end, a hug would not ordinarily be appropriate at these times, but a brief touch which emphasizes a point being discussed would be.

Self-touching

Finally, people may touch their own bodies during a conversation on the exact spot and in the manner in which they would *like* to be touched by another person. Nervous self-touching, such as scratching or pinching, is *not* included here. (In fact, research suggests that these acts sometimes reflect hostility or guilt, although, obviously, they may simply show discomfort or the need to scratch an itch!) Yet, when people stroke or caress themselves in the presence of others, it often suggests an unconscious desire for sensuous contact. I have watched couples having dinner in a restaurant when the woman would run her fingers lightly over her lips or neck as the man talked. (The message, loosely translated: "Touch me, you fool!")

Another version of this invitation is the self-comforting touch. Frequently, people who are feeling tired or physically uncomfortable will rub their own neck or shoulder. A sensitive person might reach out and touch the person on the spot they have been rubbing, or even offer a neck massage, if it will not detract from the ongoing conversation.

GUIDELINES FOR GETTING STARTED

Recent research suggests that most people want more touch than they get. My research shows that people who touch get touched. Satisfying touch communication, like all communication, is most likely to occur when other people know what you want. One way to let others know what you want is by skillfully initiating touches with them. This is true whether you want to develop a warmer relationship with a new friend, a spouse, or a family member. Since women are more likely to return touches than men (Jones, 1986), initiating touches with women is particularly successful. Yet, it will work with men, too—just give it a little time.

Here are some guidelines for getting started:

1. *Nothing ventured, nothing gained.* The best way to find out if another person is receptive to your touch is to try it and watch their reaction. If they respond with friendly behavior, you are on the right track. However, you may get an occasional neutral or negative reaction. My research shows that this happens about 15% of the time (Jones & Yarbrough, 1984), but even less often than this when the toucher communicates positive intentions and the touch is appropriate to the relationship. Be prepared for a pleasant surprise: Most people like to be touched.

2. *Start with "safe" touches.* A light touch to another person's hand as part of the act of giving them an object is acceptable to almost everyone and has surprisingly positive effects. The same is true of a brief attention-getting touch, unless the other person is deeply engrossed in some activity. Touches that provide phys-

ical assistance are always welcome when help is really needed
(catching a person who has lost his or her balance, offering a
hand to a person climbing out of a boat), but are often equally
appreciated when they simply make the task easier (helping
someone with a coat). Also, if you've already established a
friendly relationship with an acquaintance, a compliment about
jewelry or clothing, accompanied by a light touch to the object,
will also be appropriate.

3. *Use greetings and departures as touch opportunities.* Touch a
person you like, but who is not yet a close friend, on the arm or
shoulder when saying hello or good-bye. Closer relationships
may call for a hug, especially with a member of the opposite
sex and when arriving or leaving in a group. The general principle is: the longer the absence or expected absence, the more
expected the touch and the warmer it can be.

4. *Pick the right moment.* The timing of a touch is always important. Sometimes the timing is obvious because it is determined
by the situation. In a greeting, for example, the touch comes just
as we say "Hello." In a departure, the touch occurs when we
say "Good-bye" and just *before* a last parting statement such as
"Take care, see you soon" or "Have a good trip; I'll call you." At
other times, however, the touch requires a more sensitive reading of another's feelings or actions. We often feel that we are
acting on impulse when we touch, but part of our impulse is
probably a reading of the right moment. For example, we may
notice people moving slightly toward us, sitting at a closer-than-
usual distance, or touching themselves in a way that suggests
they would like to be touched. These are some of the moments
when a touch can be especially meaningful.

4

Bonding:
How to Create and
Sustain Closeness
through Touch

Television dramas are sometimes able to capture the essence of an important idea in an emotionally evocative image. In the series *Highway to Heaven*, which ran for a number of years on NBC, the hero was an angel, Jonathan (played by Michael Landon), who carried out assignments from "Above," usually for the purpose of improving human relations. On one episode of this program, shown on the day before Thanksgiving in 1987, there was a particular scene that I will never forget.

Jonathan and his partner, Mark, are assigned as teachers in a women's prison. When they first arrive, it is visiting day, and they witness a heartbreaking scene. The children and their mothers are not allowed to touch; they look at one another through a plate of glass and talk on a telephone. One mother says to her 4-year-old son, "Give me a kiss," and they press their lips toward one another, against the glass. A 1-year-old tries to reach her mother and presses her nose against the glass surface.

Later, Jonathan tries to persuade the warden to establish a day-care center in the prison for the young children and to allow contact between mothers and the older children on visiting days. The warden is adamantly opposed to the idea until Jonathan performs a divine intervention. He gives the warden a dream in the form of a nightmare in which the warden awakes in the middle of the night hearing his 4-year-old daughter calling for help. He runs to her room, where he finds the daughter sitting up in bed, crying. She says, "Daddy, I had a bad dream. I'm scared." When he moves toward her, he is blocked by an invisible shield. The next day, the warden reverses his policy and, as a first gesture, allows the mothers and their children to be united on Thanksgiving.

On one level, this is simply a story that creates empathy for women prisoners and their families. On another level, however, it is about a broader aspect of the human condition. The plate of glass is self-imposed for many parents, who act as their own wardens on the advice of well-meaning relatives or friends who cite the warning they were taught, "Don't spoil the child."

The principle that we censure our own touch impulses also applies beyond parent and child to relationships between parents and teenagers, husband and wife, and close friends. The reasons for the restrictions vary according to the type of relationship, ranging from concerns about sexual connotations to a simple fear of being rejected. The solution is to sort out the realistic and useful restrictions from the imagined and unnecessary ones and to know how to bond appropriately with touch.

In Chapter 1, I mentioned that the concept of bonding, sometimes called "attachment" in scientific writings, has received a lot of popular attention. Most people think of it as a tie of strong affection that is developed between mother and baby by means of touch occurring immediately after the birth. Some people believe it is irreversible and must happen at this time or else the chance is lost permanently. Marshall Klaus and John Kennell (1982), the authors of *Parent-Infant Bonding*, object to this literal use of the term, which they say is based on a misinterpretation of the research findings. They call it the "epoxy" view of bonding, the idea that love works like a fast-acting glue. In contrast, they define bonding as the process that leads to "a unique relationship [of affection] between two people that is specific [to the pair] and enduring through time" (Klaus & Kennell, 1982, p. 2). This broad definition is more accurate and useful than the popularized notions of bonding. It suggests that we may develop closeness with a number of people throughout our lives, that the bonding process may be gradual rather than happening all at once, and that, while long-lasting, these relationships are not always permanent.

Klaus and Kennell list "fondling, kissing, cuddling, and prolonged gaze" (p. 2) as bonding behaviors. The list is suggestive but not complete in terms of touch behaviors. We might also add to the list other behaviors such as verbal expressions of loving or liking, listening and giving rapt attention, and acts of sacrifice or caring. However, it is important that the recipient of these gestures see them as expressions of love or affection if bonding is actually to occur.

One man described to me a conversation that took place in his 30s between himself and his father, a man the son described as being "distant" and "not much of a toucher." After some discussion of past problems in their relationship, the son said, "I wasn't really sure you loved me." The father replied angrily, "I don't understand you. I went to work every day at a job I hated to bring home the bread to you and your mother." From the father's point of view, this was an act of love, but the message he intended was not received. As the primary ingredient in everyone's first experience of being loved, intimate touches continue to be important in bonding with others, and it is difficult to accept a relationship as loving if it does not include touch.

THE TOUCHES THAT BOND

The fact that bonds are not necessarily permanent suggests that they require maintenance. This means that when people live together or see one another often, touching and other forms of affectionate display must be continuous if the level of closeness is to be sustained. Obviously, however, strong bonds can survive periods of separation. Klaus and Kennell (1982) give the example that "a call for help even after 40 years will bring a mother to her child and evoke attachment behaviors equal in strength to the first year of life" (p. 2). Yet, there are limitations on how long people can stay apart and still feel close—it depends on the relationship. One estimate is that romantic relationships can only survive separation for about one year, even with occasional visits during that period of time. It is significant that when people with a close relationship have been away from one another, even for a day or part of a day, their first mutual act will often be a touch. It is not so much the sheer quantity of touch that makes a difference, however, but the quality and the use of certain kinds of touch that keep people together. Let's look at some of these kinds of touch.

The Expected Touches: Greetings and Departures

The role of touch in carrying out the theme of continual "going apart and coming together," which characterizes all close relationships, is most apparent in the case of two touch meanings, "greeting-with-affection" and "departure-with-affection." These are what I call hybrid touches—each combines two somewhat different meanings. One meaning is ritualistic; it says, "I acknowledge your presence and we can begin communicating" or "this is the end of our interaction." The other meaning is more personal: "I like you" or "I love you."

Most of these hybrid touches involve hugs or kisses or both, but less intimate contacts such as placing both hands on the other's shoulders, squeezing both hands, caressing the face, head, or neck, or patting on the lower back can also convey the meaning of affection. These touches can occur several times in the same day for people who are especially close, but the guiding principle is that the touches become more affectionate the longer it has been since the last meeting or the longer it will be until the next one.

In my research, I found that hugs and kisses were especially common during good-byes. One reason for this is that the departure touch is the last act and doesn't have to be followed by anything else. Almost everyone has had the experience of an opening hug lasting longer than expected, making you wonder what was intended. There is no such uncertainty in a good-bye. When people do not expect to see one another for a while, the last touch has particular significance because it allows them to reassure one another that the warmth will continue in their next meeting. This explains why hugs at airports just before departing flights are so often prolonged.

A particularly significant feature of these touches is that they are ambiguous to some extent. Especially when they come before or after a separation of some length, it may be unclear whether the affection is spontaneous or a response to the expected ritual. Often, the loving expression of a hug at these times is sincere, but the individual who performs it may not be able to show this affection on other occasions, so the impact is diminished, and the true feelings are not perceived accurately.

I do not mean to be cynical about affectionate greeting and departure touches. They are essential and expected in close relationships. Yet by themselves, without other forms of affectionate touching, they do not achieve the potential for bonding that most people want.

Simple But Special Touches

In a sense, almost any touch, unless it is unpleasant in some way, can serve the purpose of establishing or maintaining a connection between people. Sometimes a touch which would ordinarily carry only a mildly positive message—for example, assisting a person with clothing or grooming, the "instrumental" touch meaning—can be bonding if it's done in a particularly loving way. As part of her dissertation study, Elizabeth Anderson collected descriptions of "significant touches" from people's lives. Hugs and cuddling were the most commonly recalled kinds of touches, but some simple touches were also vividly remembered. Here is an example:

I was five, and my mother had washed my hair and was combing it out. She was being rough and swearing. My father said, "Don't do that, you're hurting her," and he took the comb and gently combed my hair. I nearly fell asleep. . . . In that moment, I understood the difference between brutality and tenderness. (Anderson, 1987, p. 67)

The Touch Meanings That Mean the Most

Although simple touches can be meaningful, there are four other kinds of touches that are more fundamental to bonding. The meanings conveyed are appreciation, support, togetherness, and affection. These messages are especially important because they are direct and clear in their positive meanings. They are gifts in the sense that they are not obligated by the circumstances, unlike greeting and departure touches, and they can be used on a daily basis to bring people closer.

The appreciation touch.

In this touch, the person expresses thanks for something the other person has done, usually also saying it in words. To be maximally effective, the touch should come at the first opportunity after the favor has been performed. Sometimes words are not necessary; a peck on the cheek by your spouse as you voluntarily start doing the dishes, for example, is clear in itself. If thanks are verbalized, the touch should come before or exactly with the words, not afterwards—which would be awkward and seem like an afterthought. (Try it out both ways for yourself to see the difference.) Generally, only an unexpected or especially well-performed favor would receive the appreciation touch, so that it is genuine and not forced.

This is usually not a highly intense or emotional touch. In fact, it is sometimes used by people in relationships that are not close (for example, a boss with an employee). Also, the touch is ordinarily brief, and nonvulnerable body parts (elbow or shoulder) are about as likely to be contacted as more intimate regions (as in a kiss or a squeeze around the waist). Yet, this is the most underestimated and underused touch in close relationships. The touch of appreciation affectionately acknowledges a freely given, unobliging favor, and giving gifts and having them recognized is crucial to bonding.

The support touch.

This touch, which nurtures, reassures, or promises protection, is more obvious as a bonding behavior than the appreciation touch. However, there are some surprising features about how this meaning is communicated. You might think the touch itself would have to be highly intimate to convey the message—perhaps holding a person close, reminiscent of cuddling a baby—but most support touches involve a limited contact of the hand, occasionally with an encircling arm, directed to only one or two body parts. The reason for this caution is that people are careful about invading the space of a distressed adult because a hug might imply, "You really aren't capable of handling this." With a crying child, however, cuddling and holding is almost always fitting.

It's the situation in which the touch occurs that is the most important in clarifying its meaning. Either the toucher knows from prior knowledge about the situation or something happens or is said that indicates that the other person needs comforting at this time. It could be a physical danger (walking out into deep water), an injury ("Did you get burned?"), or an illness, but more often it's a psychological need. For example, the toucher says "Cheer up honey," and the touch translates, "It's going to be O.K." Usually consoling words are spoken, but this is often unnecessary because the situation makes the touch clear.

The only other main feature about the way support is communicated is that the touch is almost always initiated by the person who offers comfort. Apparently, asking for support with a touch is considered "clutching." Again, children are the exception; they may just climb into a person's arms when they need comforting. Like the appreciation touch, the support touch can sometimes be offered by people who are not close.

The togetherness touch.

This is the touch that says "We're doing this together," "I'm enjoying being with you," or "We're a couple." The distinguishing feature of togetherness touches is that they last longer than any other touch except a sexual embrace, usually for at least several minutes. These touches can be rather casual, although they usually involve contact of vulnerable body parts, not just the arms or shoulders. Examples include a couple walking with their arms around one another's waists or holding hands, two people maintaining knee contact while they sit in an audience, or people involved in a conversation at a distance close enough to permit repeated brushes.

Words are not necessary to clarify the togetherness meaning. When the pair is positioned side by side, there may be no talk at all, just the continuous touch. When they do talk, they may be positioned side by side or at an angle toward one another, but they very seldom talk about the relationship or the act of being together. (They do not have to say "I'm feeling close to you"—the touch says it for them.)

The togetherness touch is obviously highly intimate because it makes a clear statement about the closeness of the relationship. People who are "just friends" or acquaintances rarely use it. Also, although it is used among children who are friends and in close adult-child relationships, among adults it is mainly used in opposite-sex relationships because of the potential romantic connotations.

The affection touch.

This touch is referred to as just plain "affection" or "pure affection" (although the other bonding touches are also affectionate or caring) because it is more unconditional as an expression of positive feelings. Its distinctive feature is that it is not tied to a specific kind of situation, unlike appreciation (which acknowledges a favor), support (which is a response to distress), or togetherness (which comes when an activity is shared). It is also "pure" in the sense that it is not connected with a greeting or departure ritual. The meaning is just "I like you" or "I love you," and the touch's simplicity makes it more intimate than any other touch of closeness.

Like the togetherness touch, which is a close second for intimacy, this touch occurs exclusively in close relationships, often involves vulnerable body parts (those other than arms or shoulders), and is consequently rarely used between males. However, the involvement created by the affection touch does not come mainly from its exclusiveness or the touch itself, but from its spontaneity.

The idea of hugging as a form of intimacy is popular now. There is a "National Hug Week," and bumper stickers include sayings such as "Have you hugged someone today?", "Did you hug your child this morning?", and "Hugs, Not Drugs." However, as positive as hugging is and as good as it feels, it is not the only way of expressing affection. In my research, I was surprised to discover that hugs, kisses, or a combination of both occurred in only about 25% of pure affection touches. Although words of endearment sometimes accompany an affection touch, they are even rarer and not essential to the meaning. A caress, pat, squeeze, or even a simple spot touch without words, perhaps as one person passes the other in the room or just as one is sitting nearby a loved one, can also speak volumes about the relationship. In the closest of bonds, especially lovers or parent-child relationships, the spontaneous use of the most intense form of affection—a hug and kiss when saying "I love you"—is both appropriate and powerful. It complements and enriches the other forms of the touch of affection.

Combined meanings.

Because the meanings of touch are affected by nuances of the situational context and what is said, it is sometimes possible to communicate more than one of the bonding meanings at the same time. This is another way of making the positive message especially strong. For example, a couple may be sitting together and maintaining contact with the sides of their bodies (togetherness) when one reaches over and gives the other a squeeze and a kiss (affection). These kinds of hybrid touches often occur at special locations. I recently attended the graduation of a Ph.D advisee and good friend who was receiving his doctorate. At the end of the ceremony, he gave me a hug and said, "Thanks for everything." Because a hug was not required by this situation, I interpreted it not just as a touch of appreciation, but also as affection for our relationship.

Touch Sequences: When One Touch Is Not Enough

There is another way of strengthening the impact of bonding touches: Repeat the same touch meaning until the purpose is accomplished. There are several situations in which this is needed and several ways of doing multiple touches.

Repeated support.

It may take a series of touches to properly comfort someone. For example, consider tucking a sick person into bed. You cannot convey the meaning by just pulling the covers up to the chin of the ill friend or spouse and then withdrawing your hands. Some other touches, like fluffing the pillow, caressing the person's hair, and patting the chest are also needed. Or, take the example provided by a mother who reported walking her 5-year-old son to his first day at kindergarten. He was anxious about the new experience of going to school, which he voiced in several ways, saying "I don't want to go to the school," "I don't know any of the other kids," "Maybe the teacher won't like me," and so forth. With each expression of concern, the mother provided reassuring words, such as "I think you'll really like it," "It won't take you long to make friends," and "I know your teacher is looking forward to meeting you." She accompanied each statement with a pat on the head, a caress to the shoulder, or a gentle rub on the back. Often, support touches need repeating until the other person is comforted.

Touch sequences at greetings and departures.

One of the ways of getting around the ritualistic limitations of hellos and good-byes is to perform the affectionate touches more than once. In the "two-hugger," for example, one person may be seeing another off at the airport at the end of a visit. After talking about the pleasure of being together, they may hug, talk about when they can get together again, hug again, and say good-bye. The message is, "This is not just a ritual—the affection is real."

Multiple affection.

Often at the beginning of a period of time that people will spend together or toward the close of a visit, after the initial greeting or before the final leave taking, multiple affection touches will be used to reconfirm the importance of the relationship. These touches may go in one direction, especially in the early part of a visit when the host or hostess is most likely to initiate touch as a way of reassuring the other person that their stay is welcomed. It can also go back and forth with an exchange of touches, especially toward the close of the visit when the visitor is expressing enjoyment about the time together. The touches in both situations say, "I just want to touch you again."

Reinstated togetherness.

One other occasion for multiple touches is when people are sharing time together, but are also involved in their own separate activities. For example, a couple may be sitting together at the library, each reading a different book. For a while, they have their ankles entwined with one another. Later, one gets up and leaves, returns to reestablish the touch, pulls away again while concentrating, and so forth. Each contact is a reminder—"I'm still enjoying being with you."

The basic "vocabulary" of affectionate touches is much the same, regardless of the kind of close relationship. How and when these messages are used, however, differs with whether the bond involves a close friendship, a romantic partnership, or one of a number of types of relationships within a family.

TOUCHING IN CLOSE FRIENDSHIPS

It is fairly easy to go from being strangers to acquaintances with a handshake. Acquaintances can become friends with a little more effort, and going from "just friends" to close friends requires yet a bigger leap. In Chapter 3, I talked about some of the transition touches that can be used to develop greater involvement. Once a friendship enters the closest phase, however, still more intimate touching is expected and needed, and it's important to know the possibilities and the boundaries. Let's start with the most problematic situation, the man-to-man bond.

Male Friends

A number of factors have been suggested to explain why men are not very intimate with one another. Summarizing the research, therapist Robert Lewis (1978) lists several of these, including the motivation to be competitive with other men, fear of homosexuality or appearing to be homosexual (homophobia), the belief that men should control their emotions, and the lack of affectionate male role models. As Lewis points out, men describe themselves as having more same-sex friends than do women, but when it comes to dealing with important personal concerns, they usually seek out a women friend for help, not another man.

Men generally deal with the issue of how to touch one another by expressing friendliness in limited ways, falling short of the more affectionate touch meanings. The most common touch, even among close friends, is a handshake greeting, although occasionally a longer-than-usual grip or one hand on a shoulder is used to add extra friendliness to the gesture. Even a brief touch to the shoulder or arm happens mainly in departures, although this same limited degree of contact can be and sometimes is used for the warmer touches of appreciation and support.

Competitiveness among men, despite its drawbacks for the development of intimacy, does provide some opportunities for greater physical involvement. Playful touches, as found in mock wresting, which are much more common among men than women, do permit contact with body parts other than hands, arms, shoulder, or upper back (the "nonvulnerable" areas). When the competition is directed toward other men in team sports, the rules of everyday interaction are temporarily suspended; hugs and even butt slapping become permissible among team members. This principle carries over to another unique situation—when men have their pictures taken together as part of another kind of "team" (political running mates, members of a fraternal organization, etc.). Posing with their arms around one another is the one situation in which the togetherness touch can be used by men; after the shutters click, however, watch the arms fall.

I think male friends could use the bonding touches (except togetherness touches) more than they usually do, especially greeting or departure hugs. However, the *first* such touch is inevitably the most difficult, and it usually requires some instigating event in a special situation that provides support for affectionate contact between two men. Often, it is an "experiential" or "personal growth" group that presents such an opportunity. In particular, the comparatively recent phenomenon of "men's groups" is a promising way such breakthroughs can be achieved. These take various forms: men's therapy groups, led by a psychotherapist or counsellor; men's consciousness-raising groups, sometimes led by a male "guru" such as Robert Bly or Sam Keen (see Bly, 1992; Keen, 1991); and less formal men's support groups. Hugging among males in such situations may emerge as a group ritual when departing at the end of meetings, or it may come about as a natural consequence of an emotional self-revelation by a group member. Often, men discover their deep-seated needs for receiving affection from other men as a result of such experiences. Here is an example from a therapy group:

> A 25-year-old group member, who was doubting his self-worth aside from what he could do for others, was directed to go around the group and communicate nonverbally with each member. As he moved to each man, he was individually embraced and verbally reinforced for his worth as a person. After completing the round, he spontaneously returned to one of the men who had given him an especially full and powerful hug. Burying his head in this man's chest, and weeping uncontrollably, he cried out, "Dad, why did you have to go. You were the only one to love me for just being me." The emotion that was released through the embrace aided this individual in grieving the death of his father and allowed him to have a new understanding of his self-doubting tendencies. (Rabinowitz, 1991, p. 575)

Most of the men whom I still hug in greetings and departures are the ones with whom I have participated in such groups. As men learn to express their feelings more openly, in part as a result of such experiences, eventually they may be able to instigate more affectionate touching with other men without needing the support of membership in a group in which special permission for touch is given.

Female Friends

Affectionate touching with the same sex seems to be less of a problem for women than men. The one period of time when this is least true is young adulthood, at about ages 18-25, when romantic relationships are the major focus. In my research with college students, I found that women were no more likely to touch other women than men were to touch men, although they did touch somewhat more affectionately. As they grow older, women can relax with one another more. Although they are still likely to engage in more touches with men, especially romantic partners, they will use the full range of bonding touches in moderation, including some hugging.

The one partial exception is the togetherness touch. It is strictly taboo in public. Two of my female students actually conducted an experiment in which they walked arm in arm on the street and in stores. They received lots of frowns and head-shaking reactions. However, heterosexual women do use this touch in private or when they are relatively isolated from others, but on a selective basis. Esther Davidowitz describes this incident:

> Clara and her good friend Lauren hadn't seen each other for a few years—ever since Lauren had to move to another city. When they

were finally united on a planned vacation, they immediately began to talk about Clara's new job; about Lauren's husband and children. They went on talking for the next few days. "And yet," says Lauren, "I felt miles apart—like there was a gulf between us." Then one day, finally, while the two friends were walking along the beach, Clara linked arms with Lauren. "It was exactly what I desperately needed," says Lauren. "After we touched, I didn't feel cut off any more. I felt connected." (Davidowitz, 1986, p. 126)

Opposite-sex Friends

There is more license for affectionate touching in opposite-sex than same-sex relationships in this culture. Yet, touching in nonromantic, nonsexual friendships between men and women can be tricky. The togetherness touch, for example, may be more comfortable for the pair in public than it would be in private, where it might suggest the possibility that a sexual advance will follow. Also, other people in close relationships with a friend can cause one to be cautious about initiating affectionate touches. For example, one woman told me that after her divorce, "I felt funny hugging the husbands in couples I had been close to, even though I had always hugged them before." Hugging can even be a problem in friendships in which neither person is involved in a romantic relationship. One solution is what I call the "cool down" sequence. It happens most often during greetings. For example, the man may be waiting at a table in a restaurant. He stands up when his friend arrives, they hug, and she kisses him on the cheek. When they sit down, they may maintain a less affectionate touch, perhaps her hand resting on his shoulder for a while—a version of the togetherness touch. It allows them to sustain the warmth without the intimacy of a longer embrace.

Another issue that may arise in close male-female relationships, romantic or not, concerns who seems to be in charge. If one person initiates touch more, he or she may seem to have more power. This may be a problem especially for men, who may be more sensitive about the fact that it is not a sexual partnership. Because men generally initiate more sexual touches in romantic relationships, when a women friend initiates more touches, it may irritate a psychological wound for the man. However, the woman may also have concerns about whether the relationship is equal. In my studies, I observed one creative solution to this problem which was especially common in male-female relationships in which each person considered the other to be a "best friend." It involved the use of multiple affection touches where the contact went back and forth, a sort of "ping pong" pattern which underlined the essential equality of the relationship.

TOUCHING IN ROMANTIC AND MARITAL RELATIONSHIPS

In these relationships, touch is particularly significant as an indicator of how things are going. One study showed that when people were shown videotapes of supposedly engaged couples, the pairs who were touching were rated as liking one another more (Kleinke & Meeker, 1974). Although this study reveals stereotypic beliefs about the behaviors of couples, which are not always reliable, this is one case in which stereotypes are accurate, as shown by another study by Ernst Beier and Daniel Sternberg (1977). They videotaped conversations of married couples. Some couples were high and others were low in marital discord. The couples with the least conflict had more eye contact, sat closer together, and touched one another more than the less satisfied couples. The lack of touching and the other kinds of nonverbal involvement in the couples with more conflict reflects the fact that they were having problems. Yet, it seems likely that the lack of certain behaviors also contributed to the difficulties. The high-discord couples actually talked a lot, but this apparently did not help to ease their difficulties. It is also significant that the husbands and wives in these marriages had more self-touching than individuals in the other relationships, a signal that suggests they would have liked more contact with their spouses. Touching and other forms of closeness messages are necessary to reassure marital partners that the relationship is solid and caring at its base, allowing effective conflict resolution at other times.

Not all couples are the same in terms of how much touch each partner would like. Generally, it is the wife in a married couple who has a greater desire for nonsexual touching (or perhaps she is just more aware of her need for touch than the husband). Of course, not all wives are the same in terms of how much touch they would like, but it is significant whether their needs for touch are being met. One study showed that marital satisfaction for wives was related to how well the touch behavior of their husbands matched their expectations (Gallehugh, 1982), although no such correlation was found for husbands. The importance of this finding is emphasized in another study in which husbands received a training program in marital communication and touch (Kuykendall, 1981). A follow-up questionnaire given several weeks later showed that the marital satisfaction of both the husbands and wives was enhanced by the training. It seems likely that the husbands who took the training met their wives' expectations better and thus raised their level of satisfaction; as for the husbands, their satisfaction may have increased because their wives were more satisfied, or perhaps they discovered that when their own needs for touch were met, they also felt more satisfied. The message for husbands seems clear: Learn how to touch your wife.

The Times Not to Touch

Despite the relational advantages of touch, there are certain occasions when physical contact by couples is highly inappropriate. The most obvious of these times is during a verbal conflict, when the initiation of virtually any touch will be seen, at best, as an attempt to avoid the issue, or, at worst, as a one-up move designed to get the other person to give in. That is, it comes off as a controlling rather than an affectionate touch, regardless of the intent.

The one possible exception to the principle that conflict and touch do not mix may be the togetherness touch. I know of one couple who sometimes work out disagreements on highly emotional topics while holding hands. It works because it's a *mutual* touch; in this situation, it says, "Even in conflict, we're in this together and we care about one another."

The other particular situation in which touch may be inappropriate is when one partner is expressing sadness or hurt, not about something outside the relationship, but rather about the actions of the partner. It might seem as though this would be the time for a support touch, but unless the distressed person specifically asks for reassurance, a touch may serve to cut off exploration of the feelings, and it may be interpreted as a one-up effort to save the person from experiencing the emotion. Rather, the person may need an opportunity to express their feelings in words and to hear the other's response. Admittedly, this is a more ambiguous situation than the one in which an argument is going on, and the appropriate response may depend on the relationship. When in doubt, simply ask, "May I hold you?"

Unexpected Pleasures: Times When Touch is Especially Appreciated

All four of the bonding touches and their variations can and should be used in a relatively uninhibited way in romantic partnerships more than any other relationship, except that of a parent and a young child. In addition, there are certain circumstances when a particular touch will have more than the usual positive impact and be especially memorable. One of my students, James Dykema (1986), conducted a study in which he asked romantic partners to recall and describe in writing a time when a touch from the other partner was unexpected, but very much appreciated. Several types of special situations emerged from the analysis.

Affection "out of the blue."

This is actually a version of the "pure" affection touch discussed earlier. The distinguishing feature of this event is that the partners were not talking or directly communicating with one another before the touch occurred. One male respondent wrote, "I was shaving and my intimate came in unexpectedly and hugged me from behind." A female wrote, "I was almost asleep, my partner came to bed very late, we briefly held hands in a very caring manner." In some cases, the couple was involved in an activity together, but not focusing on one another at the time. For example, a female said, "We were snorkeling, which we had never done together. He reached for my hand and we swam together for a while holding hands." What is important about the out-of-the-blue touches are that they show an awareness and caring for the partner, even at a time when something else is the focus of attention.

The status giver.

The incidents in this category involved a touch in the presence of others that showed that the partner was especially valued. For example, a male reported, "It was at the end of a party with a group of people who were in an exercise class together, and I was reclining on a lawn couch, casually talking to two male friends. The woman from the group I had been dating came over and slid down next to me with her arm around me. What an ego-boost!" The touch is especially meaningful when the others present are important to the person receiving the touch. One woman wrote, "We were talking to some old friends of his and he just hugged my waist." In another incident, a woman was embraced around her shoulders by her intimate as he was introducing her to his parents. The power of the status giver is that the action is intended for two audiences—the partner and the others present. It can be translated, "I care for this person and I want you to know it."

Special consideration or effort.

In this case, some quality of the touch is unique to the relationship, showing that the toucher is exerting extra thought or effort in meeting the partner's needs. For example, in one incident, the couple had just arrived home from a long and tiring trip, and both felt exhausted. When the couple had gone to bed, the woman complained of back pain, and the man massaged her until she fell asleep. The woman commented, "I really appreciated it because I knew he wanted to go to sleep too." In another case, a husband and wife were lying on separate sofas watching the news on television when he noticed she was saddened by the story reported. He turned to her and said, "I love you." After a moment, she went to his sofa and cuddled with him. He wrote, "It came after a moment of feeling especially close, and even though we were both comfortable where we were, she went of her way to show her love." The touch can also be a small gesture. One male respondent wrote, "I was lying face down on the floor, my intimate was giving me a back massage. Her face was rather close to my head, which was turned to one side. She called out loudly to a housemate, but before doing so, she covered my upturned ear with her hand."

The special support of reuniting.

Some incidents that occurred were simply unexpected support touches given when a partner was frustrated or saddened by an event outside the relationship itself. However, the more unusual and powerful touches were acts of forgiveness or reassurance after an argument. These touches ordinarily came after a period of time had passed and angry feelings had dissipated. One male respondent wrote, "She put her neck and chin against my neck after we had a distancing confrontation and she had pulled away." Interestingly, people seldom touch when they apologize because this converts what might seem like an affectionate touch into a compliance touch. (Translation: "I want you to say it's O.K.") It's the partner who receives the apology who can best offer a touch as a sign of acceptance.

TOUCHING IN THE FAMILY

Touching between parents and children and among siblings is obviously critical to their bonding and communication. In addition, touching in the family can affect the personality of the child and is probably the most important single factor influencing touching in later life. However, different amounts and types of contact are appropriate, depending on the age and phase of development of the child. I focus mainly on the perspective of the parents because their roles are so important, although most of what I say applies to grandparents and other close caretakers as well.

Touching Infants (Birth-14 Months)

It is almost impossible to cuddle, caress, and kiss infants too much. Tactilely defensive children are the only exceptions. On the basis of cross-cultural evidence and insights from studies of other animals, authorities such as Ashley Montagu (1971) and Mary Ainsworth (Ainsworth & Bell, 1969) suggest that breast feeding is also important. How long this should go on is more controversial and may depend on the personal philosophy of the parents, as well as practical considerations such as the working schedule and comfort of the mother. Some authorities suggest that eventual weaning is a significant lesson for the child and that dependency must be gradually withdrawn (Winnicott, 1984, 1987). My own point of view is that the child should be allowed to wean him- or herself, if at all possible. Continuing to nurse the child until he or she is ready to stop by a certain age, although inconvenient at times, will result in a happier child.

The central principle in all forms of affectionate touching with the infant is to provide reassurance that the world is a safe and a loving place and that he or she is worthy of being cared for. In line with this principle, there are several important specific guidelines.

Touching should be in response to the needs of the child.

At first, the infant should be held and touched a lot, well beyond simple caretaking (changing and dressing), regardless of whether there seems to be an immediate need or not. Learning to read the child's signals is especially important. Initially, sounds of distress or crying may seem undifferentiated, but soon the mother is able to tell the differences between pain, discomfort, hunger, and the desire to be picked up.

Before long, the baby will begin to communicate the desire for touch more clearly, perhaps beginning with moving toward the mother's breast for nursing and later reaching out or holding on when a hug is wanted. The impression the child gets is not only that needs will be met, but also that he or she brings about the wanted contact. In fact, one expert suggests that the mother can position herself so that the breast is available at a time when feeding would take place, so that the baby "discovers" it (Winnicott, 1987). The other side of the coin to this kind of responsiveness on the part of the mother (or other caretakers) is knowing when the child does not want touch and respecting the signals. However, it is essential to distinguish between simple distress cries, which may continue for a while after the child is held, and actions of rejection by the child, such as pulling away.

It is especially important to respond consistently and promptly to crying.

Bell and Ainsworth (1972) found in their research that the amount of time it took the mother to come when the child cried was an excellent predictor of how long the child would continue to cry. Furthermore, at a later age, the babies whose mothers came consistently and quickly during the first three months were less likely to cry and more likely to be consoled by holding when they did cry. The cry of anger or distress when a child is removed from a dangerous place or an unsafe object is taken away, which generally occurs after 6 months, may be an exception to the principle that cuddling is appropriate as a response to distress. The child can be given a replacement object or toy.

Constant contact is not essential.

Ashley Montagu (1971, pp. 220-288) noted that in many cultures of the world, infants are strapped to the mother's back or front (child front-packs or backpacks are equivalents in this country). This allows the mother to be responsive to the child's physical condition, anticipating needs almost before they occur. Authorities on American childrearing have argued that this is not essential to healthy upbringing, and there may be some distinct disadvantages to what one writer has called "sticky plaster mothering" (Nash, 1978). One disadvantage is that the child does not learn to signal when contact is desired, so constant holding or carrying children in packs may encourage passivity. The other disadvantage is that carrying the child for long periods of time is tiring and may be contrary to the nature of many American parents. In addition, although using a backpack may actually be convenient and calm the child at times, if overused after crawling has begun, it will stifle the exploration that is essential to early learning. Nevertheless, a great deal of holding of the infant is desirable, especially during the first 6-8 months. Furthermore, evidence from cultures in which constant holding at this age is a common practice suggests that these children grow up to be highly cooperative and content members of the society, a subject I discuss in more detail in Chapter 12.

The baby needs both affectionate and playful touching.

Research by Michael Lamb (1977) shows that after 6 months of age, infants tend to respond more favorably to the father's than the mother's touch, probably because fathers engage in more physical play (bouncing, swinging, etc.) than do mothers, who perform more caretaking touches (changing diapers, etc.). These particular roles of the father and mother may change in this culture as fathers assume more responsibility for caretaking, but the important point is that infants need both tactile affection and tactile play, one soothing and the other stimulating.

Touching Young Children (14 Months-4 Years)

Infancy is obviously a time for frequent touching by parents. However, I was surprised by the results of a study by Vidal Clay (1966), who observed mothers with their children at beaches and other public settings. He found that the walking children were touched more often and for longer periods of time than the infants. It makes sense that young children who are more mobile can more easily initiate and sustain interactions with the mother. In addition, fathers also tend to become more involved with children at this age than during infancy and therefore to touch them more.

The greater amount of two-way communication between parents and children beyond the age of infancy also means more controlling touches are used. Another of my students, Kim Freize, conducted a study (1988) in which she videotaped parents with their young children at the zoo. Although some touches of pure affection or togetherness were used, mainly by mothers, the most common were attention-getting touches ("Look at this") and compliance touches ("It's time to move on now"). Interestingly, some mothers patted or caressed their child briefly just before guiding them away to the next exhibit (affection, then compliance), whereas fathers tended to use plain compliance touches.

It is important that there be ample bonding contacts to counterbalance the parents' control during this high-touch period of the child's life. These touches may include a rewarding hug or pat for a job well done (appreciation), sitting with the child on the parent's lap or with an encircling arm while watching television or reading a book (togetherness), holding an injured or frightened child (support), or just squeezing or caressing spontaneously (affection).

Regular routines of touching can provide opportunities for intimacy as well as the sense of stability which children need at this age. My son Christopher, 10 years old at this writing, has always had trouble going to sleep. Every since he was 3, I have massaged his back just after his story or during a talk at bedtime. It usually works; he goes to sleep. Another important routine at this age is a departure hug when parents leave for the day or in the evening. This reassures the child of the parent's return when he or she is being left with a baby-sitter or at preschool.

Touching with Older Children (Ages 5-10)

Research by Kathleen Mosby (1978) suggests that the amount of intimate touching with parents may decline during this phase of development, even though touching with same-sex friends may increase. The child is away at school during the day and beginning to establish some independence from parents. As my son Christopher explained to me when he entered the first grade, parents do not walk "graders" to the door of the school.

How touching is done and who provides it may be significant at this age, however. Sandra Weiss (1975, 1978) studied the relationship between the child's body image—a rather good indicator of self-esteem—and parental touching with 8-10-year-olds. She found that the father's touching was especially important in the development of a healthy body image. As a partial explanation, Weiss suggests that the child at this age is starting to see him- or herself as an individual, separate from his or her parents. Since the ties with the mother are stronger, the father's touch may be less threatening and have more impact. In addition, however, the way the fathers touched was important. Those fathers who touched more dynamically—making some abrupt contacts, using longer touches, and even employing some moderately rough touches like grabbing and pulling—had sons and daughters with more positive body images. Weiss translates these vigorous contacts as saying, "I want you to know I am very much here, strongly involved with you, but that I am clearly me and you are clearly you" (1978, p. 21). Because these are the kinds of touches that are more characteristic of fathers, the implication is that fathers with a "hands off" attitude are not meeting their child's needs at this phase of life.

Weiss's findings do not suggest that more gentle forms of contact, which tend to be characteristic of the mother's touch, should be stopped altogether, or that mothers should not touch at this age. She did find that mothers who touched their girls less frequently and contacted their boys on fewer body parts had a somewhat more positive effect on body image than did other mothers. The implication is that high-touch mothers may need to curtail the intimacy of their touching at this time, especially with boys, allowing the father to take over to some extent. From the point of view of single parents, the implication is that more physical kinds of touching should partially replace other touches during this age period, regardless of the sex of the parent.

Touching with Adolescents (Ages 11-18)

This is the time in life when touching hits bottom, both in quality and quantity, again judging from the research of Kathleen Mosby (1978). Touching by parents especially declines sharply. Surprisingly, contact with same-sex peers actually increases in junior high school and levels off in high school, according to studies by Frank Willis and his associates (Willis & Reeves, 1976; Willis, Reeves, & Buchanan, 1976). However, Willis found this touching is seldom very intimate or affectionate, and a lot of it is rather aggressive, even between girls. Opposite-sex touching may or may not increase, depending on whether the teenager is part of the dating scene or has a steady romantic partner. In general, this is often a period of unfulfilled needs for touch, and not just needs for sexual touching.

Two explanations have been offered for the comparative lack of physical contact between parents and teenagers. One is that the "incest taboo" prevents touching, even between a parent and child of the same sex. While this may be a factor, it is not the most important reason because most touches do not have sexual connotations, assuming there is no history of sexually suggestive touching in the family. The other explanation, which pinpoints the overriding influence, is that the teenager has a need to establish him- or herself as an independent person. Affectionate touching may be a reminder of earlier periods of greater dependency, and controlling touches, especially the vigorous ones which were appropriate in the previous phase, are likely to be taken as a challenge.

Touching by parents does not have to stop altogether at this time, although it virtually does in some families. The solution is for the parents to make a transition, probably to less touching, but more importantly, to using different kinds of touches. This will be difficult for some parents who fondly remember earlier periods of greater affection. The guiding principle is to touch the teenager in ways that are appropriate to what he or she is becoming—an adult—rather than what he or she was—a child. Thus, the touches that will work best are the ones used in developing friendships. It makes sense if you consider that parents and teenagers are actually negotiating a new basis for their relationship.

I counseled one single-parent father who was frustrated by the fact that his 12-year-old son often rejected his touches. I asked him to keep a record of touches with his son for one week, writing them down as soon as he could without being noticed and making sure to record all rejected touches. It turned out that affectionate hugs and touches, in which the father was holding on while asking the son to do something, were the major offenders. As homework for the following week, I recommended that he touch the same way he would with a good male friend. Affectionate touches became a casual pat on the shoulder, and compliance touches were only spot contacts. The rejections disappeared.

Touches that suggest a one-up or power position for the parent are definitely inappropriate. These include pats to the head (which go out of acceptability somewhere at about age 8) and tickling, picking the other person up, or other kinds of overpowering physical play. Even touches that suggest a psychological advantage through a dominant physical position, such as touching from behind or above, may be risky. Hugs are likely to be rejected also—but for a different reason; they are overwhelmingly affectionate. Also, the togetherness touch is virtually taboo, especially with the opposite sex because among adults and adolescents, this is the only bonding touch in which sexual connotations are salient.

Touches of limited physical contact may be good for starters—a simple touch of greeting at the end of the day or a helping touch such as showing the teenager how to hold a golf club or perform a tennis stroke. Moderately affectionate expressions such as the "reference-to-appearance" touch can also be used. For example, I observed a father touch his sunbathing teenage daughter lightly on her arm and say, "Are you getting burned?" (Translation: "I care and I want to touch you.") The next step might be a warm pat of appreciation on the back or an unexpected caress of affection on the arm. In addition, when mutual confidence in the relationship has been built, a hug (with father) or a hug and kiss (with mother) might come at a greeting or departure, especially when a period of absence from one another is involved.

One other solution for teenagers and their parents is a group touch, which is less threatening than other kinds of contact, especially if it is established as a family tradition. It might be a "touching round" involving all of the family when one or more members are arriving or leaving for a trip. Some families have also adopted an in-group ritual in which any member can call a "touch alert," a request for touches that everyone can exchange and share. In fact, even on a one-to-one basis, asking for a touch tends to give special permission for both persons, since this places the asker in a vulnerable rather than a dominant position.

Touching Young Adult Children (Ages 19-25)

A seemingly miraculous event occurs when young people have moved out and then return for a visit: They find that they can hug their parents again and feel good about it. Mosby's (1978) research shows that this is a high-touch life period, exceeded among adults only by touching between somewhat older adults. Contacts with romantic partners are especially frequent at this age, but touching with parents is also on the rise. This is a time for rebonding between parents and their children.

Touching Among Siblings

Loving touches from older siblings can supplement the parents' touching, especially for infants and young children. At age 6, my son Christopher carried his 1-year-old brother, Trevor, around much of the time, also engaging him in mild physical play, to his younger brother's delight. At that time and continuing through until Trevor was 5 years old, Christopher has also been part of the bedtime ritual of kissing Trevor goodnight. Sibling rivalry can set in and result in aggressive touches, especially when young children are close in age, but unless touching with the older child drops off dramatically when the new one arrives, this can be largely avoided if the parents give strokes—both compliments and appreciation touches—for doing a good job in caring for the baby.

Young children learn to touch one another from the way they are touched by their parents and by watching touching between the parents. Hugs of comfort and affection are easy to imitate. Appreciation and togetherness touches are more adult, but can be used, especially the supportive togetherness of leading a young sibling by the hand. "Announcing-a-response" touches are common as a way of expressing excitement ("Guess what we're going to do?"), and playful touches tend to replace affection touches as the children grow older.

When the teenage years are reached, touching is likely to decline between siblings who are close in age, just as it does with parents. One of the surprising findings of my research was that togetherness touches— walking arm and arm or with arms around one another, maintaining contact while sitting together, and so on—virtually disappear from the time the children reach the teenage years and thereafter, either between parents and children or between siblings who are near one another in age. Maybe this is another case in which the incest taboo is in effect, or it may be that families are self-defined as a unit at this point, so the members don't need this particular kind of reassurance. Direct expressions of affection between siblings are also less common after puberty and until sometime in the early adult years. However, these touches may be partly replaced by subtler kinds of contacts which imply a secondary message of affection or togetherness. For example, one young woman who was home from college reported braiding her teenage sister's hair while talking to her about her date that night and how nice she would look. The older sister translated the touch to mean, "This reminds me of the old days."

CHOOSING TO BOND WITH TOUCH

Americans like to think of themselves and their close relationships as being unique—and to some degree they are. However, when it comes to touching, it is more the amount of contact than the way touches are used to communicate that is different from one friendship to another or from one family to another. The need to bond is biological and shared among all humans. The means of bonding with touches in different types of close relationships are largely determined by a cultural code. The degree to which touch is used to realize the potential for bonding is where individual choice making comes into play.

Sometimes it takes persistence to establish the bonding relationship you want. Greg Risberg, a professional public speaker who gives talks around the country on the importance of touching, jokes about his low-touch Swedish background (personal communication, 1988, January). "I'm surprised Swedes reproduce," he says. He also tells a story about how he got started touching his father at a late age. Risberg's father had been rushed to the hospital, and the doctors thought he was dying. "My father was lying on a stretcher, and I scooped him into my arms and told him I loved him." Later, after the father had recovered, Risberg was determined to continue the touching, even though he received resistance. After some months of effort, Risberg says, "One day I rushed out of his house and was almost to my car when I heard my father calling to me. I went back and saw him standing at the top of the stairs. He said: 'You forgot to do that, that,' gesturing with his hands" (as though he were hugging someone). "If there is hope for a 76-year-old Swede," says Risberg, "there is hope for everybody."

5

Touch and Sexuality: Attracting and Finding Pleasure with a Partner

JOHN, A MAN in his 20s, called in to a radio talk show when I was being interviewed. He related an incident that occurred in a disco when he was talking to another man. "A woman came up and touched me on the back," he said, "and I went into a back-up mode." He went on, "If I want to touch, I'll do the touching."

John's apparent reading of the situation was accurate in certain ways. He was right in assuming that a touch from a stranger of the opposite sex in this setting usually carries sexual connotations. His surprise was also to be expected since a touch would not ordinarily come this soon. Yet, his interpretation of the situation also illustrates certain common misconceptions. One is that it is the man who ordinarily initiates flirtatious communication in a disco, bar, party, or other such setting; in fact, the woman is usually the first to signal interest, although she is likely to do this with such subtle nonverbal behaviors that the man has the impression that he is the initiator. The other misconception is that the man will be the first to touch in these circumstances; in fact, it's usually the woman.

In general, there is no aspect of touching that is more misunderstood than its relationship to sexuality. For example, some men (and a few women) believe that virtually any touch between a man and a woman has sexual implications, when, in fact, very few touches between the opposite sexes are sexual.

To be sure, some touches are closely linked with sex, so much so that a definite and predictable sequence of touches can be specified. Desmond Morris (1971, pp. 74-79) described the following steps on the path to sexual intimacy, and only the first three do not involve touch: (a) eye to body, (b) eye to eye, (c) voice to voice (initiating conversation), (d) hand to hand, (e) arm to shoulder, (f) arm to waist, (g) mouth to mouth, (h) hand to head or face, (i) hand to body, (j) mouth to breast, (k) hand to genitals, (l) genitals to genitals.

Morris may have left out some possible steps in between some of these, but the progression is clear. The steps are well known, as is the risk that the other person may abruptly end the encounter if steps are skipped, especially between people who are not already sexual intimates. The sequence is familiar to most teenagers, although not necessarily from firsthand experience, and when a young man brags about "how far" he got, he is talking about these steps.

Much less well known is how to get from one step to another in a way that is satisfying to both people. Acquiring skill and sensitivity is not just a matter of how many times a person has been through the sequence. Experience is not always the best teacher, and practice does not necessarily make perfect.

THE VOCABULARY OF SEXUAL TOUCHES

Sometimes people are confused about whether or not a touch is "sexual." One person may be aroused by a touch, but this does not mean that the other person had sexual intentions. Also, a sexual touch is not always meant to arouse; it may be simply be an expression of potential sexual interest for the future or a reminder that a sexual relationship already exists. There are several variations on the sexual theme in touching. Let's start with the most obvious messages and work our way toward the subtler versions.

Explicitly Sexual Touches

These touches involve contact with one or more of the sexual body parts—the breast area for women and the abdominal, pelvic, upper thigh, and buttock areas for both sexes. Ordinarily, these touches occur when people are alone or when it is assumed that other people are not watching. These features in themselves do not make a touch sexual, however. For example, lovers, close friends, or family members may make contact with sexual body parts (but not with the hand) in a frontal hug of affection. One of two variations identify explicitly sexual touches.

Type #1: The casual sexual touch.

In this type, one person simply reaches over and touches the other on a sexual body part, usually the buttock. The touch occurs almost exclusively between people who are already sexual intimates; otherwise, it's an invitation to rejection. Words are not necessary, and if they are spoken by the initiator, they seldom have anything to do with sex or love. The touch simply conveys the message "I like your body" or "I can touch you here because we have a sexual relationship." It's the fact that the hand touches a sexual body part that distinguishes this touch from the casual touch of affection.

Type #2: The intense sexual touch.

In this type, both people mutually and continuously touch one another on a number of body parts, usually during a hug and usually with hands wandering over one another's bodies. Obviously, kissing or repeated kisses are also common. Such touches may cause arousal, especially if the hands caress sexual body parts or mouth-to-mouth kisses are prolonged, but they do not necessarily lead directly to further sexual intimacy. Like the casual sexual touch, they constitute a statement about the nature of the relationship. Even a hug with hand caresses to the other person's back or extensive kissing also conveys the sexual meaning. That is why if two close friends are hugging hello or good-bye, and one person begins caressing the other or extends a kiss beyond a second or two, the effect is shocking. It transforms an affectionate touch into a sexual one. Unlike the casual sexual touch, when words are spoken, they are either expressions of love or else they are statements of sexual intent—"You feel so good," "Let's take a shower and go to bed," and so forth.

Seduction Touches

There is no ambiguity about the sexual message in the explicit touches described above. However, as an opening move, they usually occur only in established sexual relationships. Seduction touches are slightly more ambiguous, although the intent to get the other person involved sexually is usually read accurately. The difference is that the touch is transparently masked as a nonsexual touch.

A common example would be one person asking a date to engage in what seems to be a togetherness touch: "I'm tired. Why don't you lie down here on the couch with me?" Or, it might involve the offer of a "helping touch": "It's been a long day for you. How about a massage?" If this strategy works, more explicitly sexual touches may follow.

Flirtation Touches

Picture this situation: You are sitting at a table in a restaurant with a group of people. Sitting next to you is an acquaintance. You become aware that he (or she) has positioned a knee so it touches yours, and the touch is not removed. If this were a close friend or a lover, this touch would express togetherness (translation: "I'm enjoying being here with you"). But in this case, it seems flirtatious (translation: "I'm physically attracted to you").

The flirtation touch is much more ambiguous than the seduction touch. Its ambiguity stems from a combination of two features: (a) on the surface, the touch seems just warm or friendly, but (b) it's too warm or friendly for this particular relationship. Unlike the seduction touch, this one very seldom involves extensive body contact, and it may occur either in private or when others are present. As with other kinds of flirtatious behaviors—a coy glance, for example, or a joking comment about wanting sexual involvement with someone—the cautiousness of the ambiguous message allows the initiator to test the water without jumping in. As the first move in a courtship, any kind of flirtation is risky. However, the flirtation touch is somewhat more risky—and more titillating—than other approaches.

The most common and clear-cut example is the subtle form of the togetherness touch, illustrated in the restaurant example above. With a mere acquaintance, holding hands at a party is a bolder move, as is a minimal affection touch—a caress to the arm or a squeeze to the shoulder. A hug or a kiss in a relationship other than with a good friend is nearly off the scale, but as part of a greeting, it could pass as acceptable flirtation.

With a person you have just met, subtler moves might be more appropriate. The reference to appearance touch—"Gee, that's a nice ring" or "I like your shirt"—will work. Even subtler is the "announcing-a-response touch"—a mock slap when the other person has made a funny or teasing remark, for example.

In fact, with a stranger in the context of a bar or party, almost any touch will do, since we do not ordinarily touch people we don't know. Certain touches may be too fainthearted even for this situation, however. An attention-getting touch for the purpose of a brief request, an incidental contact when handing an object to someone, or a brush that appears accidental could each occur with anyone, so the flirtatious message might not be conveyed. An interesting exception occurs when two strangers pass each other in a crowded place so that they have to turn sideways to get by. If the woman turns with the front of her body toward the man rather than the more common back turn and contact occurs, it could be a come-on.

Some flirtatious touches are clumsy or objectionable. Touches that are overly long for the intended purpose, such as an attention-getting touch in which the hand just stays there, are awkward. In a business or professional context, especially when initiated by a man to a woman, this kind of touch is insinuating and unattractive. If a boss or supervisor is suggesting the possibility of a raise or some other reward or favor, the overlong touch implies coercion. Finally, an explicitly sexual touch with a person who is not a sexual intimate is not flirtatious at all. It's a direct proposition, whether or not it is stated in so many words.

The "This One Is Mine" Touch

Certain touches between romantic partners are intended primarily for the benefit of others. In effect, they say, "Notice that we have an intimate relationship." The togetherness touch in the presence of others is one type. A couple entering a room of people while holding hands or with arms around one another are clearly conveying this message. If a woman is talking with a man and her partner walks up and puts his arm around her, he may also be implying to the other man, ". . . and don't interfere." If used too persistently, the togetherness touch will ward off not only prospective suitors, but practically anyone who might approach.

The "grooming" touch has a less extreme effect than the togetherness one, but it also carries the "this one is mine" connotation. This touch involves correcting the appearance of the other person in some way— straightening clothing, rearranging hair, removing debris, or cleaning up the other person in some way. Especially when others are present, grooming conveys a possessive message. Parents do it with children in public, and no one thinks much about it. Adults who are romantically involved often direct this touch to a partner as a subtle means of "staking a claim" to their "territory." On the other hand, if a boss or a supervisor does it with a subordinate, it becomes an insulting assertion of authority. Perhaps the one exception to the implication of ownership may be when the touch is used between people who have just met; it becomes a form of flirtation since it is obviously too early in the relationship to claim possession. (It's amazing how much lint gathers on men's clothing when they are talking to a woman in a bar.)

Generally, the grooming touch is acceptable between married or long-term romantic partners, but this depends on whether the person being touched is willing to accept the implication of belonging to the other person. Consider this "Dear Abby" letter I received from a woman who had read about my research in the newspaper:

> For the past twelve years I have been deeply involved in a relationship
> with a man who is 61 years old. Five months ago he decided that he was
> bored and restless with this relationship and wanted to be free of it. . . .
> We have continued to see each other about twice or three times a month
> since then and it has always been warm, pleasant and caring. . . . I sup-
> pose I should tell you that the other half of this relationship seemed just
> as satisfied as I was so it came as a huge shock to me when the following
> incident happened and I am still puzzling over it. We were at dinner and
> Bill [name changed] actually recoiled from my touch when I started to
> wipe away salad dressing the waiter had accidentally spilled on his belt
> and just very slightly below the belt. He actually moved bodily a good
> three inches away as though my touching was taboo. I have never
> encountered anything quite like the awkward moments which followed
> with neither of us saying a word, yet both being aware. Thereafter, I
> refrained from touching him at all, and he acted afraid of touching me.
> So please explain what this could have meant.

This woman's gesture was a grooming touch, and the fact that it involved an intimate body zone made the sexual implication doubly strong. In my letter of reply, I suggested that the man may have been embarrassed by an open statement of their relationship in public, especial-ly if he was considering withdrawing from the romantic involvement. Although the woman responded spontaneously and was apparently unaware of the meaning of the touch, the man's reaction demonstrates the significance of the grooming touch as an intimate gesture.

COURTSHIP AND FLIRTATION

How does a sexual relationship get started? The various shadings of mean-ing of sexual touches I have described in the previous section play a criti-cal role, but they occur in the context of other messages. Let's back up and look at the whole process.

"Courtship"—literally "paying court"—is an old-fashioned term that connotes caution, politeness, and a certain amount of formality. "Flirtation" is the more modern term and implies a more casual approach to sex. Courtship is a good word to keep in mind, however, since it sug-gests the need to go through a gradual sequence of communications.

Courtship and Quasi-Courtship

The distinction between courtship and quasi-courtship makes all the differ-ence in reading the first signals of sexual interest. Courtship suggests serious romantic or sexual interest, while quasi-courtship, which is more common, implies attraction, but without serious intent. Quasi-courtship is the kind of flirtation that can occur between the husband in one marriage and the wife in another when their spouses are right there. It happens in offices when no office romance is intended. Salespeople use it with clients to get their interest with no desire or intent to go further. Quasi-courtship can even occur in subtle forms between members of the same sex who are heterosexual.

It is important to read these two kinds of flirtation signals accurately. Even though they do not always involve touching behaviors, they are the opening messages that tell a person how to proceed with touching later (if at all). So, I will take a brief digression here before we return to the subject of touching in potentially romantic relationships.

What is confusing is that the two kinds of flirtation look a lot alike. Courtship involves behaviors designed to show attraction to another person. Quasi-courtship involves some of those same behaviors, but accompanied with qualifying messages that say, in effect, "Don't take my flirting seriously." What do each of these forms of communication look like in practice?

Courtship signals.

It all begins with "courtship readiness." Body tonus and alertness improves. The woman might cock her head to one side and look at the man with overly wide eyes. The man might stand erect with his chest slightly pushed out and feet spread slightly apart. Some self-preening will also occur. For example, the man may unconsciously adjust his tie or touch the front of his hair as if putting it in place. The woman may play with her hair at the side of the head with her palm out toward the man or stroke her neck lightly. If things progress far enough, the two people will go beyond "readiness" to "acts of invitation" (to the "dance" of courtship). The woman may stand with her hand on a hip, as if to emphasize the curve, or, if she is seated, she may cross her legs so the knee and some of the thigh show. He may place his thumbs in his belt so that the fingers point toward the pelvic area.

Quasi-courtship signals.

So far it looks pretty sexy. Yet, if it's quasi-courtship, the qualifiers will come soon, and they may have been there from the beginning. The main clue is that positioning of the body will not be very direct, at least not for long. In direct contrast, when the courtship is serious, the couple will progressively face each other more directly and maintain a lot of eye contact, effectively shutting out any possible intruders. In quasi-courtship, the man may let his eyes stray to watch another woman go by, and the woman might do the same for a passing male. Either person might lose eye contact to look around the office or at his or her romantic partner across the room, as if to say, "Notice where we are." If a woman is flirting with her eyes, but her hand is on her husband's elbow next to her, it is equivalent to saying, "Don't take my eyes too seriously, buster." In the absence of the partner, either person might alter the situation by talking about their spouses or children.

The immediate situation itself may be all the qualifier that is needed. Albert Scheflen (1965), the psychiatrist and nonverbal researcher who developed the concept of quasi-courtship, originally discovered it while watching films of family psychotherapy sessions. Here he saw flirtation behaviors between one of two male psychotherapists and a female in the group, the mother on some occasions and the oldest daughter on others. Obviously, this could not be real courtship because of the situation. It's similar to other circumstances in which flirtation happens between two people whose partners are present. What was going on?

After closer observation, Scheflen noted that the psychotherapists initiated flirting behaviors when one of the females in the group was losing interest in the discussion. For example, the therapist might turn and look toward her, adjust his clothing, and brush past his hair with his hand, and she would respond with similar behaviors toward him. After a while, the female would "decourt" by ceasing the display of courtship signals, turning toward the rest of the group, and paying closer attention to the conversation.

Wherever it occurs, quasi-courtship is a way of getting attention and creating involvement. It spices up conversation, but it's not a way of exploring sexual possibilities. It's also not the same as teasing, when one person courts without qualifiers, and then withdraws suddenly. Some people do not know the differences, so without necessarily having bad intentions, they nevertheless get themselves into embarrassing or awkward situations.

Love Between Strangers: The Courtship Sequence

Quasi-courtship usually occurs between people who know each other, often in situations that are not conducive to serious courtship—an office where others are present, a party where both people have come with someone else, and so forth. When a man and a woman who are strangers meet at a party or bar, unaccompanied by partners, the scene is set for courtship. That doesn't mean anything will happen, but the possibility is there.

Timothy Perper and his research assistants (Perper, 1981) spent many hours observing singles in bars. As a biologist, Perper was interested in mate selection. One of his more intriguing findings was that, contrary to popular myth, it was the women and not the men who were doing the choosing, at least initially. Perper also found that the courtship ritual involved a highly predictable sequence of events, a discovery that has been verified in research by other investigators (McCormick & Jones, 1989).

The preliminaries.

A certain number of courtship readiness signals may be broadcast before any approach occurs. These may include some clothing choices made in advance—a low-cut blouse for a woman, for example, and tight jeans for a man. Readiness may also include certain behaviors. For example, a man may stand with an erect posture, spread his feet apart somewhat, and cast his eyes about the room. A woman who is open to an approach may engage in even more readiness signals, for example, "lip licking, 'dancing' in the chair, and head tossing" (Moore & Butler, 1989, p. 209). It may be advisable not to overdo these signals, however. A man who acts too macho may scare off prospective partners. A woman who sends off too many sexy signals is likely to attract some suitors she will have to reject (Moore & Butler, 1989).

If the woman sees a man who interests her, she may make her move. She can just stand or sit next to him at the bar. Or, from a distance, she can glance at him several times. When she catches his eye, she may sustain the glance for several seconds and then look away. In the coy version of the glance, she looks down after making eye contact, and if she looks up again, the message cannot be missed (Moore, 1985). Despite the fact that the signals are fairly clear, they are subtle, and the man who decides to approach may think it was his idea in the first place.

There is one other preliminary. His approach must be acknowledged. It will usually happen before he says anything; she will simply look in his direction when he moves in. However, a man who approaches a woman without prior signals from her may be setting himself up for rejection. She may cut him dead with a quick glance and no smile or by looking straight ahead. Assuming all goes well, however, the first formal step in the courtship sequence can begin.

Stage One: Talk.

Conversation begins. "Mind if I sit down?" "I don't think I've seen you before. Do you live around here?" The opening line is a lot less important than most men believe. After all, she has already agreed to talk. Back-and-forth conversation allows both people to gather some information about one another, while preening and other courtship signals reassure them that the interest is continuing. The two people are likely to be positioned at a slight angle to one another at this point, looking away from time to time to think of something to say.

Stage Two: Turn.

At some point during the conversation, each person begins to turn toward the other—first with the head, then with the upper body, and finally, at stage two, the bodies of both people face one another directly. They may also move in toward one another. If they are seated, she may even place her feet between his, allowing greater closeness.

Stage Three: The touch that makes or breaks.

At any point in the sequence, if one person fails to play his or her part, the courtship is over for all practical purposes. If one talks and the other does not, it's over. If only one turns, it's over. As Perper points out, however, the touch is especially critical. First, it accelerates the intimacy of the communication. Second, it is easy to tell if the touch is rejected. Pulling away or failing to respond is a rejection. Failing to return the touch has the same effect.

The woman is usually the first to touch, but this icebreaker will usually be minimal in contact and quickly withdrawn—a touch to the man's hand, arm, or shoulder to communicate "Listen to this" or "That's a funny remark," for example. This is a time for flirtation touches, and almost any contact at this point carries a flirtatious message. Later touches may be more overt—a caress or even a hug or kiss—often in response to a comment by the other person, so as not to be overly intimate. Even so, these more intimate contacts may not begin until the next stage.

Stage Four: Synchronization.

Somewhere along the way, the pair begin to move together in synchrony. Actually, synchrony is characteristic to some degree of any involved conversation. For example, one may may nod his or her head in rhythm with a gesture by the other. At this stage in courtship, however, full-body synchrony begins. From time to time, the couple are likely to unconsciously imitate one another's postures, as though they were looking into a mirror. They may lean in together and then back at the same time. One person may reach for a glass, take a sip, and place the glass down, and the other will do the same actions simultaneously. It is as though the two people were dancing together or practicing the movements of sexual intimacy in abbreviated form.

Touching will continue during this stage and may accelerate in frequency and, to some degree, in intimacy (although explicitly sexual touches would be rare). Touching can even be part of synchronization; one person may match the touch of the other with a similar return touch, or both may engage in a mutual touch such as a quick announcing-a-response hug which punctuates a shared reaction to a comment.

Do they leave together and go to "your place or mine"? Maybe, but not necessarily. One person may suggest going to another bar or party.

The evening may end with him seeing her home and asking for a date. Or, when they are alone, they may make love. The last stage sets the stage for further involvement of some kind.

The stages overlap one another. The new activity of each stage is added on, but the earlier activity continues. Talk goes on throughout. The turn stays there once it has occurred. Touching continues into synchronization. The entire process may take 20 minutes or several hours, although Perper warns that it is more common that the sequence falters at some point, rather than going all the way to completion.

A study by Naomi McCormick and Andrew Jones (1989) suggests one additional qualification: The touching in the courtship sequences may change hands at some point. They found that although women do more touching early in the encounter, men do more touching later. Apparently, touching is the bottom line of how far the relationship goes, and women get it started but allow the man the final decision about further romantic intimacy.

To some degree, the courtship sequence reflects traditional sex roles. The women emerge as subtle influencers. The men appear to be more aggressive, at least in making the initial approach and perhaps toward the end of the stages. In the future, men and women may switch their roles more. Perhaps men will sometimes be the ones to stand at the bar waiting to be discovered or glancing at a distance to encourage the woman to approach. In the meantime, although much of the traditional sex roles are still found in courtship, it is nevertheless a far cry from the macho fantasy in which the man does all the choosing, makes all the moves, and finally wins over the reluctant female. There is a good deal of equality in the courtship sequence. Either party can end it at any time.

SEXUAL INTIMACY

Something similar to the courtship sequence occurs—or should—even between people who have known each other for some time. In dating relationships that are not yet sexually intimate, the preliminaries of picking each other out and agreeing to spend some time together are over. They may have gone all the way through the courtship sequence on their first meeting. Or, it may have happened more gradually over a series of meetings in a classroom or office, at parties, and so forth, perhaps going at least as far as the initial touching stage several times before one person asked the other out.

When the couple actually goes out together, they will need to repeat the courtship sequence to some degree. The stages might unfold gradually, or they might occur more rapidly than before. In either case, it's a way of reaffirming attraction. The need to repeat the courtship sequence applies even to long-term intimates or married couples, at least from time to time. The steps may be so minute that talk, turn, touch, and synchronization occur almost simultaneously, but failing to court at all is one of the traps of established romantic relationships.

Despite the relative equality of the courtship sequence, when it comes to deciding whether or how to have sex, both people may fall back into traditional sex roles. Let's consider how and why this happens before considering the alternative, emotionally fulfilling love making.

Sexuality as Role Playing (and How to Break Out of Roles)

Research shows it is not a myth that there has been a sexual revolution in progress since the 1960s. Early sexual experience and promiscuity have been on the rise (Zellman & Goodchilds, 1983, pp. 57-59), and even the recent threat of AIDS has not radically curtailed this trend. All this freedom may be difficult to handle emotionally, however, and people may seek security in staying with certain established cultural scripts for how men and women are supposed to behave sexually. This may be true not only when the couple is deciding whether to enter into a sexual relationship, but also well after.

The script for the couple's first sexual encounter.

Let's assume that a couple has arrived at his or her apartment at the end of the evening, and they are alone. The traditional roles specify that he be the pursuer, she the pursued. So, according to the script, he is supposed to try to get her to have sex, and she is supposed to try to avoid it, or else to give in passively.

According to research by LaPlante, McCormick, and Brannigan (1980), the script is well known. Both men and women identified 10 seductive strategies used mainly by men, and 10 avoidance strategies characteristically used by women. What is more, at least among the college students these authors studied, men and women report that they generally stick to the script in actual sexual encounters.

Some of the strategies involve talking the partner into sex or giving reasons for refusing. For example, one person might argue that the relationship has become close and it's the right time to have sexual intercourse. The other might say it's still too early in the relationship or that the person cannot get involved because another relationship has just ended and it's too soon.

Nonverbal strategies are more common for inducing the person to have sex, however. The approach might begin with one person turning the lights low and putting on some music. The next step could be seduction touches, followed by explicitly sexual touches, and finally intercourse. If both people are following the script, the man will be expected to initiate each move. The woman may respond favorably to the man's advances, or she may pull back from the touching and give reasons for not going further.

Let's suppose that she responds favorably, and perhaps the couple have intercourse. Later on, there is still another script which could be played out. One study suggests that as touches become increasingly intimate, women tend to see the relationship as becoming much more "committed" than do men (Johnson & Edwards, 1991). The result may be that the pursued becomes the pursuer and the pursuer the pursued. This scenario is dramatized in the movie *About Last Night* in which, following a "one night stand" after the couple meets in a singles bar, the woman seeks greater closeness and involvement, whereas the man becomes concerned that things are "moving too fast" and withdraws. Depending on the individuals and their needs for commitment, these roles could be reversed, but this is the more common script.

The script for sexually involved couples.

Assuming that the couple has passed the first and second hurdles (bringing relief that it's over, if not sexual fulfillment), they may become committed to a continuing intimate relationship. Now still another script may take over. The new script is different, but it resembles the initial one. The question of whether they will have sex has been decided. However, the couple may settle into a pattern in which the man largely determines when they have sexual intercourse. He may also determine how they make love, including the positions taken. Or, the man may literally be expected to be on top (McCormick & Jesser, 1983, pp. 83-84). Also, in following the script, the woman will set limitations. She may determine how often they will make love and how much experimentation will be allowed. Unfortunately, playing out this script can go on for the lifetime of a relationship.

Breaking out of roles.

Despite the fact that the role-playing scripts are often followed, there is evidence that many men and women are beginning to break out of traditional sex roles. A study at a southern university showed that men responded favorably to a request for a date or to a sexual proposition from a woman who came up to them and said, "I've been noticing you around campus. I find you very attractive" (Clark & Hatfield, 1981).

Similarly, there is evidence of changes in seduction behavior. Interviews reported by Timothy Perper show that women are more frequently taking an active role. For example, some statements made by women about how they would go about enticing a male include (Perper, 1981):

I'd try to snuggle up to him or lean against him because then he'd put his arm around me. If I wanted to be kissed, I'd make the first move and kiss him. I like to have control over any intimate situation. It makes me feel more receptive. (pp. 134-135)

If I wanted to influence this guy to kiss me, I would probably sit close to him as he talked to me and smile a lot so he realizes I am turned on and liked him a lot. If he started to kiss me I would maybe try to prolong a simple kiss into a french kiss with maybe a little body pressure putting my arm around his neck. (p. 135)

Invite [him] up to apartment, turn down lights, fake TV watching or put soft music on. . . . Kiss neck. Try to lay down on couch, floor. Kiss more intensely. If other person has arm around you casually move so that hand can touch your breast. Rub back or thigh. While laying down roll to a position for pelvic thrusts. (p. 133)

If these seem like examples of aggressive role reversal—the woman playing the man's part with exaggeration—try reading the descriptions again as though they were written by a man, with a few changes of words so that the genders are switched. For example: "I'd try to snuggle up to her or lean against her so she'd put her arm around me. . . ."

The changes I am talking about are not role reversal, but role flexibility, allowing either sex to be assertive in ways that were formerly reserved only for men. Traditionally, men have felt freer than women to be assertive about their sexual interests and desires, but more women are learning to express their needs as well.

There is also another kind of assertiveness—being able to refuse the opportunity for sex when the conditions are not right. Women are usually better at this than men because it fits with their traditional role. More men are discovering that living up to the playboy ideal is actually unassertive in this second sense. Sometimes this realization doesn't come until the man has been around the circle once—bachelor to married man to single again. For example, one divorced man said:

It took me three years to get it through my head that I didn't have to screw every woman I took out. I used to make an all-out try with every one of them—and let me tell you, if I didn't find the gal appealing, it could be a rough trip, and afterward I'd be furious with myself. But somehow I had to. I felt if I didn't come on like the superstud of all time, they'd think I was a fag, or hung up, or something. (Hunt, 1974, p. 251)

This man's language choices reveal the anger he feels about his own behavior and also suggest he has not quite given up on the male script. The next step might be for him to soften his approach and look for a satisfying relationship, not just a desirable object.

If you are single, you may be saying to yourself, "Where are these liberated men (or women)? I haven't run into them." The answer is that they are in hiding—inside their roles. Each time one person sticks with the familiarity and safety of the scripts, the more likely it is that the other person will do the same. But the converse is also true. The more one person is willing to risk stepping outside a traditional role, the more likely the other person will be to reciprocate.

Here are the guidelines for breaking out of roles while enhancing courtship skills and sexual experiences:

1. Become familiar with courtship behaviors and the courtship sequence. A good way to begin is to reread the section in this chapter on courtship and flirtation and then to observe others from a distance. A bar is a good place to start observing. Then, imitate the people whose approaches you admire. Even if you feel you are pretty good at courtship, observation will sharpen your insight. Putting it into practice will also increase your choices (more people to pick from) and your chances of finding the right partner.

2. Don't court with someone just for "practice." Unless you are both attracted to and potentially interested in a romantic relationship with someone, your heart will not be in it. Men sometimes feel obligated to flirt if a woman seems interested, and women are often fearful of bruising the male ego, but it's better to end it sooner than later. If you are attracted at first, but find your interest dwindling as you get to know the other person, the courtship sequence can be ended by failing to play your part in entering any stage. Also, it's useful to remember this in reading the other person's signals. If you are attracted to someone you know, but not interested romantically, quasi-courtship can be a nice way of expressing it; it's ego building but not risky for either party. If your quasi-courting intentions are often misperceived by others, your courting signals may not be qualified clearly. Finally, do not attempt to quasi-court with strangers in bars, since the situation itself tends to override any qualifiers, and you are therefore likely to be misunderstood.

3. Do touch; but do not be in a rush. In courtship, a touch at the right time is critical to the continuation of the relationship. For the first touch, it generally works out best if the woman initiates and the man reciprocates. However, this applies mainly to the

initial encounter between strangers, when the woman may need
to reassure herself that she can maintain some control over the
man's advances. After that, either person may initiate.

4. Don't get involved sexually if the conditions are not right.
   Conditions are anything you know from past experience to be
   necessary to you in order to have a satisfying sexual experience.
   Bernie Zilbergeld (1978), sex therapist and author of *Male
   Sexuality*, says that the most basic condition is never to try to
   have sex if you are unaroused or anxious. Other conditions will
   differ with the individual. Zilbergeld specifically recommends
   making a list of your conditions. Some you can take care of
   yourself; others may require communication with your partner.
   Personal conditions might include liking the other person,
   spending a certain amount of time together before having sex,
   making sure no interruption can occur, having a certain degree
   of foreplay, receiving a particular kind of physical stimulation,
   and so forth. Cultural scripts often get in the way of recognizing
   and communicating conditions. This is especially true for men
   who are following the script for what Zilbergeld calls "The
   Fantasy Model of Sex," a set of ideas that include the belief that
   a man should be able to make love at all times. Female scripts
   also cause problems for women, especially the belief that it is
   unfeminine to make requests in the act of love making.

5. Treat the sexual encounter, especially the first one, as an opportunity for exploration and communication. The role-playing
   scripts described earlier say that the man should initiate.
   However, whether or not the couple is familiar with one another's sexual responses, it makes more sense for both parties to
   feel free to initiate touches. Whoever is initiating at the time will
   need to read the reactions of their partner. Nonverbal messages
   may be all the information that is needed: Tensing the body or
   pulling away means "stop," "it's too soon for that touch," or
   "that's too rough;" relaxing of the body, groans of pleasure, or
   movement toward the initiator means "keep going;" reciprocat-
   ing with a similar touch means, "I really like that (and I want
   you to experience it too);" moving the initiator's hand with
   one's hand signals a request. The responses can be explicit and
   verbal, if they are not overly used: "That feels good;" "Wait a little (for that touch);" "Would you touch me here?;" "Tell me
   what would feel good to you."

With couples who are committed to a long-term sexual relationship, establishing equality and doing away with stereotyped sex-role

behavior is even more important. The equality I am talking about is a commitment to one another's sexual pleasure and gratification. This deserves a separate section.

Sexuality as Emotionally Fulfilling Sensuality

Let me begin with two assumptions: (a) The best sex occurs in long-term, loving relationships, not in one-night stands, and (b) sensual pleasuring involves putting certain basic principles about intimate touching into practice.

Sensuality and sexuality.

In order to make the principles work for you, it is important to recognize the relationship between sensuality and sexuality. Sensuality literally means pleasing the senses by stimulation. In art, it's primarily the visual sense; in music, hearing; in gourmet cooking, smell and taste. Although several senses are involved in sex, touch is primary. Sensual touching is the enjoyment of tactile experience in its own right—touching that is not necessarily sexual. Sensuality becomes sexuality when it is accompanied by the idea of consummation in orgasm, a thought which is most clearly communicated by genital contact.

The connection and the difference between sensuality and sexuality is confusing to many people, a confusion that may result in anxiousness about touching. Sexual experiences can be distinguished from simple sensuality in one of two ways: (a) It's the thought that counts. If a person is touching, and the idea that this could lead to orgasm occurs and persists, even in fantasy form, it becomes a sexual experience. The thought might be blocked, or it might never occur. That is why a mother can enjoy nursing her child, and having the child fondle her other breast, without it being at all sexual. Part of the reason why making love with a sexual partner can be so gratifying is that it is similar to the earliest experiences of being held and caressed by a parent, but it is the interpretation that differs. (b) Action also counts. People can have sexual thoughts, but be clear about having no sexual intention. They might be aroused by a hug from a friend and simultaneously decide, or just recognize, that they are not going to do anything about it. Momentarily, it's a sexual experience, but it's not sexual touching, and the experience is likely to return to simple sensuality.

Sensual touching does not have to lead to sex, but it's essential for satisfying sexual experiences.

Having sex for the wrong reasons.

"Wrong reasons" does not refer to ethical or moral issues. Rather, I am referring to the fact that many people decide to have sex for reasons that make it unlikely that their experience will be as satisfying as it could be (see DeAngelis, 1987, pp. 197-199). There are a variety of wrong reasons, ranging from complex to simple motivations. Some common ones for women are: (a) it seems so important to him; (b) he expects it; (c) to keep him from getting restless for other relationships; (d) to be held; (e) to have a baby; or (f) my diaphragm was in. Common ones for men include: (a) to prove I'm a man; (b) to prove I'm not getting old; (c) I've gone too far to stop now; (d) to have an orgasm; (e) to give her an orgasm; or (f) to encourage her to wear sexy nightgowns again in the future. Other reasons may be just as common for one gender as the other: (a) the kids were asleep; (b) to help me go to sleep; (c) it wasn't time to go to sleep yet; (d) we haven't done it for a while; and so forth. The list could go on.

The right reasons are simple, straightforward, and closely related to one another: (a) it feels good and I feel like it at this time; (b) it seems to feel good to my partner; and (c) it's a way of expressing loving feelings toward the other person. The first two reasons are essential to mutual satisfaction and require that the person stay in the here and now. When these are the only motivations, it can be described as "friendly" or "fun" sex. When the third motivation is also present, the potential for a satisfying experience is greatly enhanced for both persons.

Principles of sensual love making.

Understanding the importance of sensuality and having the right reasons makes it possible, as Alex Comfort (1972) expresses it in *The Joy of Sex*, to make sex a "gourmet feast." Just as there is an art to excellent cooking and even gourmet eating, preparation and attention to detail contribute to joyous sex.

The recommendations made below are not intended primarily for people with sexual problems. When a couple is experiencing sexual difficulties, sex therapy under the guidance of a competent counselor can be extremely helpful (see Brown & Field, 1988; Schnarch, 1991). However, there is a considerable overlap with sex therapy approaches, simply because the principles described here are relevant for any couple wanting to enhance their sexual relationship.

1. *Love making does not begin in the bedroom.* The bonding touches I discussed in Chapter 4 not only bring people closer together, but also create emotional security in the relationship. This, in turn, makes sex safer emotionally, since the partners will not depend entirely on sex to meet their needs for touch. Sexual touching can contribute to bonding, but only when there is a foundation of bonding touches and other intimate behaviors such as sharing feelings with one another and giving each other

attention. Because one thing can lead to another, and sensuality can unfold into sexuality, affectionate touching is also the best way of leading into foreplay.

2. *Arousal does not need to lead to immediate intercourse.* What happens if kissing and hugging, or even just affectionate caressing, brings about arousal, but it's not a good time for sexual intimacy? One person might be enjoying the affection but not be aroused, or both might be aroused, but only one develops an intention to make love. One person might be thinking about a job that has to be done, the fact that there isn't much time, and so forth. Occasionally, one person will decide to forget about the job for the time being, or both will decide to alter their schedules—a nicely spontaneous moment. Yet much of the time, the answer is "nothing happens," at least not right then.

Being aroused and letting it go can contribute to greater enjoyment the next time the couple has intercourse. To borrow a phrase from advertising, it "builds excitement." Too much tension without release is obviously undesirable, but a certain degree of anticipation can be healthy. I am not talking about teasing, when one person stimulates the other and then pulls away, since this is manipulative and has implications of one person controlling the other. Rather, I am referring to mutually acceptable stimulation without completion. My research shows that many couples practice not only highly affectionate, but also explicitly sexual touching at times when sexual intercourse does not follow. In fact, sex counselor Barbara DeAngelis (1987, p. 227) suggests institutionalizing this practice in a "twenty-second kiss" three times a day. After each kiss, the partners return to whatever else they were doing, but their thoughts frequently return to their partner during the day.

Twenty-second kisses or some other version of mild-arousal-without-completion touches are desirable for any couple, but they are especially useful for those who have what I call the "confused signals" problem. It is most common in relationships in which there is little touching unless the couple is alone and in which the affectionate touching which does happen is often followed by intercourse. Neither may be sure what a touch means, especially at bedtime or other times when sexual intimacy might occur. The woman may be afraid her touches will be misunderstood, so she is cautious about touching unless she wants to make love. The man may think when his embrace is accepted it means she is receptive to intercourse. The roles could be reversed in terms of these misunderstandings. The solutions? Touch affectionately more often, including when others are present. Learn to communicate more effectively when touching occurs in privacy, including saying, "I'd just like to be held tonight" or "I think I'd like to make love." Eventually, complete clarity will not be necessary and love making will regain some of its spontaneity.

3. *Time management for "spending time together" is essential to intimacy.* For busy couples, time for sensual involvement may present a problem, so planning is essential. Advance discussion about each person's schedule, having a baby-sitter, and unplugging the phone could all be part of the preparation. Does this spoil spontaneity in sex? Not necessarily so.

A couple I know uses the term "spending time together" to refer to planned periods when they will be alone, usually in bed. They might make love; or, instead, they might listen to music, read aloud to one another from a book on couple communication, or just hold one another. There are only two rules: to stress positive feelings toward one another, avoiding discussion of conflicts or scheduling problems, and to touch. In this situation, the time together is carefully planned and scheduled, yet, the open-endedness of their expectations means that sex can still feel spontaneous.

4. *Rediscovering sensuality is the key to sexual fulfillment.* Most adults have forgotten the pure pleasure of sensuality that they knew as children. That is why it makes sense for couples to practice touching together, each person relearning about his or her own responses as well as those of their partner. They could simply agree to experiment with caressing one another in new ways, but it helps to have a systematic approach in order to avoid falling back into old patterns—especially rushing on to intercourse. In the book *Touching for Pleasure*, authors Adele Kennedy and Susan Dean (1986) describe a series of exercises for exploring sensuality, each of which takes about an hour. In order to stress sensuality, the exercises begin with such touches as hand-to-hand caresses, proceeding very gradually to more intimate contacts. Most people know that satisfying sexual experiences take time, but it's another thing to be convinced of this through experience.

5. *Effectiveness of communication about the sexual experience is a matter of timing.* In everyday life, each different touch meaning is communicated in distinctive and generally understood ways. In sexual intimacy, however, individuals may differ widely in what is the right touch for them, as well as the circumstances in

which sexual touching will be pleasurable. Therefore, communication of one's needs to one's partner is essential. During the act of touching, much of this can be done nonverbally, but talk will also help to increase clarity.

Discussion of the conditions necessary for each person to have enjoyable sex is especially appropriate early in the relationship, sometimes before there is any intercourse at all. If intimate touching proceeds to the point of one person being aroused while the conditions are not right for the other, it will have to be discussed then, but the best time is usually a separate occasion when the partners have agreed to talk. Since this kind of communication is based initially on past experiences with other partners, both people should be open to the possibility that the conditions will change in this particular relationship.

During intimate touching, two kinds of talk can enhance the experience. One is a spontaneous expression of love or pleasure: "I love you," "You look so beautiful," "You feel so good," and so forth. These messages come primarily from the right side of the brain and are more like nonverbal than verbal communication. Assuming the words are positive in appreciation of the partner, these expressions serve as exclamation points in the flow of love making.

The other kind of in-the-moment talk consists of requests about the partner's touching and I-statements about one's own experience. The definition of a request is asking for something in a way that suggests no negative consequences if the request is not fulfilled: "Would you touch me here (or in this or that way)?" An I-statement tells about the individual's own experience and may imply a request: "I'm getting really excited (and feel like going to completion now)," "I'd like to slow down a little," and so forth. Both kinds of messages can have a very positive effect once the partners are accustomed to the practice of talking while making love. The kind of talk to avoid is the "you-statement," which often carries with it an evaluation of the other person: "You're going too fast," "You're too rough," and so forth. An additional precaution is not to overuse requests or to use a tone of voice that suggests a command (with negative consequences for noncompliance) rather than a request. This in effect is taking the role of what Barbara DeAngelis (1987, pp. 152-157) calls "the traffic cop." The effects on the sensual experience of the partner can be devastating.

Talk about the sexual experience after it's over can also be valuable. For couples who are not used to doing this, going through sensual awareness exercises like those suggested by Kennedy and Deal can establish a norm for this kind of communication and make it more comfortable for the partners. Again, the emphasis should be on requests and I-statements, not criticism. Also fitting would be expressions of love or appreciation for the partner, and, at times, talk could be omitted altogether.

6. *The biggest wave comes after smaller ones.* I have placed a lot of emphasis on the "preliminaries" to orgasm and for good reason. The surfer who can enjoy the little waves will enjoy the big one more when it comes, and the same is true for lovers.

In their pioneering research, Masters and Johnson (1966, pp. 3-8) identified four phases of the sexual response cycle (see Figure 1).

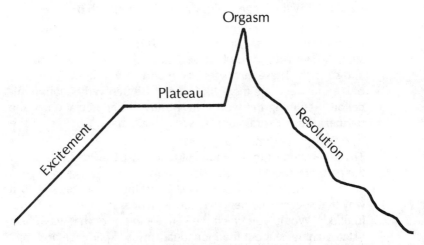

Figure 1. The Sexual Response Cycle.
Figures 1-1 and 1-2 adapted from p.5, W.M. Masters and V.E. Johnson, *Human Sexual Response*, 1966. Reprinted with permission of W.M. Masters.

In scientific terms, the excitement phase involves the gradual enlargement of the sex organs (breast, nipple, clitoris, penis, scrotum), a process that continues after intercourse begins. In the plateau period, the excitement levels off briefly at a high level, after which orgasm cannot be resisted. Resolution is the cool-down phase, emotionally and physically, in which the organs return toward normal size.

As important as it is, Masters and Johnson's research may have been hampered by the process of scientific observation. Their findings may also represent "normal" behavior, in the sense of being typical. A number of sex counselors and therapists have suggested an alternative model of the response cycle which, although it may not be the most common pattern, is nevertheless possible for couples who are practicing the kind of sensuous love making I have been describing here (see DeAngelis, 1987, pp. 188- 191; Kennedy & Dean, 1986, pp. 107-108). Diagrammatically, the alternative model could be pictured as a wavy line that progresses uphill until a peak at the point of orgasm, and then proceeds downhill in the resolution phase, again with a slightly wavy line of up-and-down feelings.

The alternative, "sensuous love-making" diagram of the cycle can be interpreted in two ways: (a) a series of rises in excitement, each followed by a brief "rest period" of delay while enlargement of the sex organs is retained, followed by orgasm; or (b) a similar pattern, but with the lower points representing some decrease in erection of the sex organs, "dutumescence," and the high points representing a regaining of erection, eventually climaxing in a peak of orgasm. Still another diagram could be constructed with the wavy, uphill line ending in a series of two or more peaks of orgasm, with brief declining slopes of excitement between each, before the final resolution. This multiple-orgasm conclusion, however, is rare, occurring for some women on occasion and among men even less commonly—and then usually only for young men (sex therapist Eva Margolis, personal communication, November, 1988). Potentially, all three of these kinds of cycles could occur in the same act of love making, although not necessarily on each occasion when the couple has intercourse.

If Masters and Johnson's curve represents average love making, the alternative versions describe exceptional love making. In a relationship of emotional security, in which there is a commitment to mutual sensual pleasuring and open communication, the exceptional pattern can become more common, even among people who do not consider themselves to be "sexually talented." A husband, who described himself as having had sexual problems earlier in his life, reported the following incident which stood out in his memory because it was the first time he had experienced the kind of love making described above:

We were spending time together in bed while the children were with a baby-sitter. We had decided to look at catalogues together to pick out Christmas toys for the kids. Since time was growing short, I had about given up on the possibility that we would make love.

I felt the need for play and suggested that we take a break and "just neck" a little. She said, "Move your mouth around some, like when you were a teenager." I was surprised at how erotic the kissing was and decided to get in some "petting" as well, at first just stroking her back and hips. I remembered reading somewhere about caressing the front of the body without touching the breasts or between the legs as being especially sensual, so I tried it. After a while, I couldn't resist touching elsewhere and she was fondling my penis, all as we continued kissing.

When I entered her, I had this sense of wanting the touching to go on for a long time. From time to time, when I was getting really excited, I stopped and just held her, kissing and telling her how much I loved her. Several times she moved against me and I could tell that she was having an orgasm each time. When I finally climaxed, I had an image of shooting through warm water with her, and then, to my amazement, I experienced another surge of excitement, a milder but exquisite second climax. After that, I kept holding and stroking her. I had never felt more relaxed and loving in my entire life.

Such experiences are unlikely to occur on every occasion, nor should they become a standard for performance, but when they do happen, they are one of the potential serendipitous bonuses for adventuring into the realm of sensuous love-making.

7. *Afterglow: Having time to be together at the end of a sexual experience is important.* Athletes need a cool-down period after exercise, and a meal is more enjoyable if it ends with dessert or an after-dinner drink. Similarly, a sexual experience requires a sense of completeness, although much more is involved. The nonverbal messages that follow intercourse are especially significant in defining the meaning of the experience. If one person gets up immediately to go back to work or rolls over and goes to sleep, it says, "Well, that's over—now back to business." The more the couple has practiced the principles of sensual pleasuring—acts of caring in themselves—the less likely this is to happen. They will not want come apart just yet.

Above all, this is a time for a return to bonding touches—holding one another for a while and caressing. The waves of excitement might come again after a period of rest, or they might not come until another time. Afterglow reestablishes a continuity of warmth and trust in the relationship. The act of love making comes full cycle and can begin again.

6

Touching in Fun and Sport: How to Play with Touch

T WO FIRST-GRADE boys stand looking at each other on a grassy area outside their school at the end of the day. One smiles and says, "I can throw you down." The other smiles back and says, "No you can't." The first boy runs over and throws the other down easily. They get up giggling. The second boy says, "I can throw you down." The other says, "Betcha can't," and then he does. There is more giggling.

One man approaches another who is sitting on a stool at a bar and grabs him around the neck while saying, "What do you think you're doing?" The other responds with a light punch, and they spar with one another for a moment. The one who had been sitting on the stool then pulls the other up to the bar and says, "Bartender, this man needs a drink."

A waitress in a restaurant comes up behind a male co-worker, puts her arms around his waist, says "Hi" with a laugh, and then tickles his ribs. He pulls away and tries to tickle her back.

These events have two things in common: (a) The touches resemble something different from what they actually are. In the first two incidents, the touches seem aggressive; in the third incident, affectionate or sexual. (b) The meaning of the touch is qualified and clarified by a "play

105

signal," a behavior that says, "Don't take this seriously"—an exaggerated statement, a smile, a laugh, a bizarre touch, or a combination of these messages. These two elements are the defining features of playful touches.

Why do people play with touch? One reason is simply that it's fun. Playful touches can relieve boredom or take some of the seriousness out of the competitiveness, sexuality, or intense involvement in a relationship. A playful touch can also allow a person a way to try out certain kinds of touching without risking the usual consequences. For example, children can use it as a way of practicing for the "real thing" (as in the "fight" sequence described above); adults can use it as a way of flirting before risking a direct statement of interest in another person. One other less obvious but important motivation for using playful touches is that they provide an outlet for touching which might not happen otherwise in a particular relationship.

THE VARIETIES OF PLAYFUL TOUCH

There are many creative ways to play with touch, but they all fall into two broad categories: playful affection and playful aggression. Some cases overlap, as playful affection can be tinged with aggressiveness to reduce the risk of being affectionate, and there is a good deal of affection in even highly aggressive play. The examples that follow are actual incidents from my research (Jones & Yarbrough, 1985, pp. 31, 40-41).

Playful Affection

These touches tend to occur primarily in close relationships or in relationships that are becoming closer, in which the basic positive feelings are clear. We do not kid about liking or loving someone if it's in doubt, although people sometimes joke as a way of hinting at stronger feelings of love or desire. The most lighthearted version of this touch involves simple affection combined with a play signal. For example, a mother greets her teenage son, saying "Hi sweetheart," while touching his nose with a cold soda can. A male says to his girlfriend, "How's about a kiss?", and a quick, mutual lip-pucker kiss follows. It's a kind of shorthand for saying, "I like (or love) you, but I'm not being intense about it right now."

A somewhat more intense and complex version involves a touch that would be sexual if it were not for a qualifying signal. I include it under playful affection because it is more a comment on the closeness of the relationship than an expression of sexual intent. Sometimes the context is part of the qualifier. For example, a woman has announced her intention to go home and finish a task and is leaving her boyfriend's apartment. He says, "Wait, I think I want to make passionate love to you," and bends her over for a Valentino-type kiss. She says, "Sure you do," pats him on the chest, kisses his forehead, and leaves. Her playful "that's a good boy" pat allows her to reject his equally playful sexual advance without rejecting him. Sometimes the sexual, playful affection touch is just ribald humor, so an exaggerated touch is the play signal. For example, one entry in a male's touch log in my study reads, "She bares one breast and I grab it." Role reversal and privately understood jokes can also be part of the kidding: A woman pinches her intimate on the buttock when passing by him, saying, "Hi, American cutey," a reference to their past discussions of her experience of being touched suggestively by male strangers while traveling in Italy.

- Warning: The playful affection touch with contact to sexual body parts occurs between people who already have an intimate relationship. Do not make the mistake of including these touches in your repertoire of early flirting behaviors.

The playful affection touch can also be a way of touching affectionately with a member of the same sex, while avoiding any homosexual implications. Here the touching will be cautious. For example:

- A male actor, who is playing the part of a gay male in a Shakespearian play, is dressed in a rather effeminate costume. Backstage, another actor says, "Oh, I like your outfit," and gives him a light punch to the arm.
- A male puts his arm around his close male friend and roommate who is finishing the dishes, in the presence of several other people in the kitchen, and says, "You would make a good wife." The onlookers, the joking statement, and the limited contact combine to make it clear that this is only play.

Sensitivity to the other person is obviously essential in playful affection touches with sexual implications. A person would not kid someone about being gay if he or she thought there were some truth to it and if the other person might become upset. Similarly, joking about sex with an intimate would be inappropriate if there were some problem in the sexual relationship.

Among men, affectionate play can move in the direction of aggression, as the above examples illustrate, so that the boundary between aggression and playful aggression becomes blurred. In fact, many playful affection touches between men involve mildly aggressive contacts that suggest cautiousness—a gentle shoulder bump or a light punch accompanying a joking comment.

Playful Aggression

Playful aggression requires less caution than playful affection, so it can be employed in a wide variety of relationships. Nevertheless, there are two versions, one safer and the other more risky.

The less involving type employs aggressive words combined with a play signal touch. For example:

- A waitress says to a customer, "Do you want the check?" The male customer says, "No, tear it up," and then touches her on the arm.
- A female says to another female, "It's about time you came to work," while delivering a light punch to her arm. (Translation: "I'm just kidding.")
- After a long visit, a male nudges his son-in-law with an elbow and says, "Maybe we'll stay a few more days."
- A female passes a male classmate who is sitting in the library looking off into space and says, "Get to work!" while lightly hitting his head with a newspaper.

In each case, these touches are minimal—a spot contact, a pat, a nudge, and so on.

The riskier type of playful aggression touch is likely to involve more body contact in a rougher way. It's an aggressive touch, usually accompanied by playful words, and it calls for a slightly closer relationship. The touches include "half-nelsons," "pulled" punches, grabbing, rough tickling, pushing, slapping, and so forth.

- A male says, "Let's wrestle," to another male and then grabs him.
- A husband says to his wife, "I'll have to pinch you to remind you," and then pinches her on the buttock.
- A female who is receiving a lesson from her male intimate on a handball court stands on his toes while saying, "Is this fair?"

It's all in good fun, but one caution should be kept in mind: It's essential to let the other person know right away that you are only playing. In other words, the play signal—usually a joking comment, but at least a smile or a laugh—must come before or simultaneously with the touch, not after it's begun. Otherwise, the touch may be perceived as truly aggressive, at least momentarily. The other person is already on guard and unable to join in the play by the time the late play signal clarifies the meaning of the touch.

Males and Females: Who Plays More With Touch?

My research suggests some rough approximations:

- Playful affection: 80.5% between males and females, primarily initiated by males; males with males, 19.2%; females with females, 0%.
- Playful aggression: 50% between males and females, again, primarily male-initiated; 38.5% between males; 10.5% between females.

Contrary to most other kinds of touching, men feel more comfortable with playful contact than do women. It's one of the few ways most men feel comfortable touching one another.

TOUCHING IN SPORTS: A WHOLE NEW BALL GAME FOR MEN

Picture this scene: The cameras are rolling. One man is standing on a small hill. Another man runs up to him, lifts him in the air, and they fall to the ground. It's not a fight, but a hug. Other men rush in from all sides and pile on, all holding and squeezing one another. Is it a Roman orgy scene? A movie about encounter groups in the 1960s? No, it's the New York Mets celebrating. They have just won the 1986 World Series.

The exact same scene can be be seen on television early in October in any year. In 1987, it was reenacted by the Minnesota Twins; in 1988, by the Los Angeles Dodgers, and so on.

If the playful touch gives men permission to touch, the play of sports takes it one giant step forward. The only play signal other than the referee's whistle in sports is the situation of being in a game on a ball field or other play arena. Perhaps all that tossing around and wrestling that fathers do with sons is a preparation for this activity.

Sports are an advanced form of playful aggression, but the emphasis is often on the aggression. Professional athletes, high-level amateurs, and many recreational players obviously take sports seriously, sometimes to extraordinary extremes. When players are heavily invested in winning at any cost, competitiveness can easily become aggression. Some coaches are noted for teaching their players to go for extra violent contacts as a means of intimidating opponents. These intimidation tactics sometimes erupt into fighting among the players and even violence among the spectators.

Is it play at all? It can be a toned-down version of warfare, but it does not have to be. I like the comment attributed to Willie Stargill, the baseball great who played for many years with the Pittsburgh Pirates. He was asked how he was able to go on for so long, playing at such a high level. "You listen to the umpire," he said. "When he says 'play ball,' you play. It's not fun if you aren't playing."

Let's take a closer look at the touching that goes on in specific sports. You can verify my observations on your own. Simply videotape sports events and replay them several times, noting the touches that occur just before or after a play.

Touching in Team Sports

Frequent touching on the field and on the sidelines supports winning in two ways: (a) it gets and keeps the players fired up; and (b) team members feel closer to one another. Many professional athletes I have talked to, especially football players, argue that a lot of continuous touching is essential to any championship team. Touching also meets strong individual needs. Tactile expressions of joy, encouragement, and comfort from teammates counteract the stimulating and often painful contact with opponents.

One generalization applies across sports: Touch promotes touch. The more contact is a part of the game, the more varied and constant the touching when a play is not going on.

Football.

This is a good place to start because football is the highest contact popular sport in the United States. As a result, nearly every variation on touch in team sports is illustrated in football. The padding worn by the players may encourage more and rougher touching among teammates because it reduces the intimacy of contact and also requires more impact to be felt, but the main factor affecting the degree of touching in football is the sport itself. Here are the main kinds of touches:

Individual congratulations. The proverbial pat on the back becomes a slap in football, a reward for individual performance. Slaps on the shoulder, upper back, helmet, or, for special emphasis, the butt, are typical expressions of appreciation for a good-but-not-exceptional play. It might be a clean tackle, a ground-gaining short run, or even a crucial block. The helmet slap also suggests playfulness, a variation on tousling the hair or patting the head of a little kid, as if to say "good boy." It's often given to placekickers ("Nice kick, little guy"). With an opposition player who has just missed a pass, the helmet slap is not a compliment, but a teasing gesture ("Ha! Missed it!").

A more spectacular or important individual play—a long completed pass, a great catch, a tackle that prevents a long run—may bring the handslap. Here, the player may actually request appreciation for his feat by extending one or both hands for a slap. A collaborative effort by two players, such as sacking the quarterback before he can get the ball off, calls for a mutual handslap: One player puts both hands down with palms up, the other player brings both hands down in a slap, and then they reverse hand positions ("We did it together!"); or, they each raise their arms above their heads and both slap simultaneously.

The bigger the play, the more exaggerated the gesture. When Denver Bronco quarterback John Elway completed a pass that set up a game-tying field goal kick in the Denver-Cleveland play-off game in 1987, he ran off the field with both arms extended high, the "gesture of triumph," to receive slaps from teammates on the sidelines. Similarly, a play that literally turns things around—a pass interception or a recovery of an opponent's fumble—is likely to bring a hug from a teammate who grabs the congratulated player around the hips and hoists him high off the ground.

Group congratulations. Winning a close or significant game is an occasion for the "group grope," the whole team hugging together or piling in a heap. This happens in other sports, but it is especially common in football. In fact, in football, any major team effort, such as stopping opponents on the one-yard line or scoring a touchdown, is sufficient reason for the group grope.

Encouragers. These are touches intended to fire up teammates before a play. The huddle itself, if players have their arms around one another or hold hands around the circle, is a subdued version. Players slapping one another on the way to the line of scrimmage, or the coach or team members on the sidelines slapping substitutes as they go into the game, are more stimulating variations.

Support encouragers. Except in the case of an injury, comfort is not given easily in football, so a "support" or reassuring touch is often combined with an encourager touch. In the 1987 Fiesta Bowl, billed as the national collegiate championship between top-ranked Miami and second-ranked Penn State, a Penn State pass interception in the closing minutes virtually killed Miami's chances. One player, who had fumbled earlier, sat crying on the Miami bench. Teammates put their arms around him and then pulled him up, as if to say, "It's OK, come on, don't get down." In other cases, I have seen a teammate embrace a discouraged player, while jostling him or slapping him on the body. The message is, "Don't give up."

Support. When all is lost, or a player is completely dejected, just simple support may be given. I have a remarkable picture that shows a line coach holding one of his college players, nestling the player's head into his shoulder. It happened near the end of a close game Colorado lost to higher-ranked Oklahoma. That kind of touch is seldom seen between men off the ball field.

As the list of variations shows, there are more options for touching when a team is doing well, and being ahead also makes it easier to keep up the enthusiasm. In a 1986 game in which Colorado upset favored Nebraska, the Colorado players were "pumped up" from the start and doing a lot of touching, whereas the Nebraska players, who were apparently not expecting a problem, had less contact with one another. As Colorado pulled ahead, the Nebraska players virtually stopped touching altogether. When a team is behind and is making fewer good plays, it's especially important to keep the touching going.

Not all touching in football is confined to teammates. Although there is some unnecessary pushing and jostling of opponents as players are getting up after a play, there are also some positive touches: helping opponents up, pats of apology for a rough tackle, slaps of congratulations to individuals on the other team for a good play, and handshakes to the winners or touches of support to the losers at the end of the game. I have also seen opposing players who used to be on the same team seek each other out after a game to hug hello and good-bye. The comradery of being in the game together can carry across the line of scrimmage.

Baseball.

Compared to football, there is less touching among teammates in baseball, probably because they are often separated by considerable distances in the field, and batters come up one at a time to hit. Another reason for the less frequent touching in baseball is that it is more a sport of individual accomplishment than football. This difference may account in part for the fewer touches, and especially for the rarity of team hugs. The batter faces the entire opposing team alone. The pitcher, with help from the catcher, deals with one batter after another, and no one else can help out much until the ball is hit. Nevertheless, there is a good deal of contact in the game itself—ball to glove, bat to ball, and glove to body when tagging an opponent out. Body-to-body contact with opponents is rare, but when it does occur, it is often hard—as when a runner slides into home, and the catcher tries to block him.

My theory is that baseball players want to touch each other more than they can. All that tactile stimulation creates a need for encouraging and supporting touches. There is some touching between teammates when the opportunities are present. For example, a batter may receive encourager touches as he approaches the plate. If he hits a single, the first-base coach is likely to step out and pat him on the behind. If he makes it to second base, he is out of reach, but at third base he can be touched again by a coach, a congratulations for getting that far. Finally, when he crosses home, he will get brief handslaps from teammates. When the team is going out to the field or into the dugout at the end of the inning, a player may be touched in recognition for an earlier play.

The problem is that the moment for joyous hugs has passed. Furthermore, the player who deserves the touches of congratulations most—the one who got the hit that drove in the run—is not available for hugging because he's standing on a base. The one opportunity, of course, is when someone hits a home run; then he is likely to be hugged by several teammates as he crosses the plate.

Evidence of the need for touch comes from the fact that baseball players use certain substitutes for touching one another. For example, after a good defensive play, the infielders will often toss the ball around to one another. Perhaps it's practice, but it's also a way of making contact with one another. Even more obviously suggestive of the need for touch is the extraordinary amount of self-touching which goes on in baseball. Most batters have an elaborate, individualized ritual of self-contact which they perform just before going up to the plate and which may be repeated between pitches. It's a way of establishing a rhythm, getting yourself pumped up, and calming anxiety. Similarly, the pitcher may pull on the bill of his cap, tuck in his shirt in the back, and pull up on his belt—and he will do it the same way before every pitch. Even the signals the coaches give are enormously complicated forms of self-touching.

When an important game is won, all this energy may burst forth in a group pile-up which rivals those in football. In addition, because of the emphasis on individual feats, the star of the game, the pitcher or a hitter, may be hoisted on the shoulders of the players as they walk off the field in triumph.

So far, I have concentrated on touches among teammates, but the manager can be both a role model and a significant giver of tactile support. Take the 1988 Los Angeles Dodgers as an example. Sports writers called them the weakest team ever to play in a World Series. The Oakland As were overwhelmingly favored to win. Some managers stay in the dugout, even after an important win. The message is, "I make the decisions, but team morale is up to you." However, Tommy Lasorda, the Dodgers' manager, is not one to stand aloof. At the end of the fourth game in the series with the As, when the Dodgers went ahead 3 games to 1, Lasorda first ran out to the mound to hug his pitcher. Then he hurried over to the sidelines to greet each of his players with an embrace as they came off the field. The players literally lined up to get their hugs. In the last game, the impossible became predictable. The Dodgers won the World Championship, 4 games to 1.

Despite the uplifting moments, there are more fights in baseball than in football. At first glance, this does not make sense; after all, football is supposed to be the more violent sport. One explanation may be the relative touch deprivation in baseball—too much tactile stimulation without enough supportive touch from teammates. Another possible cause is suggested in an observation by the noted expert on animal behavior, Konrad Lorenz (1966). He pointed out that the tendency of humans to commit acts of violence is greatly increased by their tool-using abilities. It is easier to dispatch a member of one's own species by means of a club than by fists, teeth, or claws. It is not accidental that people use the expression "playing hardball" as a verbal equivalent for getting tough or aggressive. Much of the equipment necessary to the game of baseball is dangerous, and most fights occur because of the supposed or actual malevolent use of these tools—a batter hit by a pitched ball, or a baseman struck by flying cleats.

Hockey.

To carry the theme of weaponry in sports further, hockey deserves comment. It is a fast, exciting game with considerable contact, and some of the hugging and other supportive touches of football are found here also. However, the players are also armed—at close range—with hockey sticks, and players can be hit by a fast-flying rock-hard puck. As a consequence, fighting is even more common than in baseball, including acts of the most extreme violence found among the participants in any sports.

Basketball.

Contact in basketball is restricted by the rules of the game. Although there is a certain amount of continuous bumping and pushing as players jockey for position, the referees must make judgments about when touching is excessive and then call fouls. Too much or the wrong kind of touching with opponents results in a penalty—losing the ball to the other team or giving them free throws.

The effect is that players also restrict their touches with teammates. Handslaps of congratulations are found, as well as occasional hugs. On the whole, however, the players on the same team avoid touching one another, just as they are required to avoid touching their opponents.

I watched the National Collegiate Championship game in 1986 with interest to see what kinds of touching would occur. At the end of a close contest, there were a few limited kinds of touches among the winners from the University of Indiana. I saw only one brief hug, which occurred between the top two scorers on the Indiana team. On the other hand, the losers from the University of Syracuse lay about the floor in dejection, not touching one another at all. It was much the same when Duke won their second straight NCAA title in 1992. The coach of the winners hugged his star player immediately after the victory, as the other players waited to do the same, but there was no spontaneous group hug. The losers from Michigan, who had every right to be proud of their effort as all five starters were only freshmen, were too despondent to offer one another support touches.

There is some touching for encouragement in basketball, but I think the potential is underutilized. A notable exception was the 1988 Detroit Piston team, whose members engaged in considerable slapping and hugging with one another throughout the season. This may have been the critical factor that carried them beyond the favored Boston Celtics in the play-offs and all the way to the seventh and last game of the championship, when they were finally defeated by the highly favored Los Angeles Lakers.

Touching in Individual Sports

Generally, in sports in which individuals compete against one another, contact with opponents is infrequent or nonexistent during the contest itself. Included in this category are track and field events, swimming, gymnastics, golf, and tennis. These sports can be organized as team efforts, but with the exception of relay races, it is a team effort only in the sense that the points made by individuals on the same team are added together at the end. The coordination required between teammates is usually minimal. In terms of my formula, which says that more contact in the play itself leads to more touching, individual sports are at the low end of the scale.

The primary exceptions are those individual sports in which contact with an opponent is the essence of the contest—boxing, wrestling, and the martial arts such as karate. However, in these sports the nature of the contact is highly regulated by the rules, both in the contest itself and on the sidelines. In boxing, for example, touches such as holding and blows beneath the belt receive penalties. In Olympic boxing, the rules go even further. The number of clean blows landed by each fighter, as well as the number of illicit forms of contact, are literally tallied up as positives and negatives in determining the winner. In boxing and the martial arts, there are specific territories designated where the opponents must go between confrontations. Extra touching during the match itself is confined to "handlers" on the sidelines.

Touching before competition in individual sports other than those involving aggressive contact is restricted by informal rather than formal rules. Teammates and other supporters generally avoid touching a participant prior to an event for fear of interfering with his or her concentration.

It seems the message is just "I want you to feel free to concentrate without being distracted by anything I might do."

Touching in these kinds of individual sports comes primarily at the end. However, these touches carry a lot of meaning because they summarize the entire event. At this point, teammates, coaches, and friends may touch or be touched in congratulations, appreciation, or comfort. For example, the winner of a track race may be hugged by teammates; a loser may be held and cuddled. Touches between opponents tell how they feel about one another and the contest. Some of the most emotionally inspiring moments at the Olympics come when a winner embraces the runner-up from another country, as if to say, "You were great" or "Thanks for pushing me to do my best."

Tennis is representative of the extremes in non-body-contact individual sports because the players are forbidden from invading the opponent's territory on the other side of the net. There is no one to touch but yourself in singles, and while some players perform rituals of self-contact before each serve, reminiscent of baseball pitchers, the rules do not allow much time for even this form of touching. The opponents pass one another without touch or comment when they exchange sides. Doubles is the only team event, and here only rare handslaps between partners are seen.

Nonetheless, there is considerable tactile exchange in hitting the ball back and forth, and the players may feel like touching one another at the end of the match. The first touch is the handshake, and because it's obligatory, it does not usually carry much meaning, although there are some exceptions. When Jimmy Connors and Andre Agassi played one another at the 1988 U.S. Open, Connors had criticized Agassi in a press interview prior to the match for his practice of kidding around with audience members at times when he was ahead. In the match itself, both players looked grim and somewhat angry during the play, and when it was over, the handshake was done in a very quick, curt manner, with neither player looking at the other.

However, it is ordinarily the second touch that tells the story. If it occurs, 9 times out of 10 it's the winner who touches the loser, not the other way around. Why? Because it's a support touch. It is especially likely to happen after a close match when the winner knows the loser is disappointed, and it says, "Too bad, good try." The winner who performs a second touch assumes that there are no hard feelings on the other person's part at the end of the match. Sometimes, however, the gesture may be rejected by the loser. For example, in one of the last times that Martina Navratalova defeated Steffi Graff, Navratalova had objected to a number of calls during the match, and Graff was obviously bothered by this. After the handshake, Navratalova attempted to touch Graff on the shoulder, but her opponent sped away and out of reach. Having been left with her hand in mid-air, Navratalova shrugged her shoulders in surprise. Occasionally, there will be a third touch, usually a return touch from the loser, signaling congratulations. Between players who are good friends off the court, there may be an embrace across the net immediately after the handshake.

In moments of high emotion at the end of a match between players who respect one another, the very first touch may be a spontaneous hug. Such was the case when Andre Agassi defeated Goran Ivanisevic in an exciting 5-set Wimbledon final in 1992. Neither player had ever won a Grand Slam event, and each was acutely aware of the other's longing for the win. After the last point, Ivanisevic jumped the net to meet Agassi, and they immediately hugged one another in a lengthy embrace. In his press interview after the match, Agassi nicely summed up the feelings and the desire for touch which reigns in such a moment when he spoke of the "bond that you develop out there." "You are both fighting so hard to kill the other one," he said, "yet you have so much respect for the other one fighting back" (Vecsey, 1992, p. B9).

In tennis, as in other individual sports, when the contest is over, the emotions of the competitors can also be dealt with in touches to and from well-wishers in the audience. These might be touches initiated by others to the loser in support or the winner in congratulations. Or, they might consist of contacts initiated by the athlete to a coach or another person in thanks for their continuing support; some of these touches are particularly emotional. Pat Cash's father handled all of his son's business affairs and traveled with him on the tour. Cash won the 1987 Wimbledon title, defeating top-ranked Ivan Lendl. Immediately after the handshake, Cash climbed through several rows of boxes, as the crowd watched patiently, to hug his father in love and appreciation.

Touch Among the Spectators

Watching touching makes people want to touch. It's a natural imitative response, and here again, the more the contact and touching in the sport, the more touch there will be among spectators. Back slaps and hugs in the bleachers are obvious examples, but touches also occur frequently among spectators watching the sport on television, especially when there are many people watching in a public setting. If you doubt this, spend some time in a sports bar or even the lobby of a hotel when *Monday Night Football* is on.

There is also a dark side to the effects of watching highly tactile sports. Whereas the players leave the field exhausted, the spectators may not have had enough emotional release to satisfy them. Football crowds are known for being rowdy after a game, and there are numerous incidents in which fans of a losing visiting team, dressed in the team's colors, have been attacked by the home team's supporters. Apparently, winning is not enough. For the fans of the losers, lack of release may be combined with frustration. In Denver, CO, incidents of domestic violence increase when the Broncos lose, and I assume this statistic holds up in other localities as well.

To the degree that watching or participating in sports allows people to enjoy touches that would not otherwise occur, it's positive. Similarly, playful touching in other contexts can serve the function of breaking down barriers because it can be used with nearly everyone except strangers and the most remote of acquaintances. Although women seldom feel comfortable using playful touches with other women, this kind of contact provides a good way of relating to men and children—and to the child in the man.

Milt and I are especially friendly acquaintances. We used to play tennis together until he developed tennis elbow. The other day, as I was waiting for my son in a recreation center, I felt a finger in my back, an arm around my shoulder and chest, and Milt's voice saying, "Hold it, this is a stick-up." It was corny, but it was a good ice-breaker for the conversation that followed. Whether or not we become better friends, I appreciated this touch. Whereas a more affectionate touch would not have fit the relationship, this touch managed to say "I like you" and "I like to have fun with you."

7

Power Touches:
How to Persuade
with Touch (And How
to Recognize "Moves"
by Others)

A YOUNG woman recently appeared at my door saying, "Hello sir, I'm in the neighborhood demonstrating our product," while extending her hand for a handshake. In her other hand was a spray bottle which was labeled something like "Miracle Cleaner." I hesitated, but shook her hand and said, "I'm sorry, but we're not interested." She said, angrily, "But you don't even know what it is!" She then turned on her heel and marched away.

I realize that door-to-door sales can be hard on the salesperson's ego, and I was abrupt, but I did not like this touch, and it affected my reaction. I was forced to choose either being obviously unfriendly to a stranger by refusing the offered hand or engaging in a mutual contact. In addition, the manipulative intent of the handshake was obvious. Because we ordinarily shake hands with people we know or when we are being introduced, the implication was that I should treat her like someone I know and invite her in.

We are constantly being asked by strangers to sign petitions, buy products, donate money, or answer questions. With people we know, we may be asked to do a favor, make a deadline, or give our time. Are we more likely to be influenced if we are touched, and, if so, under what conditions? When should we be aware of being influenced by touch? What is the right touch if we want to influence others? Research is beginning to give some answers to these questions.

ARE ALL TOUCHES DISPLAYS OF DOMINANCE?

It is a common belief that the person with more power in a relationship is the one who will initiate touch, and some social scientists have adopted this notion as a theory to explain touching in general. The idea is that people with more power use touches as "status reminders" to the less powerful, and that when lower status people do touch, it's supposed to be a bid to raise their power (cf. Henley, 1973, 1977; Summerhayes & Suchner, 1978). In an earlier chapter, I discussed "the myth of male touch dominance," the assumption that men initiate more touches in opposite-sex relationships as a way of emphasizing their more powerful position in society. I also pointed out that this version of the theory has been refuted by research. In general, women touch men more than the other way around. Yet, what about other forms of status? What if the man is also the boss in an organization? What if the boss is a woman? Does initiation of touch reflect status?

One of my students, Brenda Longacre (1987), observed touches within a public health organization. The group studied was a detoxification clinic, a place where alcoholism is treated. This was an ideal setting in which to study status, sex roles, and touching. There were four levels in the hierarchy of this clinic, going upward from volunteers, to attendant counselors, to counselors, and finally to the supervisor. In addition, although there were some males working in this office, most of the employees were women, some of whom were in positions of authority.

Longacre's findings showed two clear trends. First, women on the average initiated more touches to men than vice versa. Second, touching tended to flow upwards, not downwards, in the hierarchy. That is, lower-status people tended to initiate more touch to those in higher positions. Perhaps the humanistic nature of the clinic's work, the relatively egalitarian character of the organization, and the predominantly female population of the workers combined to produce these results. The acid test for the status-reminder theory should come in an organization comprised primarily of men, and especially one involving male politicians. There, status and power should be the name of the game. This is exactly the situation examined in another study.

Alvin Goldstein and Judy Jeffords (1981) observed behavior on the floor of a state house of representatives during legislative sessions. They obtained information about committee memberships, years in the system, and the ages of individual legislators to determine status. They then watched when touches occurred between higher- and lower-status persons.

The lower-status legislators were consistently more likely to initiate touches. The investigators were even able to observe conversations between the governor of the state and various legislators. Although the governor was touched frequently, he did not initiate touches to others.

These findings suggest that approaching and touching someone, even in a business or professional setting, is not necessarily a reminder of whose position is higher. In groups or organizations in which the "pecking order" is stressed, it may be that those with more power are more likely to initiate touches, and some organizations may be so authoritarian that lower-status people rarely dare to touch their superiors. For example, according to sociologist Erving Goffman (1967), in some hospitals the doctors touch nurses often, but nurses seldom touch doctors. However, in organizations in which persons of varying ranks share in the decision-making process and in which warm interpersonal relationships are encouraged, touching—and other forms of communication as well—will go in both upward and downward directions. Many of these touches will have the purpose of simply enhancing human relations; some other touches, whether initiated by those higher, lower, or equal in status, will be designed to influence.

To see how touch can be used for influence, let's start with the situation that has been studied the most. Suppose a person you have not met before or whom you hardly know wants you to do something. In this case, you actually have more power than the other person since you can readily refuse. Are you more likely to go along with what is asked if you are touched?

SUBTLE INFLUENCE: PUTTING THE TOUCH ON STRANGERS AND CUSTOMERS

A person enters a phone booth at an airport, notices a dime on the shelf and takes it. As the person leaves the booth, a young woman walks up and says, "Excuse me. I think I may have left a dime in this phone booth a few minutes ago. Did you find it?"

These people did not know they were part of an experiment conducted by psychologist Cheryl Kleinke (1977). As planned, some people were touched lightly on the upper arm by the woman, whereas others were not. Those who received the touch were more likely to return the dime.

Joel Brockner and his colleagues conducted a similar experiment, this time alternately using either a man or a woman to approach and ask about the dime (Brockner, Pressman, Cabitt, & Moran, 1982). The touch worked for both the male and the female. So did maintaining eye contact rather than looking away, even without a touch. Apparently, the principle is that being involved with the other person in some subtle way is the key to successful influence.

Will a touch help to bring compliance when more is requested than simply returning a small amount of money that does not belong to the other person in the first place? Frank Willis and Helen Hamm (1980) conducted two studies, one in which students were asked to sign a petition, the other in which shoppers were asked to take the time to fill out a questionnaire. The touch, used with half the people in each study, was a brief hand contact to the upper arm just before the request. Eighty-one percent of the students signed the petition when they were touched, 55% when they were not. Seventy percent of the shoppers complied when touched, 40% when not.

In a study by Patterson, Powell, and Lenihan (1986), students who had signed up for a psychology experiment were asked by the experimenter to spend time scoring some personality tests filled out by others. It was made clear to the students that they could leave whenever they wanted. On the average, students who were touched on the shoulder along with the verbal request spent more time on this rather boring task than those who were not touched.

Sometimes the most effective touches are ones that do not seem to have the purpose of persuading. The person who touches does not have to ask directly for something. People will give it freely. April Crusco and Christopher Wetzel (1984) had waitresses touch some restaurant customers briefly on the hand or shoulder just after returning their change. It seemed like a touch of "thanks" or just a friendly gesture, and not a specific request. However, this "Midas touch" increased the size of the tips.

It works for salespeople, too. Marcia Bartusiak (1983) reports that super salesman Barrie Stern discovered the power of touch simply from his own natural tendency to touch customers in a friendly way. It seemed to help sales. He expanded on this insight by training members of his sales staff to touch and found it worked for them as well. Since then, he has established his own company, "Skinetics," which trains doctors, dentists, insurance salespeople, military recruiters, and others to use the technique.

One financial planner told me his method for heading off "buyer's remorse" when a client has just decided to make an investment. He walks the person to the door, pats him or her on the back, and says, "You're doing the right thing." Although the planner believes the decision is a good one and his purpose is persuasion, the touch itself communicates support. It establishes a personal, caring relationship, not just one of professional advice.

The effectiveness of touches with strangers and customers relies on subtlety. The touch itself is likely to be very brief, consisting of a spot touch or perhaps a pat, and it is usually limited in contact to a nonvulnerable body part (arm, shoulder, or upper back). After all, only a minimal touch is justified in these relationships. When the most subtlety is exercised, no direct request accompanies the touch. Nevertheless, these kinds of contacts can suggest interest, liking, or maybe even a compliment. When a person has just made a difficult decision, a brief touch of reassurance from an expert advisor can also reduce anxiety. In other words, the touch makes people feel good and thus more inclined to do something for the other person. It works in situations when more obvious appeals would fail.

The simple willingness by a persuader to be tactilely involved can be persuasive in itself. Politicians understand this principle well; that is why candidates for office spend long hours on street corners shaking hands with every passerby.

CONTROL TOUCHES: THE BASIC MEANINGS

Although some touches persuade by appearing not to ask for anything, there are three specific kinds of touches that make direct requests. These meanings vary in intensity and the degree of response sought.

Level One Control: The Attention Getter

This kind of touch says "I want your attention." This minimal request for involvement requires only a slight touch—a quick pat or spot touch with the hand directed to one body part. The toucher then immediately asks a question or directs the other person's focus toward something. Although it is not very demanding, a demand is nevertheless made, and the touchee can hardly refuse. Translations of the touch include "Look at me," "Listen to this," or "Look at that."

These touches are so unobtrusive that they can be used with anyone, but the cautiousness of the approach may thinly disguise another motive. In the studies I described in which the stranger was asked about the dime left in the phone booth, the touch was actually an attention getter because it was done before anything was said and was then followed by an "excuse me," an apology for the interruption. However, it was soon clear that the person was touching not just for attention, but also to get back the dime. Between people who know one another, the attention getter can also imply a request for a change in attitude: "Pay attention;" "Concentrate on my idea;" or "Be present with me."

Level Two Control: Announcing a Response

This touch escalates the control by explicitly requesting a certain attitude. The toucher's words simply express a feeling, but the touch itself says "share my reaction," or, at the least, "show some reaction." Here are some examples:

- A woman says, "I'm so excited about today!" while touching her male companion on the side. (Translation: "Get excited with me.")
- A woman touches her boyfriend's knee and says, "I'm glad just the two of us decided to come!" (Translation: "I hope you are too.")
- A husband touches his wife's shoulder and says, "Guess who called this morning?" (Translation: "This is interesting, and you should be interested, too.")

Not surprisingly, these touches occur mainly in close relationships because they ask for more than the simple attention getter. In addition, a request for the adoption of the "right attitude" may imply action as well, the next level of influence.

Level Three Control: Compliance

More than the other two control touches, this one deserves the label "power play" because it involves a straightforward attempt to influence the other person's behavior. Even so, the persuader is likely to exercise some caution in what he or she says. Commands are rarely verbalized in a direct way ("Give me that"), but are more often implied ("We better get going;" "You gonna do the dishes?" "Can you have this done by 5 o'clock?"). The touch itself delivers the command—"Do it."

Perhaps surprisingly, the compliance touch usually works. Why? One reason is that touching makes a request personal—in effect, "Do it for me." It relies on the strength of the relationship, so it's not surprising that compliance touches occur primarily in close personal relationships, although occasionally they are used in just good working relationships. The other reason is that the touch itself is low-key. Usually, only the shoulder or upper arm is contacted, and although holding is common, a simple spot touch occurs just as often. Pulling, pushing, or grabbing is rare, and even a pat may be too much. As one office worker put it, "When a person wants something and pats me on the back or shoulder, it's like saying, 'That's a good doggie.'"

POWER MOVES: PROGRESSIVE TOUCH STRATEGIES

When my colleague Elaine Yarbrough and I began studying the vast amount of data we had collected by having people record their daily touches, we had not anticipated finding that many touches would be related to one another in a series (Jones & Yarbrough, 1985). In particular, we were surprised to discover that some of these touch sequences consisted of progressive strategic moves. Each started out looking like one kind of message, but ended up with a surprise move. They are the tactile versions of what psychiatrist Eric Berne calls "games," interactions in which one person has an ulterior motive (Berne, 1964).

Affection to Compliance

In this sequence, one person softens up the other with one or more affection touches and then touches while asking the other to do something. Examples include:

- A couple was watching television together on a couch. The female first cuddled against the male. A minute later, the male kissed the female. Several minutes later, the commercials came on, and the male put his arm around the female and said, "Will you get me some water, sweetie?" The female, who complied, translated the male's final touch as, "I know you will 'cause we're getting along so well."
- A daughter arrived at home for a visit. She greeted her father with a hug. He then kissed her on the cheek and led her toward her stepmother, saying, "Say hello to your mother." The daughter then kissed the stepmother, who did not respond, emphasizing in her translation of the father's touch, "I kiss at my father's request."

The manipulative intent of the final compliance move in this kind of sequence is underlined by the fact that it resembles an affection touch—a kiss, hug, and so forth.

The Irritate-and-Mollify Sequence

This one is somewhat the reverse of the affection-to-compliance strategy because it starts with a demanding touch—which is rejected because it interrupts the other person—and ends with an affectionate touch. The supposed purpose of the second touch is to mollify the other person for any negative feelings created by the first touch. Actually, however, it's a ruse. The effect again is control—this time to get someone's attention when they do not want to give it. Here is a typical example:

- A woman has told her male partner that she has to get a project done and does not want to be bothered. After waiting patiently for several hours, he approaches her from behind while she is writing, gives her a hug and says, "How's it going, honey?" She pulls away with annoyance, saying, "You know I have to finish this." He then sits on her lap with his arm around her shoulders and says, "Aw—I like you so much." It works; she abandons her work for a while.

The Seduction-and-Rejection Game

This sequence resembles the game Eric Berne (1964, pp. 125- 126) calls "rapo" (pronounced "rape-oh"). In the "third-degree" version of the game as described by Berne, one person seduces the other and then, during the sexual act, yells "rape!" In the milder and more common version of the game, one person simply flirts with another and then rejects the other's approach, and this is what happens in the seduction-and-rejection touch sequence. Here is an example:

- A formerly intimate couple have decided to try to transform their relationship into "just a friendship." He is visiting her, and, on a particular day, they have gone skiing together. At the top of a slope, she approaches him from behind by sliding one ski between his skis, gives him a full body press, and says, "I'll race you down the hill." He reaches back and touches her on the buttock and says, "Only if I can follow you down." She immediately jumps back and says, "You know I don't want that kind of relationship!"

Here is the pattern: One person initiates a sexually provocative touch, and when the other responds with a return sexual touch, it's rejected.

Men initiate this game as well as women, as the following example illustrates:

- A woman is preparing to go to work, and her male partner hinders her from getting ready, hugging and kissing her and saying, "I don't want you to go to work." Finally, she gives in, turns and embraces him, and says, "O.K. I'll go in later." He pulls back and says, "Hey, I've got to be someplace in 30 minutes."

The Power-Matching Move

This sequence is different in that one person starts it (with a power-play touch), but the other person finishes it with a countermove:

- At a party, a male approaches a female acquaintance and greets her with a mildly aggressive punch to the arm, saying, "Hi, how ya' doin'?" She recovers from her surprise after a brief pause and returns the same kind of blow to his arm, saying *"I'm just fine."*
- A waiter who had forgotten to bring a dessert order approaches a woman just as she is about to leave her table, grasps her shoulder, and says, "Hey, lady, do you still want this cheesecake?" She grasps him back on the arm and says, "O.K. I'll take it."

In each case, the aggressive or condescending first touch creates a power imbalance that is equalized by the return touch. In fact, the power matcher often looks much like the first touch, as if to say, "Notice what you just did." A possible advantage of this touch game is that a person who touches inappropriately may gain some self-insight by experiencing the countermove. Before using it with your boss, however, consider whether he or she has a sense of humor!

Are these kinds of strategic touch sequences good for relationships? Probably not. If you are the victim, your most uninhibited response might be to clobber the gamester. Assuming you resist this temptation, however, there is another approach to dealing with the various kinds of strategic sequences: Call the name of the game and explain why you object. This could result in a good discussion. (If the other person does not believe you, have them read this chapter section.)

If both people are aware of playing a certain game, it might be a way of having fun together. I know one couple who engage in seemingly unending games of playful aggression touches, each waiting for a chance to surprise and get back at the other. They say they enjoy it, but I think there may be a cost. If overused, power sequences can undermine more positive forms of touching in a relationship.

POWER TOUCHES: SHOULD YOU USE THEM?

Clearly, touches can be used effectively to influence others. Subtlety is the key with strangers and customers. More direct approaches such as announcing-a-response and compliance touches can be used with people you know well. On the other hand, the strategic sequences described above, which are used primarily between people who are close, are not recommended because they are manipulative in a way that may damage the relationship.

Power touches, like other forms of touching, are subject to the most fundamental principle of tactile communication: Touches should not be heavy-handed, either in the sense of physical aggression or social one-upmanship. Used too often or in highly forceful ways, power touches are objectionable. However, used in moderation and in a way that is appropriate to the relationship, they can be a way of establishing connections between people.

Section III
Touch Gone Astray

8

Seven Taboos
of Touch in the
United States

A TABOO is a forbidden behavior in a particular culture. The incest taboo, for example, is nearly universal, although there have been times in history when it was not a taboo in certain societies. Other taboos are less obvious and therefore present more of a problem for foreign visitors to a country where they do not know the rules. In certain Middle Eastern cultures, for example, it is taboo for women to smoke in public, and showing the sole of your shoe to a man is an insult. While reading through a list of *ryokans* (traditional inns) where one can stay in Japan, I ran across this statement: "American visitors are welcome but must follow Japanese customs." The message was clear. I looked for reading materials on how one should behave in a *ryokan*. I did not want to naively violate taboos.

Because touch is an intimate form of behavior, it is obvious that there would be some taboos surrounding it in any culture. In addition, because touch behaviors are often habitual and unconscious, violations are likely to occur unintentionally. I have yet to find a tourist handbook that gives detailed instructions on how not to touch in a particular country, something that would be helpful for foreign visitors. In fact, given that rejections of touch occur rather commonly on a daily basis in the United States culture—about 15% of all touches, according to my research—a guide to American touch taboos could be helpful for Americans as well.

A common misconception is the notion that there is a general taboo against touching in the United States. In popular magazines, and even in academic journal articles, I constantly run across references to "the touch-taboo most of us learned in childhood" (Jourard, 1966, p. 221), "the rigid sanctions surrounding touch in our culture" (Major, 1981, p. 15), and so forth. These kinds of statements are misleading. Not only is there no general taboo against touching in the United States, but there also are no strong negative sanctions for most mistakes in everyday touching. It's just that Americans do not touch as much as people in some other cultures. Women are involved in about 12 touches a day, on the average, and men in about 9 (Jones, 1986, p. 234). Nevertheless, there are some specific kinds of touches that are taboo.

Even for people who feel they have some idea of what touches to avoid, there are two good reasons for becoming more aware of touch taboos: (a) It is helpful to know that you are not alone. People often think that when they do not like a touch, it's because of their own personal idiosyncrasies, so they may feel unjustified in objecting. In fact, most touches that are likely to bother you are objectionable to others as well—they are violations of touch taboos. (b) Keeping the real taboos in mind is a shortcut for learning how to touch more effectively. Knowing which touches to avoid builds confidence.

FORMAL AND INFORMAL TABOOS ABOUT TOUCH: KNOWING WHEN A LINE HAS BEEN CROSSED

There are two kinds of touches that are so universally objectionable that the taboos they violate have become formalized, written down in laws, or in the rules of organizations. One is the taboo against unwanted sexual touches. The clearest case is a touch to a sexual body part of a nonconsenting adult. It can be the basis for a sexual harassment or molestation suit. Less obvious touches that only imply a sexual advance can also bring about a formal complaint or legal action. I read recently of a case in which a male hairdresser was charged in court with molestation for allegedly kissing a female customer. She testified that he kissed her on the lips while she was waiting for her hair to be fixed and her eyes were closed. He claimed she had come in complaining about a haircut, he had agreed to redo her hair, and that he had merely placed his two fingers on her lips while her eyes were closed, simulating a kiss to calm her down. The judge ruled the actual nature of the contact was irrelevant. The point was that the customer was made to feel that a sexual liberty had been taken, and he fined the hairdresser.

The other formal taboo is the one against a threatening or physically aggressive touch. In many states, "a touch in anger" is the legal definition of assault. It does not require that the toucher actually hit or physically abuse the other person, only that a threat be implied by the touch.

The most frequently violated taboos are informal—they are generally understood, but not acknowledged in laws or in the rules of organizations. Some of them are also very subtle, making them easier to violate unintentionally and making violations harder to recognize immediately. In fact, almost everyone violates informal taboos at times, and almost everyone receives some touches that are taboo violations.

How can you tell when a line has been crossed? Informal taboos are enforced by personal reactions. Most of the time, when a touch is rejected, it means there has been a taboo violation. According to my research (Jones & Yarbrough, 1984), the odds are about 7 to 1 that if you feel like rejecting a touch or you notice even a slight negative reaction when you touch someone else, it's a taboo violation.

However, it is true that occasionally people will reject a touch for private, personal reasons. A common one is that the person is in a bad mood because of something that happened before the toucher encountered them; no approach would be welcomed under these circumstances, but a touch forces a reaction. Other common reasons are that the touch is interpreted as flirtatious when the receiver is not interested or that there is something wrong in the relationship. Finally, some people have private taboos, touches they would not like from anyone. For example, I know one woman who cannot stand to be touched on the top of the head. She takes it as a reminder that she is short.

An additional complicating factor is that the absence of an obvious rejection does not always mean no taboo has been violated, since people sometimes hold their rejections inside. The most common reasons for keeping a rejection secret are: (a) fear of reprisals from a high-status toucher, perhaps the boss; (b) concern about embarrassing a toucher who may be naive (children, especially); (c) ignoring the violation in the hope that it will go away; and (d) not wanting to seem like a bad sport, since the toucher was joking. Even in these situations, however, it may be better to go ahead and reject a touch if you are the receiver, explaining your reaction to naive people and taking your chances with the boss. Otherwise, the touch will likely happen again until you do react. Consider also that if you were the toucher and your intentions were good, chances are you would rather know the other person's reaction than to have them hold it inside.

Accepting your own reactions to touch and being aware of the reactions of others are important keys to becoming a more sensitive communicator. Since rejections are not always a sure guide, however, it also helps to know the specific taboos.

THE SEVEN MOST COMMON MISTAKES IN TOUCHING

It took some detective work in my research with my colleague Elaine Yarbrough to figure out the touch taboos (Jones & Yarbrough, 1984). First, out of the descriptions of hundreds of touches recorded in the daily experiences of the people who volunteered to participate in our research, we picked out for special study touches that were rejected, either directly or secretly. We also examined "repairs," cases in which the toucher apologized for the touch because an apology suggests that the toucher knows he or she has done something wrong. Then, we compared these incidents with the larger number of touches that were accepted, especially examining situations that looked similar to those in which touches were usually rejected. This allowed us to qualify the rules and find exceptions. For example, at first it looked as if all touches between strangers were taboo because they were usually rejected, but then we found a number of circumstances in which touches from strangers were entirely acceptable. Touches that were sometimes rejected for private reasons rather than as taboo violations stood out because there were more cases when such touches were accepted than rejected.

I start with the more obvious taboos and go progressively toward the ones in which the violations are more subtly aggressive.

Taboo #1: Strangers

- Strangers should avoid touch with one another unless they are being introduced or unless a minimal touch necessary to give or request aid is used.

In this culture, the only untouchables are the people we do not know. In tight spots such as crowded elevators, we stand with our hands tucked in at our sides or in front, stepping gingerly out of the way if someone in the back has to get out and then snapping back into our spot. If it's so crowded you cannot avoid touch, chances are you will wait for the next elevator.

We do sometimes collide with and brush against strangers, but even if it's an accident, it's a taboo violation. In fact, we are supposed to be so alert in avoiding these contacts that both people frequently mumble an apology; even a person who receives a bump from someone else may apologize. Both people usually reject an accidental touch by pulling back, although there are some exceptions in which the brush is so minimal that we just ignore it. Even then, if the offender says nothing, we may wonder, "What's wrong with that person?", and occasionally we wonder if that person was trying to tell us to get out of the way. A purposeful touch by a stranger, without a very good reason, is a bigger violation and is much rarer than the accidental brush. The male who approaches a female in a bar, puts his hand on her shoulder and asks, "Can I buy you a drink?" is courting rejection.

Yet, there are some good reasons for touching strangers, circumstances in which the taboo is null and void. The obvious exception is when people shake hands when being introduced—a symbolic statement that they are no longer strangers. On rare occasions, when the introduction is between persons who are "close-by-association" (for example, meeting your future sister-in-law), a brief hug might be acceptable, although not expected. The other exceptions have to do with strangers aiding one another. When we need help, we can perform an attention-getting touch with a person we do not know, after which we would ask for the favor (although holding on for several seconds would make it a compliance touch, which would be crossing the line into objectionable behavior). When someone else needs help, even if it's only getting back change, we are also entitled to touch. We can also catch someone who has lost their balance or gently guide someone in the right direction.

None of the exceptions give license for intimacy. The principle is that only the minimal touch necessary to get or give help or be introduced to a stranger is warranted. It applies even to doctors, who generally confine touch on a first visit to those body parts that must be contacted for the purpose of the physical examination. In exceptional circumstances, however, a person in a helping role might also give a support touch to a stranger. For example, a woman told me this story:

> After I had miscarried, I had to go in for a rhogram shot. There was a new nurse in the office. She touched my arm for an extended time after giving me the shot, saying, "This is really hard." I deeply appreciated her sensitivity and found myself grateful to have had this "stranger" with me, because I doubted that the regular nurse would have shown this kind of support.

Although there are important exceptions to the rule, and a touch from a stranger might be especially appreciated when it is needed, Americans generally do not like involving forms of communication with people they do not know. It's an offshoot of the values of individualism and privacy, and by their nature, touches are the most involving kind of communication.

Taboo #2: Harmful Touches

- Accidental hurtful touches must be avoided at all times.

It is considered a nice gesture to apologize when we accidentally but harmlessly invade the space of someone we know, bumping the other person's foot or brushing them as we get up to go. It's as though a touch should mean something, and the apology is the equivalent of correcting oneself after making a grammatical error or saying something in a confusing way. Yet, it's not a taboo violation unless the people are strangers, and the touch often gets rejected, whether or not there is a subsequent apology.

On the other hand, accidental touches that inflict pain or damage (even soiling clothing) cross a line regardless of the relationship. Even if it's your mother who touches you on a sunburn, backs into you roughly, or steps on your foot, you are likely to say, "Ouch, watch what you're doing!" and she is sure to apologize. It's the one taboo that young children are expected to obey as soon as they are old enough to understand adults' objections. (When my 3-year-old stepped on my bare foot, I reacted immediately and told him to "be careful!") Like the accidental touch with strangers, harmful touches are something we are supposed to be alert to avoid at all times.

Taboo #3: Startling Touches

- One should avoid surprising another person with a touch.

It happens often: We walk into a room where someone has his or her back turned to the door and is concentrating on something; we make a comment; and the other person jumps, saying "Oh—you startled me!" However, if we lay a hand on the other person before our presence is noticed, we are likely to get a stronger reaction—a pull away with a look of surprise and then a frown.

There is something primitive operating here. Perhaps in our Neanderthal and Cro-magnon past, the individual who did not respond immediately and aggressively to an unanticipated touch had a weaker chance of surviving to pass on genes to the next generation. As much as we may feel safe in most environments today, the automatic negative reaction is still there. Even a brief attention-getting spot touch from behind may cause it, but a firmer grip or an encompassing hug without warning will bring a stronger response. Besides the unpleasantness of being startled, there is also a secondary, socially conditioned reason for rejection: The touch temporarily destroys the victim's social composure.

Compared to the other taboos, the startling touch is not a very serious violation, and often it does not get rejected openly, only privately. That is why some people think the startling touch is OK as a way of kidding, and unlike the stranger and harmful taboo violations, it's sometimes done intentionally. One person sneaks up and tickles the other, or, late at night after watching a scary movie, one person may place a cold hand on an unsuspecting victim's neck. It's the tactile equivalent of the teasing remark (translation: "Ha, ha! You're jumpy!"). However, unlike verbal jousting, there is no way the victim can come up with a surprising countermove, and some individuals object to the startling touch strongly, whether or not they mask their reaction as humor. The startling touch is popular with children—and a few adults—as a way of attracting attention, but there are better ways of getting attention.

Taboo #4: The Interruption Touch

- One should not touch in such a way as to interfere with another person's involvement in an activity requiring primary attention.

When I told one man that I do research on touch communication, he said, "I've got one for you I've never understood." He reported that when he arrives home after a day's work, he is happy to see his family and frequently hugs his wife or one of his daughters to say hello. The puzzling part was that they frequently pulled away. I asked him what his wife or daughters were doing when he hugged them, and he said his wife might be doing the dishes or his daughter might be studying her school books.

The taboo violated in this kind of incident is subtler than the first three taboos. Although the touch itself is intentional, it's misuse may be unintentional. It's a matter of misreading the situation before the touch that causes a problem. Erving Goffman, a sociologist who has studied the fine points of daily communication, has called attention to the fact that people frequently carry on two activities at the same time, one primary and the other secondary. The primary activity is the main focus, the purpose for being there. The secondary activity can be done on the side as long as it does not detract from the main focus, or it can occupy the person's time while he or she is waiting to complete the primary activity (Goffman, 1963, pp. 43-63). In the doctor's office, you may have a conversation with the person next to you, but when the nurse says, "The doctor will see you now," you go. Similarly, a conversation before a meeting can be interrupted by the chairperson when the meeting is called to order, but a whispered comment within the group should not disrupt the meeting itself.

It's the same with touches. They should not interfere with a primary activity. The man who throws his arms around his wife while she is doing the dishes is in violation of the taboo, despite his good intentions. Similarly, in my research, one woman reported being annoyed when her romantic partner began kissing her while she was trying to watch a television program. Especially bothersome are touches that call attention to themselves while the person who is touched is involved in a conversation with someone else. One businesswoman described a situation in which she was talking with a male co-worker she was trying to impress. Her boyfriend joined them, putting his arm around her waist. Later, she took the boyfriend out into the parking lot where they could be alone and told him, "Don't ever do that to me again."

Not all interruptive touches are taboo violations: It depends on whether the touch interferes with a primary activity. For example, a father sat down next to his daughter while she was watching television and touched her lightly on the arm as if to say, "Hi, I'm here." The touch was minor enough to provide no distraction, and there was no rejection. In another case, a waiter was talking to a friend just prior to serving food at a banquet. Another waiter touched him and said, "The food is here." Again, no rejection, this time because a secondary activity was interrupted for the primary one, not vice versa.

Taboo #5: Moving Others

- One should not communicate by touch alone that another person should move out of the way.

Violations of this taboo bring surprisingly strong rejections. Some violations are quite obvious. For example, a person who is in a hurry may pick up and set a child to one side, or grab a spouse by the shoulders to move into the other's place at a kitchen counter, but these are unusually aggressive touches. Most violations involve only a nudge or a light bump, but it's enough to bring an objection and sometimes resistance to being moved.

As with the startling touch, there may be a primitive basis for this taboo. Part of our animal heritage is the tendency to defend territory. Ordinarily, people will only defend spaces they have clearly marked off as theirs with objects, signs, or boundary markers—the seat you saved at a concert with your personal belongings, for example, or the property where you posted a "no trespassing" warning. Personal space, which does not have a clearly marked boundary, is seldom defended; if someone moves too close, we usually back off. However, there is something especially perturbing about being physically jostled from the very spot on which we stand, even when it's done subtly, and consequently our defenses go up.

The obnoxiousness of this touch also stems from the fact that it's easy to avoid violating the taboo. The phrase "by touch alone" is significant in the rule. A person who touches and says, "Excuse me, I have to get by" or "Careful, coming through with hot coffee!" will not receive the negative reaction. Even the husband who touches his wife and makes a demand—"Move, honey, I have to sit here to type"—probably will not get rejected. A brief apology or a verbal warning will usually get you off the hook. Similarly, I found in my research that it was common for people to actually move others physically without rejection—but only if the toucher was going in the same direction as the other person was being moved and only if the toucher also offered an explanation: "Hurry, let's get across the street;" "Let's go over here and sit down;" and so on.

Personal space becomes personal turf only when these precautions are ignored.

Taboo #6: Aggressive Playful Aggression

- A playful aggression touch should not seem more aggressive than playful.

Playful aggression in the form of mock fighting can be fun. However, there are two ways that these kinds of touches can cross over into just plain aggression from the point of view of the touch recipient, regardless of the intention of the initiator. One way is for the toucher to fail to send a clear play signal before or just at the beginning of the contact. The problem with grabbing someone around the shoulders and then saying, "Let's wrestle," is that the words do not come in time for the other person to join in the play. The aggression is done to but not *with* the other person. Consequently, the first split-second perception of the receiver is likely to be that the attack is real, and once there has been a negative reaction, it's too late to turn back.

The other way that would-be play can go too far is when the touch itself is too aggressive. Then, it does not matter if the play signal comes in advance or not. Occasionally, this happens when the play gets out of hand and becomes a fight, most commonly between two males, but this is rare. More often, it's similar to the situation reported in my research in which a male said, "Come on and hit me" to a female, and then proceeded to deliver a punch to her stomach. In another incident, a male performed a prolonged mock strangle to a female while saying, "I'm gonna get you."

Taboo #7: The Double Whammy

- An aggressive or critical verbal statement should not be accompanied by a touch that strengthens the negative message.

In the violation of this taboo, it is clear that not only the touch is intentional, but so is the negativity. One person makes a condescending, insulting, or commanding remark to another while touching in such a way as to emphasize the one-up message.

Often, the remark may seem like a joke and be accompanied by a chuckle. It's similar to the kind of playful aggression in which one person makes a teasing comment and then touches to let the other person know it was not meant seriously. The difference can be subtle, but the nature of the comment, the timing of the touch, and sometimes the nature of the touch itself are tip-offs that the touch is meant to emphasize rather than nullify the negative comment. Here are two examples:

- One man was telling his male cousin about having made a mistake in a business deal. This serious revelation was met by the cousin with a clutch to the shoulder, followed by the comment, "Boy, you messed up on that one, didn't you?" The man escaped from the touch by taking a full step away, making his reaction clear.
- A mother touched the stomach of her 20-year-old daughter, who was suffering from a hangover, and said, "How's little Jean?" (Translation: "You really aren't a big enough girl to handle liquor.")

Sometimes no pretense is made that the comment is a joke:

- A woman straightened her niece's hair while saying, "Your hair is in your face."

In the above examples, the touch itself need not be physically aggressive, since the words clearly convey the aggressive message. In another version of the Double Whammy, however, the accompanying verbal statement is a command rather than an insult, but the touch itself escalates the aggressiveness. Examples include:

- A female said to her sister, "Give me that paper!" while hitting her on the leg.
- A female said to a male, "Go walk her to the car," accompanying the words with a slap on the arm.
- A male, who was working on a stereo set, struck his younger brother on the foot for standing too close, saying, "Get out of here."

The inappropriateness of the Double Whammy is especially

apparent in cases in which the offender comments unfavorably on a body part while touching it:

- A male pinched the thigh of his girlfriend who was beginning to eat a dessert and said, "Fattening. . . ."
- A husband vocalized "Pssst" while pressing a finger into his wife's stomach. She translated the touch, "You're getting too fat."

Both literally and figuratively, such touches "rub it in."

Multiple Taboo Violations

Occasionally, touchers approach spectacular naivete or clumsiness by combining two or more taboo violations into one. This could happen because the violator does not know the rules. In one case, a male foreign student who had just met a woman at a party approached her from behind while she was talking on the telephone, threw his arms around her, and said, "It was nice to meet you." Perhaps he was misled by observing that Americans touch the opposite sex more freely than in his country, but the poor fellow managed to violate the Stranger, Startling, and Interruption touch taboos, all at the same time.

For people who should have some idea about what is inappropriate, committing a multiple violation suggests purposeful aggression. In one instance, a male casino official, who did not think a woman was old enough to gamble, grasped her roughly by the shoulder and arm and led her from the room, saying, "Young lady, come with me." The taboos violated include touching a stranger, the Double Whammy, and possibly the Harmful Touch.

TABOO VIOLATIONS AS POWER PLAYS

As we move from Taboo #1 through Taboo #7, it seems more and more likely that the touch is a calculated action, not just an accidental or habitual behavior. However, this does not necessarily mean that the toucher is aware that he or she is violating a rule. That is, from the point of view of the violator, the touch could be innocently intended. In some cases, the offender may have feelings of hostility of which he or she is unaware; for example, not all accidental bumps are accidental at an unconscious level. In other cases, like that of the father who threw his arms around family members when they were busy, the violator may be totally innocent. It is not always easy to tell the difference, but at least it can be said in favor of both kinds of violators that they are not consciously trying to put the other person down.

On the other hand, in some situations the offense is consciously motivated. The purpose is to intimidate or dominate. Males are more often guilty of this, but either sex could be implicated. Although it is not always possible to separate the naive from the knowing offenders, certain circumstances and touches rather clearly indicate the conscious use of an aggressive strategy.

Potentially, any of the taboos could be violated with purpose. For example, the male who brushes his body against a female stranger in a bar—even though he could maneuver by without touching—knows what he is doing. One woman, who is short and has trouble moving through crowds, told me gleefully that she touches others on the back to get them to let her through—a minor but intentional multiple violation of the Stranger, Startling, and Moving Others taboos. The two most common purposeful violations, however, involve either the Aggressive Playful Aggression or the Double Whammy taboos.

Wherever sheer physical strength is highly valued in a group, aggressive play violations, often combined with startling touches, are likely to occur. This is common on sports teams and in workplaces where heavy physical labor goes on. Football players and others who play contact sports tell me that being grabbed from behind without warning goes on so frequently that it rarely draws notice. Sometimes this kind of touching goes a step further, bordering on sexual as well as physical aggression. Male factory workers, for example, sometimes "goose" unsuspecting co-workers. These touches may be taken in stride by the victim, but sometimes they result in a fist fight.

Intentional aggressive play can also become ritualized, involving a set of expected behaviors. I recall that in junior high school there was a game played among the boys called "flinch." The idea was to fake a blow to another person. If the victim pulled back, the aggressor was entitled to deliver a punch to the upper arm. To keep the facade of play alive, there was also a rule that the puncher had to "wipe it off," and if he forgot to do this, the other person was entitled to a punch in return.

The purposeful Double Whammy is even more common since it can be used in more situations. In a local restaurant in a rural area, I observed one man grasp another at the back of the neck, placing his face very close to the other man's, saying, "Hey, Bill, you've been in here all day. You better get to work." At a meeting of salesmen in a company, I observed two men teasing a third about a crease in his pants, asking him, "Is this one of your wash-and-wear suits?" The two men were holding on to him on either side, and he looked as though he wanted to get away. Comments of a sexual nature, usually directed by a man to a woman and accompanied by a prolonged touch, are another version of the purposeful Double Whammy.

Some may claim such touches are all in fun and an acceptable form of social interaction, but the leering smiles of the aggressors and the looks of sadness, confusion, or anger on the faces of the victims suggest otherwise. My research shows that even when people do not openly complain about such offenses, inwardly they object. Their feelings are not usually expressed overtly out of a concern about revealing their vulnerability or a belief that others expect them to "be a good sport." Also, they may be uncertain of how to respond in a way that does not make their predicament worse.

We might wonder why people would engage in touches they know are going to be rejected, privately if not openly? Sometimes it's a way of getting attention, however inappropriately. Other motivations include: (a) testing people to "see if they can take it;" (b) hinting to a person that something is wrong with his or her behavior, a message that the individual is somehow in violation of an unspecified group norm; and (c) establishing a pecking order in a group.

Even if these motivations are validly prompted in some circumstances, there is a price to be paid for pursuing them in this way. Because touch is the most intimate form of communication, violating the tactile code deteriorates human relations.

HOW TO RESPOND TO TABOO VIOLATIONS

The first and most basic principle is to reject the touch in a way that will be noticed, at least by the offender. Sometimes there is a reluctance to do this, especially if the violation seems unintentional. However, it is important to remember that even the innocent violator needs the information that his or her touch was not accepted. Unless you are willing to forgo reacting to the violation in order to save face for the other person, at least a nonverbal reaction is called for. Where you go from there depends on the situation, especially your reading of the other person's motivations.

Dealing with the Unwitting Violator

Start with the assumption that the other person has made a mistake, unless that is obviously untrue. The nonverbal rejection—pulling away, frowning, and so on—may be enough to get the message across. However, a verbal assertion which describes your reaction and what causes it has the advantage of making your objection clear and is especially needed if the same violation is repeated by the same person. The best assertions begin with a

personal statement of a feeling—an "I-statement"—and then go on specifically about the objectionable behavior: "I don't like to be surprised with a
touch" or "It bothers me to be nudged out of the way like that." In phrasing the objection as an I-statement, the person takes on a certain amount
of responsibility for his or her own reaction, which tends to decrease
defensiveness on the part of the other person.

The opposite of an I-statement is a "You-statement," such as "You
are always touching me aggressively," which is easy to fall into and is
more likely to create defensiveness. Such an assertion will let the other
person know what he or she has done that is objectionable, but it's unnecessary with an unwitting violator. In addition, be aware that you may lapse
into using "fake-I-statements," which are You-statements in disguise, such
as "I *feel* that *you* touch aggressively."

You may also want to avoid discouraging the person from touching in the future, in which case even more caution must be exercised in
the phrasing of your objection. You can do this by adding a qualifier that
gives guidance about what kinds of touches are acceptable to you: "It's
OK if you touch me, but make sure I know you're there first" or "I like the
fact that you touch when you say hello, but its distracting when I'm busy
with something." However, do not apologize for your reaction: "I know
it's silly, but I don't like to be touched when I'm being kidded," and so on.
The apology makes it seem as though you are the offender, and the other
person will not get the point.

Dealing with Purposeful Violators

An I-statement may or may not work with purposeful violators. For the
hard-core game player, it may provide an opportunity to come back at you
with the accusation that you are "being touchy." A strong but controlled
nonverbal rejection is often surprisingly effective in these cases. A look
with a frown or disgust expression and no comment gets the message
across. Look for a second or two and then look away. A neutral expression
with a look also conveys annoyance and can be even more effective. For
repeat offenders, a simple but direct command may accompany the look:
"Don't grab me from behind" or "Don't do that again." The idea is not to
give what the power player is looking for—submissiveness, on the one
hand, or a defensive overreaction, on the other. For most people, however, an I-statement will do the job.

Dealing with Your Own Mistakes

Recently, I was talking with another professor after a meeting. He was on
the other side of a table. I had said I thought I was a "tough grader" (con-

sidered a positive trait among college professors), and he teased me by saying, "That's funny. The students say you're easy." Later in the conversation, he confessed that he had given rather high marks in one course this term. I rounded the corner of the table while saying, "Gee, Phil, you're getting soft." He stepped back a full three feet to avoid the touch he saw coming. I had to laugh at myself. He had managed to escape my Double Whammy.

Almost everyone who touches makes mistakes. Knowing the taboos of touch can give you a certain objectivity about your own behavior and help you to take rejections less personally. A brief apology— "Oops! Sorry"—when another person has rejected your touch can actually be a powerful way of relating. Even if the rejection was only nonverbal and an apology was not necessarily expected, it shows you are aware of what has happened, are able to acknowledge it, and that you care.

Awareness is the key in dealing with your own and other people's objectionable touches. In fact, just as a result of reading this chapter, you will probably notice that your behavior has already begun to change.

9

Abusive Touch: A Subject Everyone Should Understand

S CIENTISTS AT an international conference in Montreal in 1989 made some ominous predictions about the spread of the AIDS epidemic, although there was optimism that early treatment could delay progression of the disease and that eventually a drug would be found to halt it. At the time of the publication of this book, more than 1.5 million people in the United States will have been infected with the HIV virus and over 100,000 will have contracted AIDS (Altman, 1989; World Health Organization, 1991).

There is another less dramatic and less newsworthy epidemic that has been with us much longer. Like AIDS, the other epidemic appears to be rapidly on the increase. Also similar to AIDS, it can be passed on to the next generation, and it involves children even more frequently. It is the epidemic of abusive touch.

The statistics for the occurrence of abusive touch are more impressive than those for AIDS. It is estimated that over 1.5 million children are neglected or abused physically or sexually in the United States (Watkins & Bradbard, 1982); 500,000 of these are sexually abused, although some children suffer more than one kind of maltreatment

(National Center for Child Abuse and Neglect, 1983b). Annually, about 350,000 people report at least one incident of a physical attack by a spouse, and many cases involve repeated assault (Straus & Gelles, 1986). Estimates are that 1 in 4 women will be sexually assaulted at some time in their lives (Koss, 1992; Resnick, 1983). Clearly, although abusive touch has received much less attention than AIDS, it is a serious problem which must be addressed.

I did not have to look far to find examples of abusive touch. They were right there in the headlines of my local newspaper:

- "Father Sentenced to 25 Years for Punishment Resulting in Bed-Wetter's Death."
- "Former Volunteer Counselor Confesses to Sexual Involvement with Young Boy."
- "Battering Husband Breaks into Women's Shelter."
- "Woman Raped by Four Men as Crowd Cheers Them On."

Many of the stories of abuse are extremely touching. Here is one which especially caught my attention, as told by a woman who founded a shelter for battered wives and children in England:

> Fred (aged four) thought he was a dog when he arrived and clung fiercely to me, whimpering loudly. We used to transfer him from one pair of arms to another for months. He had been badly beaten and terrorized by his father, who hallucinated, and the only member of the family that escaped beating was the dog, so Fred very wisely mimicked its behaviors. He didn't communicate with anyone except by whimpering, but after months of kissing and cuddling he slowly began to talk and play with the other children. (Pizzey, 1977, pp. 71-72)

Descriptions of such incidents can be found weekly in almost any newspaper, and many do not have even the bittersweet ending of Fred's story. Such accounts, however, can be alienating. The cases that make the newspapers are often so sad and depressing that people tend to put them out of their mind, and the details are sometimes so bizarre that they seem unrelated to the experience of the average person. It may also be hard to see what can be done about the problem, and therefore many people assume that it must be dealt with by the courts and the social service agencies.

Although the tendency to ignore or avoid the issues of abusive touch is understandable, there are some important reasons for all of us to have an in-depth awareness of this subject:

1. Even children from protective and nurturing families can be exposed to abusive sexual or physical touches outside the

home. It is important for parents and teachers to understand that there are ways of preventing such experiences without unnecessarily frightening children.

2. Professionals such as preschool and grade-school teachers, nurses, and doctors are finding increasingly that they have a responsibility for detecting and reporting incidents of abuse, and to some degree in every state this is required by law. Other adults may also find themselves in a position in which they become aware of potential abusive acts involving children, and they may not know what to do about it.

3. Anyone may find their path crossed by another adult who has recently experienced one of several types of abuse. For example, it could be a relative or friend who has been the victim of a rape. These persons need support and understanding, and those who have insight into the victim's experience are best able to provide these.

4. Finally, persons who are knowledgeable about the problems and solutions involved for the different kinds of abuse are in the best position to influence legislators, contribute to the appropriate private agencies, or volunteer their services. The fact is that legislation that is only punitive to offenders is seldom a solution at all, and it ignores the plight of the victims.

So much has been written about the sexual and physical abuse of children, spouse battering, and rape that I do not attempt to summarize it all here. In particular, I play down the drama of the many stories of abuse that are available, in part because examples of touch are most useful when they provide positive models for imitation. The specific cases are often engrossing, but the details are also sometimes lurid, and, more significantly, they can be distracting. Instead, I emphasize what can be done about the problems—the solutions that hold the most promise. I also stress an aspect of the subject that is largely ignored in other writings—the role of touch itself, or the lack of touch, in creating or perpetuating abuse. Finally, I devote attention to a solution that is so obvious it has been largely ignored: touch as a remedy for problems of touch.

CHILDREN: SEXUAL ABUSE

Of all the kinds of tactile abuse, the sexual victimization of children is the least well understood by the general public. Owing to the discomfort most people feel about this topic, it has seldom been treated in the popular media. One notable exception was *Something About Amelia*, a sensitive dramatic portrayal of a case of incest presented several years ago on ABC television (January 1984). The issues involved in sexual abuse are complex, which further contributes to the lack of public understanding. Nevertheless, child sexual abuse has been a subject of considerable research, and it is the one area in the total abuse picture in which the most progress has been made toward finding solutions.

It is obvious that the effects of sexual abuse can be devastating for children. Studies show that the great majority of offenders are well known to the child. Nearly half are parents or family members, and most others are caretakers, teachers, or someone else whom the child has been taught to trust and respect (Borkin & Frank, 1986; Conte & Berliner, 1981). With these persons, and especially in cases of repeated abuse, there are severe consequences. Documented short-term psychological effects include "eating, sleeping and elimination disturbances, school problems, excessive fears, severe depression, guilt, and suicidal tendencies" (Saslawsky & Wurtele, 1986, p. 236).

The long-range impact is even more of a concern, since the debilitating influences can stay with individuals throughout their lives. Those who are repeatedly abused as children are at greater risk to turn to prostitution, drug and alcohol abuse, and criminal activity, and they are likely to become sexual abusers themselves (Conte & Berliner, 1981; Steele & Alexander, 1981). Even a single traumatic event at an early age can have long-term psychological effects. I know of one woman, for example, who was raped at age 11 by an older boy. She reported that despite a desire to marry and have children, she was unable to form trusting relationships with men. Somewhat lesser effects such as sexual dysfunctions and the inability to have satisfying intimate relationships plague others as adults.

Although the potential effects of extreme cases of sexual abuse are serious, there is another issue to consider, one which strikes closer to home for most families. The specter of sexual abuse hovers over the touch impulses of many parents and teachers who are fearful that their affectionate touches with children may have sexual connotations. The consequence is that they hold back from contact. In addition, because authorities sometimes err on the side of protecting children's rights, there have been some cases in which adults have been falsely accused of sexual abuse. In part, these problems stem from a vagueness in the law and in many people's minds about the relationship between touching and sexual abuse.

What Is a Sexually Abusive Touch?

The National Center on Child Abuse and Neglect (1978) provided the following definition of child sexual abuse: "contacts between a child and an adult in which the child is being used for the sexual stimulation of the perpetrator or another person" (p. 2). As clear as this definition may seem, it is problematic in some ways. It requires an assessment of the adult's motives, which may be difficult to determine. What is more, it leaves open some borderline circumstances in which judgment about whether abuse has occurred is difficult.

Genital contact

One issue concerns whether the touching of genitals, either by the child toward an adult or vice versa, is abusive. Among adults, direct and purposeful contact with intimate body areas, except in the case of a medical examination, is clearly sexual touching, but the situation with children may be different. The authors of one article on this subject phrase the problem of interpretation in this way:

> Our prior work on incest revealed that most cases with preadolescent children involve grossly inappropriate sexual touching, genital kissing, and the like, and not intercourse. That finding raises the question of where to draw the line between the hugging, touching, and kissing in families we applaud for stimulating healthy growth, and abusive behavior that may traumatize children . . . . Is a mother who allows her 4-year-old son to touch her breast abusing him? What of a father who allows his 5-year-old daughter to touch his penis while they shower together? (Rosenfeld, Bailey, Siegel, & Bailey, 1986, p. 481)

In some child custody cases, occurrences such as those described in the quotation have been introduced as evidence of molestation. A recent film, *The Good Mother*, was an interesting dramatic portrayal of just such a situation.

In this story, the mother (played by Diane Keaton) is divorced and has custody of her daughter from her former marriage. She eventually becomes involved in an affair with an artist and falls in love. He helps her to become more sensual and more liberal in her attitudes, and he also develops a close relationship with the daughter. The couple is frequently nude in the presence of the daughter, but without sexual connotations. On one occasion when the mother is absent from the house, the daughter, motivated by her curiosity, asks the artist if she may touch his penis. Not wanting to be prudish, he allows it. The daughter later casually reports this to her father, who sues for custody. As the story unfolds, the clear implication of the filmmakers is that this child has not been sexually abused. Nevertheless, the court awards the father custody, not an unrealistic conclusion.

A recent study surveying upper-middle-class families with children 2-10 years of age (Rosenfeld et al., 1986) specifically addressed the question of whether contact by a child with the parent's sexual organs was

a normal practice. It seems likely that the findings are conservative estimates of the actual occurrence of such behaviors because parents were
probably cautious about reporting incidents. Nevertheless, among
preschool children (2-4 years), the parents reported that nearly 90% had at
some recent time touched the breasts or genitalia of the mother, and about
50% had touched the father's genitals. Such touching was less common
among older children, but even so, among 8-10-year-olds, 55% of the
boys and 30% of the girls had recently touched a sexual body part of the
parent of the opposite sex.

Parents were also asked how they had responded. Some gave immediate negative reactions like "No, please don't touch me there," although
most responses ranged from mildly negative (making the child stop after a
short time) to mildly positive ("I let him touch, but not play or become part of
a game"). The authors conclude that "if all children who touched their parents genitals were removed from their homes, we would have a lot fewer
children living with their parents" (Rosenfeld et al., 1986, p. 483).

It seems obvious that preschool children will be curious about
sexual organs, just as they are curious about the rest of the human body,
and they will want to touch. In addition, parents will sometimes touch the
genitals of children as part of bathing them or in brief incidental contacts
when playing with or cuddling them. Although parents should not allow
extended contact of this kind by a child and should obviously avoid initiating purposeful touching of this type, they should not overreact by scold-
ing or punishing a child when a touch is simply a reflection of his or her
curiosity or an incidental contact. They can simply withdraw casually from
contact when it occurs, and if repeatedly initiated by the child, they can
explain, "I don't like to be touched there." It is good to keep in mind psychologist Sydney Jourard's (1966) suggestion that those body parts that are
never touched by parents under any circumstances may come to be
regarded by the child as "bad."

The fact that touching of the breasts or genitals of parents occurs
with some frequency among older children, particularly those approaching puberty, suggests that certain parents may need counseling about over-
stimulation or seductive behavior with children (Rosenfeld et al., 1986, p.
484). This does not mean, however, that parents should avoid affectionate
touches such as hugs, even though there may be incidental contact with
sexual body parts at those times.

In itself, contact with a sexual organ between a child and parent
does not constitute sexual abuse. The nature of the touch by the parent
and his or her reaction to a touch initiated by the child is crucial in interpreting the motivation for the touch.

Sexuality among children.

One borderline type of act which is particularly difficult to evaluate involves sexual exploration between children. It is estimated that the majority of minors engage in some kind of sexual activity prior to puberty. There is little information available on this subject, but one study has provided data on childhood sexual experiences among siblings.

Sociologist David Finkelhor (1980) surveyed college students to discover how many had had sexual contacts with their siblings and how they evaluated the long-range effects. Fifteen percent of the females and 10% of the males reported incidents occurring at some time before they left home. Mostly these involved genital touching or fondling, but there were some cases of more extensive incestuous activity. One-third of the incidents occurred only once, other experiences were repeated but not enduring, and 27% of the relationships continued for longer than a year. The ages of the children at the time of the acts ranged widely, with 40% of the occurrences prior to age 8, and 73% after that age, many at or beyond age 12 (35%).

These figures are higher than we might expect, but even more surprising is the fact that about equal numbers of the students found the experiences more positive than negative in the long run (30% each), whereas the rest were undecided. Some felt the experiences enhanced their sexual self-esteem.

How many of these acts were sexually abusive? Finkelhor found that about one-fourth of the incidents were rated as exploitative. One or more of the following characteristics of the experiences made them particularly harmful from the point of view of the students: (a) a large age difference between the two children involved (an especially important factor); (b) the use of force; or (c) extensive sexual activity (genital manipulation or exhibitionism were less negative than more extreme violations). Although the basic definition of child sexual abuse given earlier refers only to adult perpetrators, the National Center for Child Abuse and Neglect (1983) acknowledges that acts committed by minors who are significantly older than the victim or in a position of power over the child may also be included. Finkelhor's findings square with this expanded definition.

These findings should not be construed as a recommendation that parents encourage nonexploitative sex play among siblings or other children. Precocious and extensive sexual activity is inadvisable among young children and adolescents because they are not ready to deal with intimate relationships of this type on an emotional level. It is also obvious that extensive sexual activity among siblings may, in the long run, create severe relational problems within the family. Yet, it is especially important to be aware of Finkelhor's findings, since only 12% of those who had had the experiences ever told anyone about them. This suggests that parents should be aware of sexual impulses and curiosity in their children and be open to discussing sexual experiences and issues with them. In this way, both the interests of children and the concerns of parents can be handled, making sexual exploration by children less likely to occur.

Touch as seduction.

It should be recognized that not all sexually abusive touch, whether instigated by an adult or a minor, involves force or coercion. At least in the beginning, there is another pattern that may be more common. In Chapter 5, I discussed "the seduction touch." It involves the use of affectionate touching of vulnerable but not sexual body parts as a prelude to more intimate contacts. Adults usually understand what is happening when this approach is used, but children do not. In abusive touch with children, the seduction might be accomplished by the adult through a process of grooming, bathing, or other affectionate touching, proceeding to playful touching of genitals, and moving later to more extensive sex play. In effect, the child is lured into a sexual relationship (Conte, Rosen, Saperstein, & Shermack, 1985, p. 320; Deaton & Sandlin, 1980, p. 312).

When children are involved in extensive sexual experiences with an adult at a very young age, no such subtle manipulation is needed. They are seduced in the sense that they never learn the difference between affectionate and sexual touching, and they may be sensually gratified by the experience. Psychiatrist Alayne Yates (1982) has documented cases of "children eroticized by incest." She points out that we usually think of an incestuous relationship as involving passive, unwilling victims, but this phenomenon introduces a new complexity to the situation. These children were often aggressively sexual with both adults and other children.

It is obvious that such children must be placed with foster parents. However, their behaviors are so repugnant to most adults that the children are likely to be shuffled from home to home. Yates says "we need to identify and train certain foster parents as specialists. . . . [They] should be able to say to a child, 'Of course it felt good—it would to most children—but that does not make you responsible for what happened'" (p. 484).

Detecting Sexual Abuse

Recognizing the evidence of abuse in an eroticized child is comparatively simple because such children are likely to exhibit overt sexual behavior toward adults and other children (Yates, 1982), but other cases of sexual maltreatment may be harder to detect. One group of educational psychologists identified the following list of possible signs which a parent, teacher, or other adult can look for:

indiscriminate hugging, kissing, or seductive behavior with children or adults; bizarre, sophisticated, or unusual sexual knowledge or behavior; unwillingness to change for gym or participate in group physical activities; need for an unusual degree of reassurance from a parent; and excessive clinging, particularly when the offender is around (Brassard, Tyler, & Kehle, 1983, p. 242)

Another strategy for detecting sexual abuse is used by case workers who sometimes ask children a series of questions to draw out information: "Do you know the difference between a good and a bad touch?" "What is a bad touch?" "Has anyone ever touched you in this way?" "Bathing suits cover your private parts. Has anyone ever touched your private parts?" Some authorities claim an 85% accuracy rate in using such procedures (see Zales, 1988), but it is obvious that children can sometimes be led to give answers that incriminate an innocent adult. Furthermore, courts often regard children as unreliable witnesses, and leading questions are mostly inadmissible in proving a case.

To get around these problems, child psychologists have developed interview methods that involve the use of play activities. In particular, "anatomically correct dolls" (with representations of the sexual organs) have been employed. In one instance, for example, "A three year old boy . . . spontaneously grabbed the man doll, pushed the winkle [penis] into his own mouth . . . looking at the interviewer and said 'game, game!'" (Vizard, Bertovin, & Tranter, 1987, p. 22). Such acts demonstrate a knowledge of explicit sexual practices that is unlikely to be possessed by an unabused child.

Solutions

The ideal solutions to the problem of sexual abuse are those that attempt to prevent abuse before it occurs. Discussing sexual issues and the nature of sexually abusive touches with children themselves is critical. This requires that parents be informed about what to tell children and also that they overcome any resistance they may have to discussing such matters. In addition, schools can play an important role in assisting parents, and even more obviously, in preparing children to prevent or deal with overtures leading potentially to incestuous relationships within the family.

A number of educational programs designed for grade-school children have been tested and found effective in teaching information about the misuse of touch. The basic principles taught in most programs include the following: (a) body ownership—the child's right to determine who will touch what part when; (b) the difference between "surprises" (eventually told) and "secrets" (attempts by older persons to gain the child's silence about inappropriate touches); (c) intuition—teaching children to trust their feelings about touches that may be wrong; (d) saying "no" to wrong touches; and (e) support systems—encouraging children to continue telling about not-OK touches until the appropriate person is found to help (Conte et al., 1985).

Presentations employing puppet shows or other means of dramatic enactment are especially effective with young children (cf. Swan, Press, & Briggs, 1985). For example, in *Touch* (1984), a film also available on videotape, adult professional actors portray both children and adults in scenes designed to teach children about good and bad touching. Involvement and identification among viewers of the film is also encouraged by the device of including an audience of children who appear in the film at times and sometimes ask questions. Other media presentations are more appropriate for parents or teenagers (see *Child Sexual Abuse: The Untold Story; Incest: The Hidden Crime*; and *Shatter the Silence*).

Although these programs make important contributions to the education about and prevention of sexual abuse, they are not panaceas. As might be expected, educational programs are more effective in teaching concepts to older children than those in the early primary grades (cf. Conte et al., 1985; Saslawsky & Wurtele, 1986), and they are mostly inappropriate for preschool children. Past research has demonstrated that the presentations teach information about abuse, but it is usually not known to what degree they have actually prevented abuse. One exception was a study of a school systemwide program in the Kansas City area in which a 200% increase in the reporting of abusive touch by children was documented (Borkin & Frank, 1986, p.77). Finally, it should be noted that presentations should be balanced, and horror stories should be played down. In one program taught by members of a sheriff's department in a large city, assaults by strangers were overemphasized. Children were told, "There are people outside who want to grab you and take you into their cars because they want to take you away from your Mommie" (Conte et al., 1985, pp. 323-324). Such information can be frightening to children. It is also important that the positive as well as the negative aspects of touch be emphasized if programs are to do more good than harm.

When repeated abuse has been detected, the perpetrator is usually removed from the scene by the courts. This is often necessary, but there are problems with enforcing a separation when the offender is not incarcerated, and it is often difficult to secure the evidence necessary for conviction. Another legal solution is to require counseling for the offender. This was the approach followed in the fictional account of *Something About Amelia*. We do not know at present how effective this approach is. Finally, the most promising intervention may be programs in which parents voluntarily join in counseling or self-help groups designed along the lines of Alcoholics Anonymous, including Parents United and Parents Anonymous. One review of the studies reports a 70% success rate for such programs—not as high as we would like to see, but more effective than programs targeting neglect or physical abuse (Cohn & Daro, 1987, p. 438).

CHILDREN: PHYSICAL ABUSE

Because incest is especially abhorred in this society, it is not surprising that laws against it have been on the books for many years. However, the same attitude toward physical abuse of children has only recently evolved. The traditional "right" of parents to physically punish their children prevented action—and even recognition of the problem—until a certain chain of events took place.

In the 1950s, doctors began seeing a connection between numerous cases of multiple fractures in hospitalized infants. They concluded that some of these injuries must have been brought about intentionally (Gelardo & Sanford, 1987). An influential article by four pediatricians on "the battered child syndrome" appeared in the early 1960s (Kempe, Silverman, Steele, & Droggemueller, 1962), and a flurry of publicity followed. Suddenly awakened, the public reacted swiftly: "In 1963 alone, 18 bills to protect the victims of child abuse were introduced in the U.S. Congress and 11 of them were passed that year. Mandatory child abuse reporting laws were instituted in all 50 states by 1965" (Gelardo & Sanford, 1987, p. 138).

Although sexual abuse attacks the self-esteem of children and produces some long-range emotional problems, the effects of physical abuse are even more extensive. These include the obvious— physical injuries— ranging from bruises, welts, and skin punctures (about 70% of cases) to bone fractures (about 20%) and internal injuries (about 30%). Less obvious but common effects are intellectual retardation—even when brain injury does not occur—and deficiencies in simple social skills. Not surprisingly, these children are also more aggressive than their peers and more likely to become juvenile delinquents (Gelardo & Sanford, 1987).

Detection, Prediction, and Prevention

Detecting physical abuse is clearly easier in some ways than detecting sexual abuse, but there are still difficulties. Although the repetitive appearance of bruises and other physical signs are indicators, it is obvious that children can sustain injuries by accident, some being more prone to this than others, thus providing a loophole in detection for some offenders.

Sometimes parents shift abused children from school to school or hospital to hospital. Even when teachers suspect mistreatment, bringing out the facts can be a sensitive issue. In one case, for example, a mother aggressively accused preschool teachers of neglectfully allowing her child to become bruised in play activities. When the teachers eventually "wondered with her" whether these problems occurred at home, the mother confessed to being abusive, and psychological help was sought for her with her cooperation (Furman, 1986, p. 201).

Besides the physical signs, one author suggests that "personal criticism of the school, avoidance of contacts and conferences with the staff, evasiveness about the child's history and family life, and extreme touchiness about questions related to it, are not infrequent signs of parental difficulty with abuse" (Furman, 1986, p. 201).

Another approach to detection is the attempt to identify families at risk of abuse as a means of prevention. Much of the early research was directed toward discovering the causes of abuse (see Gelardo & Sanford, 1987, p. 146). We know, for example, that low income, especially combined with unemployment (leaving a frustrated father at home), is associated with abuse, although abuse occurs in more affluent families as well. Families in which abuse occurs also tend to be isolated socially, but it is not clear whether this is a cause or an effect of the problem. That is, a lack of social contacts may thrust the family together, making conflict more explosive, or abusing parents may isolate themselves as a way of avoiding detection. By themselves, such factors are not very helpful in predicting which specific families are most likely to have problems.

A newer emphasis in research is the attempt to develop screening tests for parents to find those most likely to engage in abuse. The idea is that certain combinations of factors such as hostile personality tendencies of parents, childrearing practices including little tactile or verbal communication with children, and certain characteristics of the children themselves may be predictive. This approach is promising, although the science is not yet well enough developed to make it practical and accurate in identifying families at high risk (McMurty, 1985).

How Does Touch Go Wrong in Child Physical Abuse?

Our present knowledge suggests there are two fairly distinct patterns associated with physical abuse, each involving the progressive deterioration of touch. One may be called "failed attachment," which is more common in situations in which the child was premature or there were other birth difficulties leading to early separation of the mother and child (see Gelardo & Sanford, 1987, p. 145). One study (Karger, 1979) showed that among preterm as opposed to full-term babies, there was more likely to be a problem of "synchronization" of the mother and child in bottle feeding at three months, with the mother unable to coordinate her actions with those of the baby. A pattern of miscommunication thus begins early. Later, when other behavior problems emerge, the parent may strike out in frustration.

The other pattern may be called "failed discipline," which occurs further along in the parent-child relationship, although it may be an outgrowth of failed attachment. Failed discipline occurs among parents who have a preference for corporal punishment, but who also apply it inconsistently. Thus, the same behavior by the child may be physically punished at one time but not another, or the punishment may be separated in time from the actual misbehavior. Eventually, this acts as a reward for children, motivating them to see if they can get away with the behavior, encouraging them to live up to the parent's definition of "bad," or providing them with a way to get attention (and touch) from a parent who is otherwise inattentive. The cycle often accelerates, with more aggressive and defiant behavior on the part of the child and more severe punishment from the parent (Watkins & Bradbard, 1982, p. 328).

Solutions

The most common interventions are similar to those used with sexual abuse: (a) placing the child in a foster home and/or incarcerating the offender; (b) referring the parents to self-help groups such as Parent's Anonymous; and (c) group treatment for the entire family. These approaches are directed toward long-term change and hopefully a permanent and satisfying outcome.

Given that the success rate for programs designed only for physically abusive parents (about 40% effective) is not as good as that for sexual abuse (Cohn & Daro, 1987, p. 478), it seems obviously desirable to include children in the treatment, although this approach has been rarely studied. Since children are sometimes brought into the pattern of abuse in the "failed discipline" pattern, group therapy may be appropriate for families in which older children are involved. A slightly different approach, used when the children are younger, is employed by the Family Services Program in Columbus, GA. This agency operates on the premise that child abuse is a problem that victimizes the entire family:

> While parents participate in group therapy sessions, ego-building crafts activities, and parent-education classes, their preschool children receive quality care and age-appropriate stimulation in a therapeutic nursery. A shared time with children is also a vital part of the program. Workers are able to observe parent-child interactions, and parents are given the opportunity to watch the workers model appropriate techniques of behavior control. (Watkins & Bradbard, 1982, p. 330)

The low success rate for physical abuse also suggests the need for short-term, interim support for families: home visitor networks, telephone hotlines, crisis nurseries and drop-off centers, and child-care instruction (Watkins & Bradbard, 1982, pp. 329-330).

Borderline Issues: Spanking and Bullying

Thus far, I have discussed only the most serious kinds of abuse, but there are two other topics that deserve mention—spanking and bullying. In the United States, spanking is not generally regarded as abuse. In one survey of college students (our future highly educated parents), over 60% of both males and females approved of its use (Deley, 1988). According to one study several years ago (Steinmetz & Straus, 1974), an even higher number of American parents, between 84% and 97%, actually used corporal punishment at some time. By comparison, in Sweden only about 20% favor corporal punishment, and a federal law prohibiting it was passed there in 1974 (Deley, 1988).

Most writers exclude spanking and related kinds of corporal punishment from their definitions of abuse (cf. Stacey & Shupe, 1983, pp. 5-6), perhaps in order to avoid alienating their audience and distracting attention from their cause—problems of extreme abuse. Nevertheless, these acts do involve the inflicting of pain by a person who is stronger on one who is weaker, and they could be regarded as mild forms of abuse. Let's consider the issue of spanking in terms of its effects.

There are two problems with spanking. First, it does not work in the long run, assuming the ultimate objective of parental discipline is self-discipline by the child. It brings immediate compliance, but longer-range behavior problems. Second, and more significantly, it teaches children that violence is a solution to problems of human conflict, and they are likely to put this learning into practice.

Research shows that there is a direct relationship between the frequency with which parents resort to spanking and a child's physical aggression toward members of the family. One study showed that among young children (ages 3-6), the more they were spanked, the more likely they were to attack both parents and other siblings. These children were fighting back, although not always against their punishers. Among older children, the resulting aggression was directed primarily against parents, and it was particularly strong if the parents did not also use reasoning as a means of discipline (Larzelere, 1986). One other study suggested that "positive communication" could counterbalance the negative effects of physical punishment on children's self-esteem (Larzelere, Klein, Schumm, & Alibrando, 1989), but no studies have demonstrated a positive long-term effect of spanking.

Avoiding spanking requires certain childrearing skills on the part of the parent. Among these is the technique of giving the child "time out" to think about what he or she has done, a technique that may be useful for parents to use on themselves when their anger bubbles over as well. Other approaches involve employing "natural consequences" (such as letting a child who refuses to wear gloves in the snow discover that it can be painful) and "logical consequences" (results agreed upon in advance, such as an adolescent staying home for a week after coming home late). When touch must be used to discipline, it can often take the form of simply picking up children who refuse to obey and placing them in their room where they can calm down.

Cool-headed actions require that parents master these methods, and many may be able to accomplish this simply by learning about techniques and putting them into practice (see Glenn & Nelsen, 1989; Krols-Reidler & Krols-Reidler, 1979). However, parents with quick tempers, especially abusive parents, need help in the form of training in childrearing.

The other behavior which borders on child abuse is bullying. I am not referring to psychological abuse by parents—excessive demands and constant verbal punishment—although this is also a form of abuse. Rather, I am talking about abusive touch among children—the playground bullying that many of us, especially males, encountered in childhood.

Bullies are often abused children themselves, although some are the products of marital conflict, neglect, or inconsistent childrearing (Khartoum, 1977). Their victims tend to be the smaller and more emotionally vulnerable children (Olweus, 1978). It is as though the bully who threatens or delivers physical abuse is saying, "I'm not the victim, you are."

We do not know all of the effects of bullying on children, but one of the principal ones is that the victims, who may already be shy, become even more so. It is as if they do not want to be noticed. An extreme long-range effect, which has been documented in a study by sociologist Brian Gilmartin (1987), is that the victims may become "love shy" as adults. These men are unable to participate in courtship, marriage, or family roles, despite being heterosexual and actually preferring the company of females.

Gilmartin surveyed single men who had never married, not out of choice, but rather from a fear of approaching women. One group consisted of college-age men, the other of men over 35; only 5% were not virgins. Two items of information on the questionnaire were highly predictive of love shyness: These men reported being bullied by peers as a child, and they said they had never fought back. This finding makes sense if you consider that men are taught they must be capable of protecting themselves and women in order to qualify for romantic relationships.

Some men escape this pattern by turning on the bully when they are still boys, and this was my experience. As a child, one bully threatened to beat me up over a period of many years. Finally, on one occasion he ordered me to do something and I refused. We fought in the gymnasium of my junior high school, with most of the boys from my class watching. The result was that he came away with a black eye, and I lost my reputation as the class coward.

This was a very positive experience for me in some ways, but it also left its mark. For a long time, continuing into my young adulthood, I found it necessary to confront every bully I came across, including authority figures who were using forms of coercion other than physical threats. I had to learn as an adult what I could have been taught as a child: Verbal assertiveness is often more effective in dealing with aggression—both verbal and physical—than counteraggression.

Some schools have instituted programs to deal with the problem of playground bullying. Methods include showing films and conducting discussions with students about the problem; teaching victimized children to be firm in telling bullies to leave them alone; and teaching martial arts that emphasize a philosophy of turning aside aggression, both physically and verbally (Floyd, 1985; Olweus, 1978; Smith, 1991; see also *Bully*).

ADULTS: DOMESTIC VIOLENCE

The battering of spouses is often an encompassing problem that is related to the physical abuse (and sometimes also the sexual abuse) of children. Many people are surprised to learn that women batter children more often than men. In part, this is because mothers spend more time with their children on the average than fathers. However, there may also be a stairstep effect of violence: The father or stepfather beats the mother, who in turn vents her frustration on the children. Additionally, a battered woman is less likely to defend a child against either physical or sexual abuse by the man because she herself is intimidated (Pizzey, 1977).

Is Spouse Abuse a Two-way Street?

Not all spouse battering involves the victimization of women. In growing recognition that men also are sometimes victims, the term "domestic violence" has come to replace the older term "wife battering" among experts. However, disagreement about the degree to which domestic violence is a "human problem," as opposed to a "women's issue," has created a storm of controversy in the field of social work.

This subject was explored in a heated exchange of views in the journal *Social Work* in 1987 and 1988. R. L. McNeely and Gloria

Robinson-Simpson (1987, 1988) presented statistics showing that, in conflicts between spouses, women are about as likely as men to strike their partners, they are as likely to use objects violently and more likely to use weapons, and they are equally likely to actually kill their partners. In a reply to McNeely and Robinson-Simpson, Daniel Saunders (1988) pointed out that women are far more often hospitalized than men in cases of spouse violence and that when homicide is committed, 60% of the women and only 9% of the men are responding to violence initiated by the spouse.

The original conception, that men were virtually the sole perpetrators of domestic violence, may have been caused by biased sampling in research, since most early studies were conducted with victims housed in women's shelters. It may also be that there is a recent trend for more women to fight back. In either case, and despite the controversy, it should be noted that most current studies show that women are far more likely to be repeatedly and severely abused than men (Pagelow, 1992). Acceptance of this fact should not keep us from recognizing, however, that there is more than one way that touch can go wrong in spouse abuse.

Two Patterns of Domestic Violence (and Two Solutions)

The resolution of individual cases of spouse violence requires consideration of the way the violence comes about and is sustained in the relationship. There are two primary patterns.

Aggression and submission.

This is the way most people picture spouse abuse. Usually, it is the male who is the aggressor. Each time the violence occurs, he first becomes agitated for some reason that he blames on the woman. She attempts to mollify him, but this only makes him more angry, and he strikes her, once or several times. She provides minimal resistance and tries to escape his blows as best she can. Often there is also another phase to the pattern. Later on, he feels remorseful and apologizes, perhaps bringing flowers and vowing to never do it again. She accepts his apology, and they may be especially loving to one another for a while. The cycle then begins anew on another occasion.

In a sense, both the man and the woman can be seen as contributing to the pattern, since her submissiveness encourages his aggression. Why, then, doesn't she leave? A number of explanations have been offered. At first, she may believe he is actually resolved to change. Later, she may simply be afraid to act. She may also be isolated from social contacts, often at his insistence, so that she has no one to talk to and nowhere to turn. She may have no job prospects. Moreover, she may be a victim of low self-esteem, possibly as a result of having been abused as a child, so she feels "no one else would have me," a belief the man may encourage.

The aggression-submission pattern could also involve a male as a victim, but the psychological dynamic will usually be different in this case. Assuming he is bigger and stronger than the woman, he may assume that it is unmanly to attack her. He may be afraid she will turn on the children in his absence if he fights back, or he may feel he needs a woman to take care of his needs. So he tolerates it for a while. In these cases the violence is less likely to be extreme, and he is more likely to eventually leave.

Touch run-amuk.

This is the pattern in which "push comes to shove"—the hitting goes both ways and accelerates. It may be men who initiate this pattern more often. One study showed that although men and women were equally likely to strike one another, men were more guilty of "pushing, grabbing, and shoving"—the probable first steps leading to more extensive violence (Steinmetz, 1977). Yet, violence can be instigated by either party, and a couple may trade off on who initiates violence on different occasions. That is, remembering that one partner "started it" last time, the other may make the first move the next time, and the partner "fights back." Each feels justified in his or her actions each time this occurs.

In the "aggression and submission" pattern, the battered spouse must leave to break the pattern. Couple therapy or counseling is unlikely to work and may simply place the abused person in a more vulnerable position for psychological manipulation by the offender at a later time. Couple counseling assumes that parties are equally responsible, but the aggression-submission pattern is not a two-way street. Individual therapy for the aggressor offender is an alternative possibility, but it requires admission by the offender that he (usually a "he") has problems. Even so, the prognosis is not optimistic.

Given that women are more likely to be vulnerable both economically and physically, women's shelters are an essential element in any combination of solutions to the problem of domestic violence. Incarceration of male offenders is not an alternative because the problem is too big, and when police are called to the scene, arrests occur in only 10% of the cases (Gondolf & McFerron, 1989). Whether or not children are also abused, just witnessing violence between their parents is a traumatic experience for them. Women's shelters also provide a refuge for children. Because there are some accounts of karate-chopping women abusing men, and some women are bigger and stronger than their male partners, in the future there should also be places where men can go. The need, however, is less pressing.

When "touch run-amuk" is the prevalent pattern, separation of the couple may still be the best solution, but couple counseling is another alternative that is sometimes feasible. If both people have violent tendencies, they may leave one relationship and later go into another in which the same pattern is repeated. Assuming there is some basis of attraction and affection in the relationship, including perhaps a desire to protect the children from exposure to violence, they may be able to work it out together.

Government-sponsored agencies may be able to play a role in this kind of therapy, and the "workshops for couples" I describe in Chapter 14 on "Learning to Touch" suggest an approach. We also need a national "Couples Anonymous" organization for battling adults parallel to the Parents Anonymous groups that deal with child sexual and physical abuse.

ADULTS: SEXUAL AGGRESSION AND RAPE

Although rape is in some ways the ultimate in abusive touch, it also shares much with other pathologies of touch. Females are far more likely to be the victims of sexual aggression than men. Rape more frequently involves a combination of violence and illicit sexual acts, but coercion may replace force in many situations, just as it often does in child sexual abuse. Although the image of rape that comes to mind for most people is an attack by a stranger, there is growing evidence that, like other forms of abuse, the offender is more commonly a person well known to the victim.

Seeing rape as simply another form of abusive touch has a distinct advantage. It robs it of its special status in popular misconceptions as a bizarre criminal activity that happens only to women who do not exercise proper caution. Experts say that a primary reason for the underreporting of rape is that many women who are victims do not realize that their rights as human beings and as citizens deserving protection under the law have been violated (Kilpatrick & People Against Rape, 1986). This "hidden rape" may take the form of a husband forcing sexual acts on his wife. In some states, this is not defined legally as rape, but even where it is, some women do not realize they have recourse to the law. More commonly, unreported incidents involve "date rape," when a woman may assume she is responsible for having gone out with the man in the first place or that nothing can be done about it. It is also helpful to recognize that rape is the near relative of other forms of sexual aggression (unwanted sexual touching) that fall short of intercourse or penetration. These acts also constitute abusive touch, and in many cases they are covered by laws against molestation.

Why Men Rape

One of the common misconceptions about rape is that it is primarily moti-vated by sexual desire and that aggression is simply the means the man uses to accomplish his end. However, the evidence suggests the reverse, that the desire to dominate is primary, and sexual arousal is the by-prod-uct. It seems likely that this is true even for "date rapists" who do not have a history of violence.

One study of male prisoners who were convicted rapists found that the men were more aroused by depictions of sexual acts involving violence against women than other erotic scenes. Furthermore, they were also aroused by representations of nonsexual physical aggression toward women, but not by similar acts directed at men (Quinsey, Chaplin, & Upfold, 1984). Clearly, domination of and violence toward women was erotically stimulating to these men. What is even more distressing, howev-er, is other research that has shown that similar responses could be readily reproduced in men who were nonrapists, including populations of normal college students.

One series of studies showed that depictions of violent sexual acts against women caused men to have more fantasies about rape, to be more accepting of violence toward women, and to entertain the possibility that they might use force themselves (Malamuth, 1981; Malamuth & Check, 1981a, 1981b; Malamuth, Haber, & Feshback, 1980). In another study, college students experienced massive exposure to pornographic films involving coercion or violence toward women. This resulted in men reporting less compassion for rape victims and for women in general. Even women who viewed the films were affected in this way, although to a less-er degree (Zillman & Bryant, 1982).

The solution is not to ban pornography. Pornography does not cre-ate the desire to dominate sexually, but rather panders to such impulses. Instead, the roots of the problem are to be found in societal attitudes toward women and sexuality, and this explains both why men sometimes rape and women sometimes do not report it. This point could be illustrated by exam-ples from lower-income groups, but it can be demonstrated more clearly by a look at the most common forms of sexual aggression found among those who are young, educated, and of a middle class background.

Sexual Aggression, Date Rape, and the College Student

Sexual aggression is not more common among college students than other groups, but there is more information available about illicit sexual acts in this population. Recent research shows that the problem is extensive. One survey of college women showed that 13% had experienced intercourse under force or threats of force at some time in their lives. The majority of these women knew their offender and many had been romantically involved with the man. Another 24% had been victims of attempted rape, and an additional 18% reported experiencing extreme verbal coercion to have intercourse (see Koss, 1983, p. 83). Other forms of sexual aggression are even more common. In one study of sorority women, presumed to be less likely to be victimized by sexual aggression, 51% reported forced touching of sexual body parts by men (Rivera & Regoli, 1987).

How do such beliefs interact with a man's behavior when date rape or other acts of sexual aggression occur? Who are these aggressors, especially those known to the women? Most are not men you would notice as being odd in any way. In one study, college men who were admitted date rapists were given a battery of psychological tests (Koss, Leonard, Beezley, & Oros, 1985). The results showed they were not identifiable as persons with psychopathological tendencies. Rather, they had certain beliefs or attitudes about sexuality and relationships between men and women, and they were divided into two distinct groups ôn the basis of the tests. The "adversarial rapists" view men and women as being essentially in conflict with one another. They are likely to agree with statements such as "A man's got to show the woman who's boss right from the start or he'll be henpecked," or "Most women are sly and manipulating when out to get a man." The other group, surprisingly, were "traditionalists." They are men who are conservative about women and sexuality, and they tend to agree with statements like "If a woman wants a man to marry her she shouldn't have sex with him until she's got him," or "A woman shouldn't give in sexually to a man too easily or he'll think she's loose." Each of these perspectives are obviously representative of major portions of American society.

How do such beliefs interact with a man's behavior when date rape or other acts of sexual aggression occur? Psychologists Charlene Muehlenhard and Melaney Linton (1987) have identified certain "risk factors." Incidents are more likely to occur when the man initiates the date, pays all expenses, and drives. If the couple "parks" to neck or goes to the man's apartment, or if the man feels the woman enticed him in some other way, such as by wearing "suggestive clothing," the probability of an attack is increased. Heavy alcohol or drug use may also contribute.

It is obvious that none of these conditions is particularly unusual, and at least some of them could occur on almost any date. However, when the man also possesses a certain set of beliefs, perhaps "liberated" by stimulants, the following picture of his perspective emerges: She has placed herself in a vulnerable position and therefore either "deserves" what she gets or has "led me on."

Date rape does not usually involve extreme forms of violence. Why, then, does the woman submit? Accounts of women show that the elements of surprise, disbelief, and uncertainty about what to do are major factors. For example, the following is the story of "Tori," as recounted by a female journalist who had interviewed victims of date rape:

> She and her date had dinner at his house. They kissed a bit. "We were sitting on the couch watching a movie. . . . Then he started grabbing me and trying to caress my breast and I kept saying 'stop' and he . . . he picked me up and then from there . . ." she shifts uncomfortably. "I don't want to go into it."

> Tori's pause in relating her story is characteristic for all the women interviewed for this story. To Tori, date rape is still a relatively new and seemingly taboo subject, making it more difficult to recount.

> But she continues to recall her experience. "He . . . he raped me, and after he ejaculated . . . I didn't know what had happened, but I kicked him in the crotch as hard as I could when my knees got free . . . I was covered with blood. I was bleeding so profusely. I never have known pain so bad . . ." She pauses to gather her thoughts. "He was saying things like, 'Say that you love me, you know you love me, you know you want this—you want this like I want this.' I couldn't believe he was saying that." (Chapin, 1989, p. C1)

Another woman said, "I didn't look at it like rape. I just thought, 'My God, this guy is forcing me to do something I don't want to. . . .' I thought rape was some guy coming out of bushes at you" (p. C3). These women were simply unprepared for such an experience.

Why don't women report these kinds of incidents? We know that rape is vastly underreported in general; the highest estimates suggest that only about 25% of rapes are reported to the police (Kilpatrick & People Against Rape, 1983, p. 92). The rate is even lower for college students; one estimate is that for every 10-15 rapes in this group, only 1 is reported (Koss, Gidycz, & Wisniewski, 1987, p. 168). It seems likely that the percentage of cases of date rape which is reported to the police is at least as low, and in many cases, the women do not tell anyone at all. Here again, societal attitudes and beliefs about how other people will respond are influential.

The myth that women actually want to be raped is shared by many men, but among women the prevalent myth is that a woman who does get raped was in some way guilty—of a lack of caution, if nothing else. As one older woman expressed it when her daughter told her about a friend who was date raped, "She should have known better." Many women are embarrassed or fearful they will be stigmatized if they tell about an incident, and some do not know their rights have been violated. One study showed that 48% of women who had been forced to have intercourse did not acknowledge that they had been raped at all (Koss, 1983, p. 89). Almost all such cases involve persons well known to the victim.

The Effects of Rape on Women

It is obvious that date rape is frequently traumatic for victims and may affect them for many years afterwards. As one writer put it, "when violence wears a friendly face, the damage can be devastating" (Chapin, 1989, p. C1). We know little from research about the specific after shocks of date rape, but there is considerable information available about the effects of rape in general. One study showed that 33% of rape victims reported seriously considering suicide, and 11% had actually attempted it. Most victims bear their wound alone; a bare 15% had sought psychological counseling (Kilpatrick & People Against Rape, 1983, p. 92). Even for those who have sought professional help, however, recovery may take a long time, and some never recover completely (Ellis, 1983; Lenox & Gannon, 1983). Clearly, this form of abusive touch may leave its mark indelibly on the life of the victim.

Solutions

As with other kinds of abusive touch, the response of most legislatures, especially after some dramatic event captures public attention, is to pass tougher laws. Some groups have made it their sole purpose to lobby for broader legal definitions of rape and sexual assault and more severe penalties. While there is a moral issue here, by itself, this is not much of a solution to the problem. There is little evidence that more stringent laws have any deterrent effect, and they may actually discourage juries from convicting offenders when there is any doubt about their guilt. The great majority of rape and assault cases do not result in convictions (Clark & Lewis, 1977), and many prosecuting attorneys do not believe they can win a case before a jury of average citizens (Koss, 1992, pp. 25-26).

Because societal attitudes toward rape and sexual aggression are part of the problem, effective and responsible public information about them could help. One goal should be to remove blame from the victims. This could have the effect not only of encouraging those who know victims to provide more emotional support, but also improving law enforcement by making it more likely that women will report incidents. Television and film dramatizations can be especially effective in bringing about a different mind set. A recent movie, *The Accused,* is a good example.

The story was based on a famous case in Boston in which a woman was raped in a bar as a crowd of men watched. In the film version, the rapists are not convicted, but the woman (played by Jodie Foster) goes on to sue the onlookers. Toward the end of the film, the rape itself is presented in a flashback as the incident is recounted in the trial. One woman reviewer said she was at first surprised to see how flirtatiously the woman behaved in the enactment just before the rape. By that point, however, the movie audience has identified strongly with the victim, and the message is made all the more clear: Even a woman who acts seductively does not deserve to be raped.

Preventive education programs can help as well. For women, such a program involves informing them of their rights and providing training in self-defense and assertiveness. For both men and women, sex education classes in schools and seminars and short courses in colleges and universities can provide information on what constitutes sexual aggression and what the law says. This approach seems especially useful for dealing with the problem of date rape. Although there has been some research on the effectiveness of educational programs (see Mann, Hecht & Valentine, 1988), more is needed to determine which programs and methods are most effective.

Finally, given that changing the attitudes of men may take a long time and will not be completely effective, and that some rapists do have psychopathological tendencies, the most important solution is to provide help for the victims. Just talking about it can be helpful. One study showed that victims improved in their psychological outlook as a mere result of the initial interview for the research (Ellis, 1983, pp. 484-486).

Self-help groups comprised of victims have also proved effective. They rely on a basic psychological principle for effectiveness. People who feel "different" from others because of some emotional trauma, and who may be upset by their own reactions to their victimization, begin to feel more normal when they talk with others who have had the same experience, and the trauma can eventually be overcome (Coates & Winston, 1983). Although family and friends can play an extremely important role in the recovery process, self-help groups provide a kind of support that victims may not be able to find elsewhere. In general, virtually all of the therapeutic approaches studied have been shown to have a positive effect on women in their efforts to heal the wound of sexual aggression (Ellis, 1983).

TOUCH: THE UNDEREXPLORED SOLUTION

Many causes have been suggested to explain various kinds of abusive touch. These include psychopathology, low self-esteem, lack of communication skills, lack of education, poverty, unemployment, environmental stress, alcoholism, drugs, bureaucracy, racism, sexism, and the glorification of violence. It reads like a list of most of the ills of modern society.

One theme recurs in all of the literature, however. It can be summarized by this proposition: "Tactile abuse begets tactile abuse." We know that abused children are more likely than others to become abusing parents, and children who are victimized may become victims again as adults. Often, the same pathology of touch has been traced through several generations. There is also considerable overlap across different types of abusive experiences. For example, sexually abused children are more likely to become battered spouses, and battered girls are more likely to become victims of rape as adults.

The official name for this pattern is "the intergeneration transfer hypothesis" or "the cycle of abuse." One review of the literature concludes that about 30% of sexually or physically abused children, along with those who are victims of extreme neglect in which basic needs are not met, eventually become abusive parents (Kaufman & Zigler, 1987). Considering that some abused children do not become parents, that some later exert abuse toward a spouse rather than children (Pagelow, 1992, pp. 110-111), and that neglected children are less likely than abused children to be aggressive, this is probably a conservative estimate of the abuse-to-abuse effect. Nevertheless, although 30% may seem like a small percentage, among social scientific studies on complex problems, it is a substantial figure. It is by far the single most powerful predictor of abuse that we have.

Research shows that the 70% or so who escape this cycle tend to have certain things going for them: (a) one close, supportive relationship with a parent or foster parent while they were growing up; (b) awareness of the risk that they are likely to pass on abusive tendencies and the determination not to become an abuser; (c) a current loving romantic relationship; and (d) the good fortune to avoid many highly stressful events in their present situation (Egeland & Jacobvitz, 1984).

Sometimes those who escape the pattern find a socially acceptable way to work out their frustrations and hostilities. World Boxing Council light-heavyweight champion Donny LaLonde is a case in point. Abandoned by his natural father as a young child, he was later beaten repeatedly by his stepfather. On one occasion when his stepfather was beating his mother, LaLonde jumped on his back and attacked him. At 15, he left home and made it on his own. He says, "I felt that pain was a part of life. But I also *wanted* pain. I subconsciously felt I deserved it." As a champion, he urges abused kids to believe in themselves, but he also abuses his opponents in the ring. He is aware of the paradox: "Why should a kid have to do what I did—go into boxing and put his life on the line—to get respect?" ("Jocks," 1988, p. 75).

There is another perspective to consider which is also related to problems of touch, but from a different angle. Many writers have suggested that the acceptance of violence in this culture is the root cause of abusive touch in general. One research investigator in particular proposed that the *lack* of touch at certain critical times in child development is itself the underlying cause of violence in society. James Prescott of the National Institutes of Health described his theory in an article, "Body Pleasure and the Origins of Violence" (Prescott, 1975).

Prescott based his ideas on extensive data supplied by anthropologists on behavior in tribal societies. His analysis showed that highly violent cultures are characterized by at least one of these childrearing practices: (a) a low amount of touch with infants, or (b) a high degree of repression of premarital sexual activity among adolescents. Most nonviolent societies were characterized by a high amount of physical affection toward young children, including carrying infants around constantly. In several other cultures characterized by low amounts of violence, allowing premarital sex was enough to overcome a lack of infant touch.

Prescott's interpretation of this data is that learning to associate touch with pleasure serves as an antidote to violent impulses. By analogy, he suggests that the low amount of infant touch, combined with the relatively high degree of disapproval of adolescent sexuality found in American culture, makes the prevalence of violence in this society predictable.

Prescott has been criticized for oversimplifying the causes of violence, and it has been suggested that his analysis may not apply to complex societies. Nevertheless, his ideas do dovetail with a good deal of other evidence. Not only physically abused children, but also those who are psychologically abused or neglected, are unlikely to receive much loving touch, and they tend to be more aggressive than normal children. Some of these children later engage in a good deal of premarital sexual activity, but as a means of rebellion and not necessarily with the approval of their parents. Taken together, the information suggests that a second proposition may be added to the prediction of violence from touch practices: "An absence of loving relationships between children and parents, including tactile neglect, tends to beget abusive touch."

If abusive touch or a lack of touch is part of the problem, then a remedy is to retrain people in using the right touch. There are only a few published accounts of the use of this approach, which thus far has been limited to work with abuse-prone mothers. In Canada, social workers have used the simple method of introducing hairdressing sessions into programs designed to teach family problem-solving and childrearing techniques (Breton & Welbourn, 1981). The premise is that abusive parents cannot nurture children because they have never been nurtured themselves. Hairdressing not only enhances their sense of being attractive, but it also provides a nonthreatening and caring experience in receiving touch. When hairdressing was dropped from the activities, the groups fell apart;

when it was reinstated, the groups began working again.

In New Zealand, psychologist Jules Older introduced exercises in touch as part of a voluntary education program for abusive mothers. Participants were paired and invited to explore different kinds of touch:

> The exercise has six steps. In the first, the standing person taps her fingertips rapidly and very lightly on the shoulders of her partner. This we call *snowflakes*. Following snowflakes comes *raindrops*, in which her fingers tap simultaneously and with greater intensity. Then she *glides* across her partner's back using the heels of her hands in parallel strokes. Next, with hollow palms she claps her hands across the back and shoulders, creating the sound of *horsehooves*. The fifth stage is *whirlpools*, a penetrating massage of circling thumbs. Finally the recipient of the exercise is asked which touch she preferred and is given an extra dose of that. Each stage lasts two or three minutes. When they are all done, the partners switch places, and the sequence begins again. (Older, 1981, p. 488)

This approach is cautious, but it is important to remember that these mothers are being introduced to experiences they have seldom had before, and they are also being taught to become aware of the different effects of different touches. Older has followed up with teaching these parents massage techniques. They report positive effects for both kinds of training at home, including introducing the exercises to their spouses and substituting touches such as massage at times when they are tempted to strike a child.

In Cleveland, Parents Anonymous groups have been used to encourage abusive mothers to talk about their own childhood experiences and their current problems in relationships, and the ways these affect their behavior with their own children. Touch was a prominent topic. The following is an example of a group session:

> One parent wanted to talk about her children's inability to touch each other without hitting. Someone else observed that her children also did that and she continued to suggest that perhaps it was because the children themselves had not had a lot of experience with good touching. Each member quietly and sadly agreed that that was true in their families. "But I just can't touch them, especially Michael," one parent shared. Another joined in, "I hate the way their arms feel around my neck. I feel as if I'm going to choke when they hug me." "And it's so intense," another began, "If I just touch her, she flings her arms around me and clutches at me and she won't let me go." The other group members shared their own feelings. "I hate the way his hands go around me. It feels like spiders or flies or bugs all over me." "I think sometimes I'm going to throw up when they start hugging." "That's

how it was for me as a kid. I was touched whenever my father wanted
me. It brings back all that for me when my kids hold me too tight."
(Comstock, 1982, p. 51)

In this group, parents also discussed their surprise that others
shared their experiences and their realization that their children would
have the same touch inabilities unless something was done about it. Low-
involvement kinds of contact which could be used with children were
talked about, and group members practiced "touching in passing," a simple version of what I call the "pure affection" touch.

The effects of these pioneering efforts have not been documented
with systematic research methods, but they suggest the promise of touch
as a remedy for abuse and as a way of preventing the passing on of abuse
to the next generation.

I am not proposing that retraining in touch can replace other therapies, but I am suggesting that it should be an essential part of most programs for treating victims of abuse or neglect—including the parents who
were often themselves victims. The approach applies mainly to circumstances of physical abuse, and it obviously does not apply to the problem
of sexual aggression among adults. The victims of rape need to heal, and
the offenders need to learn to control some of their impulses to touch,
although victims who experience sexual dysfunctions as a result of rape
may be helped at some point during their recovery by relearning the sensuality of touch in sex therapy.

In Chapter 14 ("Learning to Touch"), I describe the training methods for acquiring new touch skills in more detail, but here are some of the
possibilities for adaptations of those methods to the problem of dealing
with abusive touch:

1. Most important, adults who may never have known touching
    that is not abusive need alternatives. They especially need to
    learn to use bonding touches (Chapter 4), both with spouses and
    with children, and this requires practice.
2. Experience with new ways of touching through methods such as
    massage and exercises developed in the field of sensitivity train-
    ing can also introduce these adults to the pleasures of gentle
    touching.
3. In addition, parents and spouses can learn when not to touch
    (during arguments or when angered), how to recognize when to
    absent themselves from the scene for a cooling-off period, how
    to touch unaggressively to influence (Chapter 7), and how to
    discipline children without using physical punishment.
4. Most of all, physically abused children themselves need to
    experience new kinds of touching to overcome acquired aver-

sive responses. Social workers or other helpers can practice these behaviors when they are alone with children, model them for parents who observe from a distance, and observe the parents during playtimes when they are with their children so that feedback can be given to the parents at another time. For children who have experienced extreme abuse and have been placed in foster homes, it is essential that the caretakers be skilled in restraining aggressive touches from children without returning their aggression, to be patient in reinitiating gentle touches until they are accepted, and in understanding that some of these children, especially the youngest, may need to be held almost constantly until they regain their self-confidence.

Whether similar approaches can be used with sexually abusive parents is questionable, assuming parents have been conditioned to associate affectionate touches with arousal or have used such touches for the purposes of seduction. Yet, children need to learn the differences between sexual and other kinds of touches, whether or not they have experienced abuse.

Although it is true that abusive touch tends to lead to abusive touch, it is important to keep the reverse of this principle in mind: "Loving touch begets loving touch." This principle applies to people with normal touch experiences and to those with a history of abuse. It applies to everyday exchanges between parents, between children, and, most significantly, between parent and child. Children who receive parenting that is loving, caring, and consistent will have high self-esteem. As children and as adults, they will not feel the need to dominate or abuse others.

Section IV
Touch in the Workplace

10

Ten Touch Taboos in the Office

A RADIO ANNOUNCER at a Los Angeles station told me that a memo had been circulated recently in his office urging employees to avoid touching their fellow workers. It concluded with the statement, "We don't want any sexual harassment suits at this station." When I asked a woman executive what kinds of touches are appropriate in her workplace, she said, "No touching is acceptable in a business office."

Despite such concerns and attitudes, seeing touch in the workplace as a problem to be eliminated is not realistic. The impulse to touch simply does not go away when people put on a suit. In fact, in some ways the workplace environment creates special needs for touch, and, as I will discuss in more detail in Chapter 11 ("Professional Contact"), there are numerous legitimate reasons for touching in the office. The awareness of being evaluated on an ongoing basis means that touches of support and encouragement are especially wanted. Touch is also a legitimate and effective way of persuading others, and exerting influence is an integral part of work. In addition, many people see their work activity as an opportunity for social contacts that may carry over outside the office, and friendly exchanges can also enhance working relationships; both of these motivations encourage touching.

The question is not whether people will or should touch in the office. They will and they should. The question is, what are the real barriers to touch, the ones that should not be crossed?

THE TEN TABOOS

In order to discover what touches are generally objectionable, I asked large numbers of people attending seminars on business and professional communication to recall one or two experiences when they received a touch in the workplace that they considered inappropriate. Participants filled out an extensive questionnaire on each incident, providing information about the body parts that were contacted, the situation in which the touch occurred, the apparent purpose of the touch, their professional and personal relationship with the other person, why they found the touch objectionable, and so forth.

Generally, people cannot remember their past communication experiences in detail, especially behaviors that occur largely out of awareness, as many touches do. However, there are certain kinds of "critical incidents" (Flanagan, 1954) that produce what psychologists have called "Now print!" responses (Livingston, 1967a, 1967b) or "flashbulb memories" (Brown & Kulik, 1977). These events are remembered over long periods of time because they were very surprising, had important consequences, or were emotionally arousing. A particularly objectionable touch in the workplace is one of these types of occurrences. Such acts "stick in the craw"—and in our memory.

Once the reports of these events had been gathered, the next step in my research was to ask male and female executives, managers, and employees in an organization to read summaries of the cases, to sort incidents into categories, and to explain what each set of cases had in common that would make them objectionable. Finally, I asked many people from a variety of organizations to rate the incidents to determine the degree to which each type of touch was generally regarded as inappropriate.

These analyses resulted in the following list of taboo touches. They are organized into broad categories according to whether the touches involved sexual messages, excessive friendliness for the relationship, unacceptable power plays, or simply disruptions of the normal flow of communication. As you read through the descriptions of each type and the illustrative examples taken from my study, notice that, contrary to some common assumptions (cf. Hickson, Grierson, & Linder, 1991, p. 115; Tweeton, 1986), how or where on the body contact is made is seldom the sole characteristic that differentiates and renders a type of touch problematic. Rather, it is the meaning behind the touch—the total message communicated through touch, any words spoken, the situation, and so forth—that is significant.

Unwanted Sexual Touches

What was your first thought when you saw the label "touch taboos in the workplace?" For most people, the immediate association is sexual touching, in part because sexual harassment has received so much publicity lately, and in part because it is widely recognized that sexual touching has no place in the office. Nevertheless, people are sometimes unsure about what kinds of touching are sexual and the degree to which certain kinds of touches are objectionable. So, precise definitions of the different kinds of unwanted sexual touches and assessment of the difficulties presented by each type of violation can be helpful.

#1: The Coercive Sexual Proposition.

This is the most blatant type of sexual touch. In these incidents, a person in a position of power over another touched in an overtly or suggestively sexual manner; at the same time, he or she verbally implied or stated a request for sexual favors connected with a job-related reward or punishment. For obvious reasons, these cases occurred when the two people were alone. Examples include:

- During the course of an audit, a male inspector/auditor commented to a female employee that she "would want to pass the audit and not be sent back to the typing pool," while touching her thigh and crotch. She moved away, tried to remain calm, and told him she would report the incident.
- A female personnel director sat down next to a female member of her staff at a desk when they were working after hours. The director caressed the other woman's thigh and said, "You know, don't you, why you were promoted? There's another job coming open in a few weeks—it's yours, when . . ." The staff member said, "I don't want the job if this is how to get it."

The Coercive Sexual Proposition obviously places the victim in a difficult situation, but the responses given above provide good models of actions designed to insure that such intimidating touches are not likely to go further nor be repeated.

#2: The Expression of Sexual Interest.

Sexual interest or desire is communicated in these incidents, but the perpetrator is not necessarily in a position of power over the recipient, and no direct reference to a "pay-off" or threat concerning the victim's job is involved. Nevertheless, some of these cases appear to involve a rather clear sexual proposition:

- At the end of a workday, a female put her arm around a male co-worker and caressed his shoulder while repeatedly urging him to go to a party with her. "I'll show you a good time," she promised. He replied, "No, I don't want to. My wife wouldn't appreciate it."
- After a meeting held at the apartment of a male group member, when others had just left, the host embraced another male for several seconds in a frontal hug, also caressing his neck while saying good-bye. The male who received the hug did not reject it overtly, but commented in his account, "We are good friends, but I felt he had crossed a line between a hug of good friends and a hug between lovers."

In another version of this taboo violation, the expression of sexual interest takes the form of a professional put-down. It involves one person touching items of clothing or the skin of another while commenting in such a way as to imply or state that the other person's appearance is sexually provocative. The incidents reported involve male touch initiators and female recipients:

- At a coffee bar during work, the male president of a company commented about how good a female employee looked and smelled, saying "You must have a hot date tonight." During the comments, he touched her hair, tweaked her nose, adjusted her shirt, and sniffed her neck. She reacted with a surprised and annoyed expression, but said nothing. She interpreted the touches to mean "I'm sexually attracted to you and enjoy looking for a reaction because you're so serious and professional."
- A male district manager approached a female employee in a front office following a meeting both had attended and unzipped a portion of the front of her jump suit. He commented, "I couldn't resist. You shouldn't wear clothes with front zippers." The female reacted immediately, saying, "Hey! What the hell do you think you're doing?"

The intention of the offenders is less clear in these cases than when a direct proposition is made, but these touches are more insulting and can be even more tricky to handle. The woman who reported the first incident above (with her boss) commented on the difficulty of knowing how to respond:

I felt angry at myself because I was stunned and could find no words to say because I told myself, "Be a team player, don't be too female, then you'll be perceived as weak." I walked away with anger toward him, but more toward myself for my powerless position.

Although the Expression of Sexual Interest cases involving a sexual put-down may seem different from the more overt sexual propositions, organizational members classified these events together because they share the characteristic that the victim is treated as someone who is enticingly available.

#3: The Sexual Innuendo.

In this type of touch, no direct reference to sexual interest is made, but a desire for sexual involvement is suggested by the nature of the touch itself. Often, nothing at all is said, and if the toucher does say something at the time of the touch, no reference is made to sexual interest. The feature that identifies Sexual Innuendo incidents is that the touch involves a contact of the sort that would ordinarily occur only among persons who already have a sexually intimate relationship (a lingering kiss or hug, a brief contact with a sexual body part, and so forth). The remarks of the people who recounted these incidents in the study show that the intentions of the touchers were subtly masked by the deceptively casual nature of the Innuendo touch. Examples of this touch are:

- In an emergency room at a hospital, a male doctor standing next to a female nurse while they were working on a patient touched her on the buttock without comment. Although she said she did not feel confident enough of her interpretation to say anything, she was offended by the touch.
- A female pressed her breast to a male's back and shoulder while standing just behind where he was seated, asking him a question about a document they were both reading. He rejected the touch internally, but did not express his reaction since the touch could have "multiple meanings" and others were present.

For certain reasons, the Sexual Innuendo touch is less likely to be rejected overtly or strongly than a more direct approach. Because the touch is only suggestive of a sexual proposition, and other people are nearby in many cases, the person who receives the touch may be too embarrassed to call attention to the act.

#4: The "Humorous" Sexual Advance.

These touches are similar to the Sexual Innuendo touch in that contact is made with a sexual or otherwise intimate body part. They may also resemble the Expression of Sexual Interest touch in that a verbal proposition may be made. The difference is that the touch is presented as a joke, not to be taken seriously. In order for the "humorous" intent to be conveyed, there must be some kind of a "play signal" which qualifies the sexual meaning—a smile, laugh, exaggerated statement or behavior, and so on (see Chapter 6)—although this detail was not always reported in the descriptions of incidents. Some examples are:

- A female counselor was patted on the buttocks by a male coordinator, her superior. She rejected the touch by moving away and looking disgusted. She translated the touch to mean "I like your ass," but said it was meant as a joke. The male was described as a friend, but not close.
- A female was approached in the hallway at work by her superior, a male she described as a friend. He hugged her from the front with his arms around her waist, pulling her pelvis toward him and saying, "Let's fuck!" She commented, "It's happened before, I knew what to expect, it's meant in fun." Despite her resignation, she did not like the touch and pulled away.
- A female squeezed a male on his buttock briefly while passing by his desk where he was standing. The male treated it as an apparent joke and rejected it by saying, "I got excited there for a minute—I thought 'X' (another female employee) did it."

This touch can also be difficult to handle. It is sometimes done by someone who is a friend, perhaps one who secretly wishes for a more intimate relationship. The person who touches could also be a superior, making it doubly hard to object in a firm way, and the lack of a clear verbal rejection could be read as an acceptance of the touch as a way of having fun. For example, the put-down retort used by the recipient in the last described incident above could be interpreted in this way. In general, the "Humorous" Sexual Advance places the recipient in a dilemma—either going along with the joke, or, if not, possibly being seen as "overly serious" or a "bad sport."

Overly Friendly Touches

Some people feel uncomfortable about open displays of affection in the office—hugs, kisses, squeezes, or caresses—but they do happen and are generally acceptable if they do not disrupt work. That is, they are acceptable in the right relationship. However, when a touch is too warm for the relationship—a hug from a not-close friend or other affectionate touches from an acquaintance or near-stranger—it's objectionable, and overly friendly touches are by far the most commonly encountered form of touch taboo violation in the office. They are generally less troublesome to handle than sexual touches, but it is sometimes less clear when a line has been crossed intentionally because the touch initiator might conceivably feel the relationship is closer than does the recipient. In addition, there is an inherent ambiguity in such a touch: Is it flirtatious or simply an awkward attempt to get closer? Judging from the way organizational members classified these incidents, the ambiguity is ordinarily resolved by noting whether the touch is initiated by a person of the opposite or the same sex as the recipient.

#5: The Flirtatious Touch.

When this touch occurs between people of the opposite sex who are not close, it is usually seen as a way of communicating attraction. Nevertheless, the uncertainty on the part of the person who receives this touch as to how to interpret it is reflected in these summaries of reported incidents:

- A female put her arm around a male acquaintance's shoulder in his office and gave him a squeeze. The male who described the incident was not sure what it meant, but he added that she often flirts.
- Prior to a group meeting, a male who was a new employee held the hand of a female, also patting and squeezing her arm. She said he was an acquaintance whom she had met recently. While touching, he said he liked her and wanted her to "show him the ropes of the office." Her first thought was that he was flirting, but she was hesitant to make this judgment because he was an older man.
- In an open area office, a male repeatedly touched a female, caressing and tightly holding her shoulder and arm while carrying on a conversation with her. It seemed obvious to her that the touches of this person she barely knew were meant to convey sexual attraction, but since others were present in the room, and there were no suggestive comments made, it occurred to her that his behaviors might be more odd than provocative.

#6: The Relationship-Inappropriate Affection Touch.

When the overly friendly touch occurs between people of the same sex, it is likely to be interpreted as inappropriate affection rather than flirtation. The touch is regarded as unauthentic or simply confusing:

- A female was approached at a regional meeting of an organization by another female—someone she knew, but not well. The woman who was approached did a sidestep to avoid the frontal hug she saw coming and received an embrace around the shoulders, accompanied by a squeeze. She interpreted the touch to mean, "Look, we are old friends who have not seen each other in a while."
- In a hallway during a break in a meeting two males had attended, one put his arm around the other's upper back and patted him on the shoulder. Because they had just met, the touch did not make sense to the male who received it, and he was unable to translate its meaning.

Inappropriate Power Plays

Whereas the six types of touches discussed thus far intrude on the boundaries of appropriate personal role relationships, the next two types have to do primarily with violations of expectations for the performance of professional roles. Touch can be used legitimately to influence others in an organization, but inappropriate power plays push influence beyond acceptable limitations.

#7: The Status Reducer.

This type of violation involves using a touch to diminish another's status. Often there are onlookers, which makes the offense worse, but as one person put it in explaining why it's a taboo, "It's not a good idea even if no one else is present." These touches are more commonly directed by a male to a female and a superior to a subordinate, but the defining characteristic, as seen by organizational members, is that the touch comes across as "demeaning" or "patronizing" in the context of the situation. Here are typical examples:

- While he was talking to two other men, a male director put his arm around a woman who worked under him. She interpreted the hug to mean, "That's O.K.! I'll take care of you," and commented that he was acting as a "caretaker," showing an "older brotherly attitude in front of his male peers."
- A male came up to a female just as she was finishing a task she had completed under his supervision, and, in the presence of another person, patted her on the head. She translated the touch as meaning, "Nice job little pollock girl," and said it reminded her of being told that she was a "good little kid."

Men are also sometimes the recipients of the Status Reducer touch, although the one-up move is sometimes used less directly with them. In the following example, it seems as though the superior is giving a compliment, but the touch also emphasizes the subordinate position of the man who is touched while, at the same time, diminishing his status with his peers:

- During the course of a meeting, it was revealed that a male member of the group had carried out some instructions from his superior that other members of the group had failed to do. After the meeting, in the presence of other subordinates, the male superior put his arm around him while praising him for what he had done. In describing the incident, the subordinate said there was "a look of importance on the other person's face" and "I was being used to make a point for my boss."

Although a touch that emphasizes the lower organizational position of the recipient is the most common form of the Status Reducer, any touch that negates the professional role of a person has a similar effect. For example, victims can be touched in such a way as to treat them as children:

- A male high school principal pulled a female substitute teacher—against her objection—toward a vault in his office, kidding about locking her in.

#8: Affectionate Compliance.

This touch is used as an indirect way of getting another person to do something:

- A male put his arm around the shoulders of a female co-worker while asking her to do a job for him. They were friends, but not close. She translated the touch to mean, "I like you, and I want you to do this for me."
- A male approached a male acquaintance at his desk and patted him on the shoulder while asking him, "When can this job be completed?"—thereby implying he would like it done quickly. The man who received the touch interpreted it as an attempt to "get closer" as a way of "gaining favors."

The issue in these touches is not whether the relationship is close enough for the touch, or whether status is being exerted, but rather the mixed message. The touch itself—a caress, squeeze, shoulder hug, and so on—suggests affection, or possibly flirtation, but the toucher's words show it's really a compliance touch. What is objectionable is the manipulative intent. As one person put it, "He touches for his own benefit—to get you to help him look good to his supervisor." Ordinarily, it is a peer who uses this technique of influence (lacking the power of a higher position), but bosses sometimes use it as well:

- A female team leader caressed the shoulder of a female subordinate in her office, asking her to do a task. The woman who received the touch read it as "buttering me up" to make it "easier to get the work done."
- A male supervisor was telling a female subordinate that she would have to perform a task she had objected to doing. He patted her on the back while saying, "I'm sure you will see this will all work out for the best."

Disruptive Touches

The two kinds of touches in this general category are disruptive because they interfere with the normal flow of work and communication in an office, although for very different reasons.

#9: Task Interference.

This touch involves distracting someone from work activity for a nonessential purpose or the interruption of a conversation. It must be a common occurrence in the office, but it was the least commonly reported type among the workplace taboo violations, probably because it is neither highly objectionable nor highly memorable. It can be bothersome, however, especially when it's done by the same person repeatedly. Only incidents with co-workers were reported because the touch would ordinarily be acceptable from a superior:

- While talking on the phone, a female employee was approached by a female co-worker who touched her arm without speaking. The woman who was touched tried to ignore the other person, who waited at her desk. When the telephone conversation was over, the other woman told her about some news she had heard.
- While a female technician was performing a test at her desk, another female stopped by and slid her hand along the technician's arm, holding on for several seconds. The woman had to stop her work to answer a subsequent question, although it was not clear why the information was needed at that time.

#10: The Physically Aggressive Touch.

This is an extreme kind of violation, but it does occur. The examples are clear:

- During an important meeting, a male employee had made statements that a male co-worker had exposed as being untrue. When the others had left the meeting room, the employee who had been challenged confronted the co-worker, poking him several times in the chest while saying, "Wait until you need my help and see if you get any!"
- A male employee who had just made a presentation walked up to a male co-worker in the hallway afterwards, saying, "Where the hell was the pointer you promised to return to me for my meeting?" He emphasized his statement with a punch to the other man's chest.
- A female employee came to her desk where a female co-worker was using her word processor and gave her a push on the shoulder, saying "You're always here at 8 a.m. when I want to get to my desk." The woman who received the touch translated it as meaning "Get the hell out of the way."

Although verbal or nonverbal expressions of anger frequently accompany the Physically Aggressive Touch, thus reinforcing the aggressiveness of the message, nothing else need be expressed or said. This is one type of violation in which it is the nature of the touch itself that flags the behavior as objectionable, as these examples suggest:

- A male who was in charge of overseeing food and beverage preparation in a restaurant was taking a break. His superior, the general manager, walked past and slapped him on the back of the head, as if to say, "Get back to work!"
- A male and female who were co-workers were having an argument in the hallway about a business-related matter. After one statement he made, she slapped him on the front of the shoulder, but apparently not in jest. His translation of the touch was understated: "She disagreed with me."

An expression of anger without a touch would not necessarily be objectionable. As one person put it in his response to the aggressor: "Express your anger in words, but do not lay your hand on me."

DEALING WITH UNWANTED TOUCHES IN THE WORKPLACE

As with the "seven American touch taboos" described in Chapter 8, there are advantages to being aware of the 10 workplace taboos: (a) recognizing why a touch is objectionable—and knowing that there are plenty of others who feel the same way—can help you in pinpointing and articulating your objection; and (b) familiarity with the types of taboos can also help you to distinguish degrees of violation so that you can gauge your response.

Recognizing Taboo Violations

Dealing with inappropriate touches in the workplace requires some special insights. It's worth noting that most of the 10 taboos are uniquely applicable to the office environment, even though some overlap with the more general 7 taboos (Chapter 8). Number 9, the Task Interference touch, is the same as the Interruption violation. Number 7, the Status Reducer, is a version of the Double Whammy or one-up touch. However, touches such as the various kinds of unwanted sexual overtures and those that are inappropriately affectionate appear to present more of a problem in the workplace than outside. Partly, this is because people who would ordinarily have little contact with one another are thrust together in the office. In addition, power differences in organizations and the desire to influence others who are not close introduce some complications that seldom apply to more informal situations.

If you have been thinking about some objectionable touches you have received in the workplace, you may have discovered that some do not fit neatly into 1 of the 10 taboos, although most will. There are two reasons why this might be true.

One explanation is that a touch may be objectionable for purely personal reasons unrelated to any taboo. This was true for about 10% of the incidents reported on the questionnaires. Some reasons for rejecting touches are rather extreme and unusual. For example, one person said, "I prefer that people stay at arm's length and keep their hands to themselves." Another said, "The person was in a much lower grade in the organization—not my peer." More typical of the personal reasons, however, was a bad history in the relationship. In explaining his negative reaction, one person said, "I don't respect the man. A pat on the back from anyone else wouldn't bother me." You probably would not want to touch people who have these kinds of responses to you (the loss may be theirs), and you might respond negatively to touches from others for personal reasons on rare occasions, but nothing professionally inappropriate has occurred.

The other reason why a touch might be hard to classify, even if it is a taboo violation, is that it goes overboard, violating a combination of taboos. Test yourself on your ability to recognize the combined violations in each of these examples before I give my interpretations:

Incident #1:

In an open office area with other people around, a woman was hugged and given a full-mouth kiss by her male supervisor as he was saying good-bye on his last day in the office. Rumor was that he had been fired. Explaining why she rejected the touch internally but not openly, the woman said, "I wanted to be supportive to the end. I was also feeling very grateful for all the training and encouragement he had given me. I had expected the hug—not the kiss!"

Incident #2:

During a break after a meeting, a female was engaged in a conversation with a male in a higher position in the organization. She said she was trying to create an impression of herself as a "strong, independent, knowledgeable person." Shortly, her romantic partner, who worked in the same office, came up, put his arm around her, and stayed in that position. She interpreted the touch to say, "My woman. She is my property."

Interpretation, Incident #1.

If one of the taboo violations you identified was "Expression of Sexual Interest," I would agree, but it's also "Sexual Innuendo" because it's the kind of touch that should only occur in a romantically intimate relationship (although not generally in the presence of others in an office). In addition, it had the effect of a Status Reducer because it suggested that there had been an unprofessional relationship between the two people. As she put it, "Even though this was his last day on the job, it wasn't mine. The implied intimacy didn't do anything to help my credibility. Although people laughed about it [later], it was noted I was the only 'girl in the office' who got a kiss."

Interpretation, Incident #2.

The touch communicates "togetherness" (common among romantic intimates and used occasionally, but rarely, between close opposite-sex friends), but it's not Sexual Innuendo or Flirtation because the toucher was a romantic partner. Because the touch called attention to itself and thus disrupted the conversation, it qualifies as a Task Interference violation. Yet, it's also a Status Reducer because it emphasized the recipient's nonprofessional role as "girlfriend" when she was projecting a professional image, and this seems to have been the bigger issue from her perspective on this occasion. She reported that shortly after the incident, "I led him [the romantic partner] out of the meeting to the parking lot and let him know (angrily) that I felt put down and that his action had affected my credibility with the person to whom I was speaking."

Assessing the Seriousness of the Offense

Once you feel confident that a touch is inappropriate (and thus that you are not alone in this evaluation), the second advantage of knowing the specific type of taboo violation is that it can help you to select the appropriate response. In addition, such assessment can also be used by persons acting for the organization who must determine whether and to what extent disciplinary action should be taken (although this applies principally to cases in which a formal charge of sexual harassment has been made).

As I mentioned earlier, the final stage in my research was to ask a large number of people from many organizations to rate the incidents according to their degree of acceptability or unacceptability in the workplace. As expected, this information provided evidence that nearly all of the cases were identified as involving objectionable touching. In addition, this data allowed me to establish how serious the different violations were from the point of view of members of organizations.

Statistical analyses showed there were four distinct groupings. The group of touches that were rated as most objectionable consisted of the Coercive Sexual Proposition and the "Humorous" Sexual Advance. Although it may be surprising that a sexual touch masked as a joke would be considered as equally objectionable as a coercive request for sexual favors, both of these violations involve not only a highly intrusive sexual contact, but also a demeaning power move that threatens the victim's professional role. That is, both types of touches treat the recipient as a sex object and also as someone undeserving of respect—through linking evaluation to compliance in the coercive touch and through humiliation in the "humorous" advance. (The implication for would-be jokers is clear: You cannot get around harassment issues by implying you did not really "mean anything" by a sexual touch.)

The next group of touches involve either a sexual message or an extreme power move, but not both, which accounts for why they are rated somewhat lower in the degree to which they are objectionable. These include the Expression of Sexual Interest, Sexual Innuendo, and the Physically Aggressive Touch. Next in line comes the Flirtation Touch; it obviously has sexual implications, but only mild ones. The group of touches that are rated least offensive (but still objectionable) includes the Status

Reducer, Affectionate Compliance, Relationship-inappropriate Affection, and Task Interference. Apparently, the inappropriate power plays involved in the first two kinds of violations in this group receive only about the same amount of censure as the last two, which are simply awkward or uncomfortable to handle.

Assuming we are talking about 1 of the 10 taboo violations described here and not a violent physical or sexual assault, your first line of defense is to confront the person who initiates objectionable touches. The second line of defense is to register an official complaint, although there are limitations in terms of the situations in which this approach is likely to be effective. In most organizations, making an official complaint is not a viable option when the offense involves flirtation or one of the touches described above as the least offensive violations. It is true that in some organizations any unprofessional behavior, including those that involve these less serious touch offenses, could be reported to a manager or an ombudsman, but it may be that the person with this institutional role can only attempt to mediate the conflict, not to discipline the offender. Even if the offense involves repeated sexual or physically aggressive touching, it may be advisable to act immediately on your own, whether or not you make an official complaint later.

Taking Action: Dealing Directly with the Offender

The recommendation I made in Chapter 8 for dealing with taboo violations in general is also good advice in the workplace: (a) reject the touch immediately and overtly, and (b) make a statement that clarifies the specific characteristic of the touch event that brings your objection. Sometimes it is hard to have the presence of mind to do either of these at the moment, particularly if other people are looking on and/or the offender is a superior in the organization. Some people prefer to take up the matter in private. One woman wrote the following memo to her boss: "I like my job and I enjoy working with you. However, at times you touch me in ways I find bothersome. May we discuss this in private at your earliest convenience?"

However, there is a distinct disadvantage to failing to reject an unwanted touch at the moment: It may affect the way others evaluate the incident. It may also influence the toucher's interpretation of whether or not the touch was accepted.

In one study, Martin Remland and Tricia Jones (1985) examined reactions to a sexually suggestive and coersive touch. They asked raters to judge the following hypothetical incident occurring at the end of an annual performance appraisal interview between an employee, "JoAnn," and the head of her department, "Dave":

Dave rose from his chair and walked to the other side of the desk. Resting his hand on JoAnn's shoulder, he continued, "You know, with the right contacts and the proper instruction there's really no limit to your future advancement with the company." (p. 166)

Different raters were then told different versions of how JoAnn responded, positively or negatively, verbally and/or nonverbally. For example, the negative-nonverbal/negative-verbal version went like this:

JoAnn shook her shoulder trying to dislodge Dave's hand. Frowning, she stated, "I'm sure I will manage the way I've been going. I prefer not to advance through contacts or instruction of any kind." (p. 166)

The results showed that the raters were more likely to feel the touch was harassing and inappropriate, and also more likely to approve of JoAnn, if she rejected it in some way, verbally or nonverbally. This showed the touch with its implication was unwelcomed. Also, the nonverbal rejection (pulling away and frowning) was especially important because it led to further disapproval of Dave's behavior. That is, the rejection was obviously clear and authentic, and Dave should have known his advances would not be appreciated.

In short, it is best to show your objection to an objectionable touch immediately and clearly. This is true not only for sexual or hostile touches, but also for other inappropriate contacts because they denigrate your professional position. In fact, in some cases the less objectionable taboo violations, especially the overly friendly touches, are preludes to more objectionable touches that may come at a later time (cf. Hickson, Grierson, & Linder, 1991, p. 114).

Taking Action: Registering An Official Complaint

If you are satisfied with your own response (a clear rejection) and the response of the offender (perhaps an apology and a commitment not to repeat the behavior), you may want to drop the matter. However, assuming that sexual or physically aggressive touching is involved, the act is committed more than once, or other kinds of offensive acts follow, it may be wise to report the incident. This may be critical to establishing your case with an official or a review board within the organization; it might also be essential to establishing a basis for a legal claim against the individual or your employer at a later time.

The sexual harassment situation deserves special commentary here because of recent developments in the law and the fact that it is more difficult to substantiate than outright physical assault. The demeaning comment, "Don't make a federal case out of it," no longer applies to unwanted sexual approaches in the workplace. You can make a federal case out of it in certain circumstances, owing to court decisions based on the Civil Rights Act of 1964, otherwise known as the Equal Employment Opportunity Act.

How the law regarding sexual harassment has been interpreted.

Originally, this legislation was passed to make it unlawful to discriminate in hiring or employment "on the basis of race, sex, religion, national origin, or color" (Leap & Gray, 1980, p. 58). No mention of sexual harassment was made, but in time the law was applied in this area, especially in cases of harassed women, but sometimes also harassed men. There can be financial penalties for the employer, but there are qualifications:

1. The harassing behavior must be directed only against one sex. For example, a woman would have to show that men were not treated in the same way in an organization.
2. It has to be shown that the harassment had a negative effect on the person's employment. Originally, the interpretation was that a plaintiff had to show evidence of being discriminated against in a personnel decision or fired because of a refusal to submit to harassment—for example, being discriminated against for rejecting a boss's advances. Since then, the interpretation has been broadened to include situations in which the harassment created an unbearable work situation, a "hostile environment" for the employee (Faley, 1982; Webb, 1989). This change has opened up many more sexually intimidating circumstances for consideration under the law.
3. The employer does not have to have been informed or know about the harassment to be liable, if it's committed by a supervisor of the victim, or someone else operating as the employer's "agent." However, the employer is not currently liable for harassment between co-workers unless he or she knows about it (or should have known about it because the problem was widespread in the organization) and fails to take corrective action (Webb, 1989).

Touch and sexual harassment.

Touching is obviously not the only type of unwanted sexual advance in the workplace. The U.S. Office of Personnel Management defines sexual harassment as "deliberate or repeated unsolicited verbal comments, gestures, or physical contact of a sexual nature that is unwelcome" (Woodrum, 1981, p. 23).

However, touch is particularly significant in sexual harassment both for personal and legal reasons. From the personal perspective of the individual employee, surveys consistently demonstrate that both men and women make a distinction between unwanted sexual touching and other forms of harassment (Gutek & Nakamura, 1983). One study of working women (Powell, 1983) showed that the majority agreed two kinds of behaviors were sexually harassing: suggestive touch (69% agreeing) and propositions, which may or may not involve touching (81% agreeing). More women had actually experienced suggestive touching (41%) than propositions (26%). Respondents were divided in half on whether sexual remarks or suggestive gestures constituted harassment. Few regarded flirting or staring as harassment. This suggests that although organizational members are often not entirely sure about what constitutes harassment (see also Jaschik & Fretz, 1991), there is some consensus that sexual touching is prominent as a form of harassment.

Sexual touching is also considered by the courts to be especially significant in harassment cases. A law journal review of court decisions summarizes it this way:

> Claims based on exclusively verbal conduct have [generally] been denied. . . . Plaintiffs tend to prevail in hostile environment actions where they have been the target of several sexual advances involving extremely offensive physical contact (Webb, 1989, p. 264)

For example, cases in which a boss made occasional suggestive and vulgar remarks or promised a promotion for sexual favors were not considered in violation of the law. However, in another case in which verbal harassment was combined with "physical contact, including rubbing, pinching, patting and kissing," the court made an award to the plaintiff (Webb, 1989, p. 264).

Despite the widespread recognition of the importance of touch in harassment, exactly what kinds of touches are harassing has been vaguely defined in the law and in other writings. For example, it is typical of questionnaire studies that suggestive physical contact is explained only as "touching/grabbing/brushing" (Powell, 1983). This is unfortunate because it makes the identification of objectionable sexual touching appear to be a highly subjective judgment.

This tricky issue is clarified by the descriptions of the four kinds of sexual touches given in this chapter—the Coercive Sexual Proposition, the "Humorous" Sexual Advance, the Expression of Sexual Interest, and the Sexual Innuendo Touch. These behaviors can be rather easily and objectively identified. Although all four types are generally objectionable in the workplace, any question as to whether such touches are unwanted in a particular incident can be cleared up by noting whether they were overtly rejected at the time and/or whether a complaint was registered by the person who received them.

Documentation of the kind of touching involved in the Coercive Sexual Proposition, especially if it occurred repeatedly, would generally be accepted as evidence of sexual harassment in a court of law. The other three types of sexual touches might not qualify, but the law is constantly changing, and the overall trend is toward liberalization, favoring the harassed employee. So, under the "hostile environment" interpretation, repeated incidents of these types might also lead to a judgment for the plaintiff.

Whether or not a particular kind of inappropriate sexual touch is currently acknowledged by the courts, the fact that sexual intimidation in the workplace has received official negative sanction in the law changes the situation considerably. Organizations have taken notice, and incidents involving any of the four types could be reported through internal channels. All four are sexual, and all are objectionable. On the other hand, by its ambiguous nature, the Flirtation touch would not ordinarily qualify as harassment in itself. If repeated over objections, and especially if combined with any of the more overtly sexual touches, it might be considered as partial evidence of harassment within an organization.

Steps the Individual can take in cases of sexual harassment.

Let's suppose that your first line of defense has been exhausted. You have rejected approaches in a clear manner and have specifically talked to or written a memo to the harasser in an assertive way. The harasser has dismissed or ignored your objections, or seemed to agree, but repeated the behavior. You have decided that filing an official complaint is imminent.

One writer, Jo Cates (1985), has suggested a number of progressive actions you can take:

1 Document examples by keeping a diary.
2 Write a memo to the offender, citing specifics and saying you will go to a qualified authority in the organization, although you prefer not to take this action.
3. If this does not work, carry out your threat by going to someone in a higher position, a personnel manager or a union representative.
4. The next step would be to go outside the organization—to the State Fair Employment Practices Office or the Equal Employment Opportunity Commission (EEOC) Practices Office—or to use the union grievance procedures.

5. Ultimately, all other approaches failing, you can take legal action, first going through the EEOC (which has a certain amount of time to solve the problem), and then, if necessary, to your own lawyer for a Title VII suit (EEOC could file a suit on your behalf, but this is unlikely).

6. If you fail to get sufficient redress from these actions, a civil action against the employer (for monetary compensation on the basis of pain and suffering or job loss) is an additional option. A criminal action against the individual is also possible, but this would generally apply only in extreme cases such as those involving a sexual assault.

Cates warns, "if you do opt to take corrective measures . . . be prepared for the worst" (p. 25). However, she adds, submitting to the harasser is defeating to self-esteem and quitting the job can be costly (p. 26). Confronting the offender, in person or through a written warning of further action, is usually the first place to start, and you can decide how far to go from there. The problem might be resolved to your satisfaction at any point along the line.

WHAT SHOULD ORGANIZATIONS DO ABOUT TOUCH?

The following case may seem quite different from the situations described in this chapter:

> In Kentucky, two women coal miners were stripped, greased, and run out of the mine as "an initiation rite." The women filed charges of sexual harassment against their company and were awarded $2,000 each. (Woodrum, 1981, p. 21)

The harassment in this incident is especially excessive because of its violent nature, but it is similar in principle to the more common kinds of sexually harassing touches discussed in this chapter. These taboo violations are also humiliating, although to a lesser degree, and they can be nearly as intimidating, especially those involving coercion for sexual favors. The reason that a sexual touch is more objectionable than a suggestive gesture or remark is that it intrudes not only on the individual's right to freedom from unwanted intimacy, but also on the sanctity of one's body. When coercion is involved, the actions resemble those kinds of pressure sometimes found in date rape incidents (see Chapter 9). If the perpetrator is much stronger than the victim, the more extreme forms of sexual contact may suggest that there is more to come—the ultimate in unwanted touch, a physical or sexual assault.

When the sexual aggressor is male and the touch recipient is female, there is also a political implication. Sexual harassment has been used for a long time as a way of keeping women out of traditionally male workplaces, or as a means of keeping women in a submissive position once they are there. It's just more obvious in the miner incident. That is why it was inevitable, once the Civil Rights Act against discrimination was passed, that the law would be applied in cases of sexual harassment.

There is much that employers can do in a constructive way to deal with sexual harassment in their organizations. Many have already taken the following recommended steps (Woodrum, 1981, pp. 25-26; Powell, 1983, pp. 27-28): (a) articulate a clear written policy; (b) publicize it with employees; (c) establish a grievance system for complaints that protects the rights of both the complainant and the accused; and (d) act on the results of the grievance procedure, fitting the punishment, if any, to the offense.

As appropriate and overdue as such steps are, there has been an unfortunate side-effect of the current attention to the problem of sexual harassment. Overreaction by some employers to the threat of Title VII suits has created a climate of anxiety about touching and interpersonal relations in many organizations. I hear about this occurring in a wide variety of places across the country and in many types of organizations. For example, federal employees in the Washington, D.C. area report they have been told by the agencies they work for to cease touching their co-workers altogether. In a western urban college, there are posters in each hallway saying "Stamp Out Sexual Harassment." There is nothing wrong with that message, but the picture that accompanies those words shows two stick figures, one reaching out to touch and another recoiling from the contact. Translation? "Touch equals sexual harassment."

It is in the interests of both employers and employees to take a positive outlook on touch as well as to provide information on sexual harassment. Training programs at all levels of organizations should include a thorough discussion of the role of touch in the workplace. At the least, organizational members should learn to distinguish among the various types of sexual touches, other kinds of objectionable touches, and appropriate touching.

In addition, the negative emphasis on sexual harassment can be counteracted by information and skills training stressing the effective use of touch. Employers, managers, and employees should be aware that touch can further both personal and organizational objectives. This is the subject of the next chapter.

11

Professional Contact: How to Touch Effectively on the Job

C ONFESSIONS OF a male "organizational hugger":

It was at our annual retreat, and our top people from around the country had been brought together to exchange ideas, discuss innovations, hash out problems, and get current on what's happening in the company. I had always had something of an adversarial relationship with this one woman, so it surprised me when she volunteered me to head up one presentation and discussion. Toward the end of the retreat, at a dance, she came up and gave me a long hug. It said, "We're starting over, and we like each other."

When we were all leaving the next day, I was approached by another woman for a good-bye. She's a big, affectionate woman, and when she gave me a full-body hug, I could feel her breasts heavily on me. I was confused for a split second— "Is this a come-on?"—and then I realized it wasn't. There were other people present, who were also saying good-bye, and there was no caressing, just a solid hug. The touch meant, "I'm not afraid of my body or showing you how much I like you."

Are these really confessions, admissions of a person who can not keep himself out of trouble? The man who told me about these incidents is a high-ranking executive, second in charge of an extremely successful management consulting firm. He felt the touches were appropriate, and I agree. Admittedly, the nature of the work done in this organization and the special occasion on which these touches occurred are important considerations, but these incidents do suggest that touching in organizations can be much more affectionate than the stereotypes about business people would suggest.

Depending on how many years you have worked in organizations and how many different kinds of organizations you have experienced, the following may or may not be news: Virtually all of the touch meanings I have talked about in this book are conveyed in organizational settings on a regular basis. A few are inappropriate, but most are acceptable, given the right organization and the right moment. In other words, there are no special "corporate touches," but there are rules about the times and places for certain touches.

If you are a toucher or a would-be toucher, it does help to be in a certain kind of organization. You will be able to use at least some of the advice I give in this chapter regardless of where you work or expect to work, but some organizations are more empowering than others to individuals and their relationships. They are the places where professional touching can be used to the best effect.

There are a number of classification schemes for organizations, but one is especially helpful for determining the acceptability of various types and amounts of touch: the distinction between the "X," "Y," and "Z" types of organizations (see Ouchi, 1981).

The X-type, or autocratic organization, is based on the assumption that "the controlled worker is a good worker." The idea is that most people do not like to work, but with the right balance of rewards and punishments, they can be made to perform effectively. Those who rise to the top may be partial exceptions, according to this view, but even they are motivated by selfish interests. Competitiveness with one's peers and submission to one's superiors is rewarded in the X-type corporation. In nonprofit organizations of this type, especially certain kinds of bureaucracies such as government and law enforcement agencies, the name of the game is "keeping out of trouble." Authority and power, rather than strokes (tactile or otherwise), are the primary means of influence employed.

The Y-type, or human relations-oriented organization, is based on the premise that "the happy worker is a good worker." It is thought that people like to work if working conditions are favorable. Worker benefits, job security, and good interpersonal relations are stressed. Employee opinions are solicited, although decisions may be made largely by leaders. This approach rose in popularity at the time of World War II and has since waned. It is still in practice in some organizations, especially nonprofit ones which draw significantly on volunteer workers. Touching would ordinarily be common in these organizations, especially contacts that enhance friendly relationships.

The *Z-type* organization in the United States is an Americanized version of the Japanese model of management. The primary belief is that "the involved worker is both a happy and a good worker." Job security and employee input are stressed, but in combination with efforts to involve people directly in improving the way the work is done and in decision making. For example, quality circles, in which employees spend time in teams discussing ways of enhancing productivity, are one of the types of innovations of this approach. Satisfaction in group task-related activities and identification with the organization as a whole are encouraged. As in the Y-type organization, touching is likely to be common, and it will be used both to encourage work effort and to build personal relationships.

The Z-type organization is the wave of the future. It is the type of organization described in Peters and Waterman's *In Search of Excellence* (1982). Many Y-type organizations have already made the transformation, and some X-types are attempting to go in that direction. Your organization may be a combination, in which case it may be in transition. I am going to make the assumption that you are in a work situation, or are going to be, in which there is room for you to make a difference through the way you relate to others. I am also going to make the assumption that you are interested in the following: (a) individual advancement, or at least being noticed favorably in what you do; (b) the effective performance of your immediate work group and the organization as a whole; and (c) satisfying relationships with your co-workers, superiors, and persons below you in experience or rank. I will examine the ways you can use touch to advance these objectives. Let's start with the most fundamental touch of all in any organization—the handshake.

THE HANDSHAKE: YOUR KEY TO THE CLUB

The handshake is a ritual, but it's far from meaningless. There are three main occasions when people shake hands, each time carrying slightly different but related meanings (Schiffrin, 1981): (a) The introduction: "We are now available to each other. We are no longer strangers." (b) The reopening (when greeting people we already know): "We reaffirm our relationship." Another version of this is the handshake that reopens cordial relations after an argument: "We are no longer in conflict." (c) The closing: "We are parting but our relationship will continue" (literally, we will stay in touch). My research shows that the closing handshake is rare in casual, everyday situations, but it is quite common in business organizations.

All three of these uses have to do with solidarity, with emphasizing symbolically that a bond exists. Other, somewhat less ritualistic uses of the handshake are closely related in that they can be used to signify a strengthening of the bond. For example, the handshake is often used by members of work teams to say "congratulations" or "thanks." This has a slightly different connotation than when a touch such as a hand on the shoulder is used to convey the meaning. The handshake for this purpose is less personal and more group-oriented. It says, "We're in this together" or "We did this together," rather than "Nice going, you did it" or "Thanks for what you did for me."

The importance of the handshake should not be overlooked. It is the basic ritual that says, "You are important, you belong."

The Rules of the Handshake

Chances are good you already understand the rules intuitively, but it's good to know them consciously as well. One reason is that the handshake, like other rituals, takes on a special—and negative—meaning when it's left out or done in a way that takes back its meaning. Although these violations could be unintentional, mostly they are purposeful, and the victim of this subtle jab must have an in-depth understanding of the ritual to determine an appropriate response.

How to shake.

Emily Post (1940, p. 23) says the handshake should be firm, slightly more so for a close friend. The deviations are "the bone crusher" (which conveys the intent to intimidate) and "the limp noodle" (appropriate in some cultures, such as among the French, but insulting in the United States).

When to shake.

There are only two hard-and-fast rules about when to shake: (a) It's required in an introduction between two men, and more and more this is true as well when women are introduced to one other or to men, especially in an organizational setting; and (b) It's required whenever one person offers a hand.

In a reopening, you generally shake hands only if you are going to stop and talk. This becomes more expected the longer it has been since you last saw the other person. For a colleague you see everyday, or someone you have already seen that day, a nod and a smile are usually enough.

However, some organizations and some individuals are more formal than others, requiring more frequent handshakes. If the other person is higher in rank than you in the organization, when in doubt, allow the boss or superior to decide whether to offer his or her hand. He or she is also allowed more latitude about the "shake-only-if-you-stop-and-talk" principle, and might just reach out at some distance to shake hands briefly to say "Welcome back." No further conversation would be needed. The maximum would be a shake a day for each person. There could be an exception, however, if the first shake was because the two people had not seen each other for a while, and the second was on a new and special occasion on the same day.

A special occasion is any out-of-the-ordinary meeting. A daily or even weekly staff meeting would not usually qualify, but an appraisal interview would. A relatively formal social occasion apart from the workday—going to your boss's house for dinner, for example—would also be a special occasion.

A particular kind of special event is a group meeting at which people from a different organization or work team are present. This calls for a "touching round" (see Jones & Yarbrough, 1985, p. 43). Like the situation in which family and friends meet you at the airport, the rule is that everyone gets touched—in this case, with a handshake—and there will also be a closing round at the end of the meeting. Members of the same team or organization may or may not shake with one another, but all members of both contingents must shake with everyone in the other group. Visiting salespeople may not be extended this courtesy in some organizations, but generally it is a good practice to observe the rule for touching rounds in any meeting involving three or more people.

Claiming Your Key to the Club: Handshakes and Women in Organizations

The advice in this section is directed to women, but men should be aware of it too. Emily Post (1940, p. 11) says that when a man and a woman are introduced, she may decide whether or not to offer her hand. He should not initiate the handshake. This rule is going in the direction of extinction, especially in business organizations. However, some men are not sure whether they should offer their hand or not. As a woman, you might as well take advantage of the uncertainty. If you are meeting someone for the first time, go ahead and initiate. In the case in which you meet a male of much higher rank in his territory—his office, for example—you might give him a second to move in your direction, but meet him halfway. When meeting men in other situations, extend your hand first. The same is true for re-openings (with people you already know). However, be ready for the following avoidance tactics which some men may employ.

Avoidance Tactic #1: Male-only handshakes.

One person described this incident to me: A male Dean in a college entered an office, greeted a woman who was actually higher in rank, but without extending his hand, and then walked across the room to say hello and shake hands with a male in the room. The same Dean was also observed at a meeting to go around the table, shaking hands with all the men, but skipping the women.

As management consultant Susan Baile points out, this seems like an obvious insult, but it's not always easy to tell. Some men with a traditional upbringing feel it's inappropriate to offer a hand to a woman. It's more clearly a sexist behavior, however, if the man does not approach closely enough to allow her to initiate a handshake.

Countermove #1.

Fortunately, the solution for the woman in these situations is straightforward. She invokes the obligatory rule by offering her hand. The requirement to reciprocate when a handshake is offered is so widely acknowledged that in the rare instances when a man would fail to respond to a woman's overture in this type of situation, he and not she would be the one to lose face.

Avoidance Tactic #2: The flimsy handshake.

He offers his hand in this move, but it's not a real handshake. It could be the "wet noodle," but it's especially likely to be a palm-down hand; it could even be a single finger offered. The message is, "You're sooo delicate. You're not really tough enough to belong to the club."

Countermove #2.

Again, the surprise of your initiation may avoid this problem altogether. Even if the flimsy hand is already offered, you drive your hand into his palm, with the wrist turned up for the palm-down hand, and shake firmly. If he is really a gameplayer and is prepared (unlikely), he leaves his hand closed, so you shake what is there. It's awkward, but he will get the idea.

Avoidance Tactic #3: The hand kiss.

He has accepted your grip, but he may have one other move in his repertoire—he pulls your hand up for a kiss.

Countermove #3.

You cover his hand with your left, an extra-friendly two-handed shake.

In the best of all possible worlds, you would not need these techniques, but with a little practice with a supportive friend, you will be prepared. Should you also shake hands with other women? Absolutely. Should you hug other women as a substitute for the handshake? Highly questionable, although it has become more common in recent years among some women executives. The question is, do you want to join the club, or do you want to start your own club—one which excludes men?

THE SECRET OF SELECTIVE CONTACT

With the handshake mastered, you are ready to move on to other productive ways of influencing others with touch. The basic principle is this: You do not touch indiscriminately, at any opportunity. You do touch when it's appropriate and could make a difference in the relationship or in the other person's motivation. As I mentioned in Chapter 3, persons with "reward power," including those who have higher status and are respected, have more permission to initiate touch (Burgoon & Walther, 1990). Therefore, the higher you rise in the organization, the more your touches are likely to have impact, and the more important it is that you apply the selectivity principle judiciously.

The following guidelines for putting the principle of selective contact into action are phrased as easy-to-remember "touchstones."

1. Strokes, not pokes.

This is not to be taken literally. It's true that pokes are usually inappropriate, but they could be acceptable as friendly playful-aggression touches. Rather, the guideline is that you should touch only when you have something positive to communicate. Remember that touches derive their power primarily from the fact that they can be used to reinforce desired behaviors in others. This does not mean you can never criticize or disapprove, but just that you should not make physical contact at those times. Specifically, here are the circumstances in which you should *not* touch: (a) you have to tell the other person he or she made a mistake; (b) you are tempted to belittle someone while touching; or (c) you are annoyed or angered with the other person.

2. Different strokes for different purposes.

The broader your repertoire of touch meanings—the more meanings you can communicate comfortably and effectively—the more you can choose the right touch for the circumstances. If you always use touch for the same purpose—whether to get attention, express liking, or whatever—you lose the surprise element that gives your touches impact.

3. Different strokes for different folks.

People vary in their attitudes toward touch. Management consultant and professional public speaker Susan Baile tells this story (personal communication, November 13, 1991):

> I was giving a seminar on communication for business and profession-
> al women in a certain city. While I was discussing how to use touch in
> the workplace, one woman put up her hand and said, "I have a prob-
> lem. I'm in an office with twenty men, and they're all big touchers!"
> Another woman immediately shot up her hand and said, "Excuse me,
> but where do you work?"

Different strokes for different folks.

In a survey of attitudes toward touching among persons with a wide range of ages and backgrounds, Natalie Berryhill (1982) found that the great majority of people score above the neutral mid-point of the scale. This suggests that most people have positive feelings about touch. Some are extremely positive and score at the very top of the scale. However, about one-sixth of the population scores below the midpoint. Relatively speaking, they are nontouchers.

The type of person most likely to be a low or nontoucher, accord-ing to Berryhill's statistics, would be an older white male from a large fam-ily who lives in a large city. However, these characteristics are not very good predictors because there are many exceptions, and stereotypes are often wrong. In addition, research by John Deethardt and Debbie Hines (1983, pp. 144, 146) suggests that some people may be nontouchers in some situations, but more tactilely oriented in others. In particular, these authors found that people tend to make distinctions in their attitudes toward intimate opposite-sex, nonintimate opposite-sex, and same-sex touching with other adults.

There are at least two types of people who engage in little touch in the workplace. The "professional noncontact person" feels uncomfort-able about most touching on the job, but has at least a moderate amount of contact with romantic partners outside the office or with immediate family members at home. For this person, Deethardt and Hines's intimate/nonintimate distinction especially applies, although children of both sexes might be included in the intimate category along with spouses. This may also be the type of person who makes sharp distinctions between "proper" and "improper" decorum and workplace and private life. This person may limit his or her initiation of touches to handshaking at work, but may be accepting of other minimal contact kinds of touches on the job if they are directly related to a task.

The "general nontoucher" commonly does not touch either at work or outside, possibly because there was little contact in his or her original family or because of negative early experiences with touch. He or she may also be shy in general, corresponding to the "Sober Low Toucher" discussed in Chapter 2. However, this person may appreciate touches initiated by others.

If you are a high toucher, or moving in that direction, you may need to control the amount or types of touches you use with these individuals. It is not always easy to tell the difference between the two types, so it's best to proceed with particular caution, watching for the response you get. No response, especially after you have touched on several occasions, indicates that the way you have touched (although perhaps not touching in general) is unwanted by this person. However, sometimes the right touches with low touchers have considerable impact. In addition, in adjusting strokes to individuals, it's good to keep in mind that male-to-male touches—other than the handshake—fall into a particular category, requiring more caution than nonsexual, relationship-appropriate touches with the opposite sex or between women.

4. Different strokes for different situations.

Traditionally, at the moment when two politicians have just been nominated as running mates, they give one another an extended mutual hug from the side, or else they each join one hand above their heads. It's an expected gesture symbolizing their unity on a very special occasion. However, when Walter Mondale and Geraldine Ferraro received the Democratic Party nominations in 1984, they had their spouses strategically placed next to them on the podium so that all four of them raised hands together, but the two candidates did not touch. Mondale and Ferraro were not seen touching in public until the day after they had lost the election when they hugged in mutual condolence. The hands-off tactic had an obvious purpose—to make sure that no one could misinterpret their relationship as an intimate one.

Colleagues in organizations do not ordinarily have to be so cautious about their touching, but there are two similarities: (a) organizations are political, and colleagues must be aware of what their touches communicate to others who are present at the time, and (b) the expansiveness of a touch must be adjusted to the particular situation.

Organizations vary widely in their informal rules about touching. In workplaces in which appearances are considered especially important and formality is the norm, most touching is likely to be brief and constrained. Dress codes, whether explicitly stated in written rules or simply understood, are especially good indicators of the degree of attention to decorum generally expected. One attorney told me, for example, that he was supposed to keep his suit coat on nearly all the time, although he could hang it over his chair, for ready access, if he was in his office and not with a client. He added that touching was minimal in his office.

On the other hand, organizations in which people see themselves as being involved in highly creative types of work are particularly likely to have more relaxed attitudes about touching. For example, Ken Blanchard of Blanchard Training and Development is quoted as saying he expects hugs in his organization. "We're kidding ourselves that we can run around with our arms at our sides," he comments. "We shouldn't cut ourselves off at the nerve endings when we come to work. We need to act like human beings" (Oldenburg, 1985, p. B5).

Organizations do not differ so much in the meanings that can be communicated with touch as in the way the touches are done, the amount of intimacy that is acceptable. This depends partly on the type of touch, but especially on the body parts contacted. Touches become increasingly intimate in this order: (a) handshake, (b) hand to arm or one shoulder, (c) hand to upper back, (d) arm around shoulders, (e) hand to lower back, (f) kiss on cheek, (g) frontal upper-body hug, and (h) frontal full-body hug. However, whatever is considered an overly-intimate, out-of-the-boundaries touch in a particular organization, in general, the expansiveness of the gesture depends on certain situational factors and sometimes a combination of factors.

Formality of setting.

The latitude for touching increases progressively from the formal group meeting to daily one-on-one exchanges to work-group social gatherings to retreats or team-building sessions away from the organizational environment. Parties with colleagues, for example, allow more and friendlier touching than daily routines, but unlike other kinds of parties, flirtatious touching is still off base in most organizations. Retreats, especially at the end of the sessions, can be occasions for "unity touches" such as the arms-around-the-next-person team huddle and possibly some one-on-one hugs (but only when other people are present).

Relationship closeness.

As is true outside the workplace, the closer the relationship, the more intimate the touches can be. A spot touch to a nonvulnerable body part, or just a handshake, is enough for acquaintances. A pat or squeeze is as far as most male friends will go, regardless of how close they are, and the same goes for moderately close male-female or female-female friendships. Hugs and kisses are reserved mainly for the closest of opposite-sex or female-female friendships, and even they are rare. However, in most organizations these more intimate touches are ordinarily reserved for moments when people are alone, and the rules are more conservative at other times.

Presence of others.

Since it's O.K. to touch less but not more intimately than the relationship allows, touches of friends will be scaled down at least a notch when others are around in an organizational setting. In the company of others, a close friend might receive only a pat, and a moderately close friend might get only a spot touch. In formal situations, everyone gets a handshake, regardless of the closeness of their private relationship. The principle is that the closeness of a relationship should not be emphasized in a collegial atmosphere, and this is especially true for friendships between superiors and subordinates and intimate relationships between spouses or lovers.

The presence of others has a different effect on an informal special occasion. This circumstance allows touches such as hugs between close friends, and it may make somewhat intimate touches more acceptable than they would be in private, especially when others are not onlookers but participants in the touching.

Special occasions.

Hugs become more acceptable in most work environments when personal congratulations are in order to celebrate a wedding or birth announcement or some other major stroke of good fortune. A return after a long absence would also qualify. Even under these conditions, however, a hug will usually be limited to "the A-frame" (no lower-body contact). A major work-related accomplishment, especially a promotion, may be an occasion for "ritual hugs," and even acquaintances may participate. These hugs are characteristically brief, and they may be accompanied by two-handed, repeated pats on the other's back, a message that says, "This isn't going to last long." It's a nice ritual, but less meaningful than more personal affectionate touches in the workplace.

The professional relationship.

Some people advise, "do not initiate touching toward someone in a higher position. With the exception of handshakes, the boss should always make the first move" (Tweeton, 1986, p. 347). This is generally good advice, but there are many exceptions, depending on what the touch means. I will take up this issue in the next section.

ADJUSTING TOUCH MEANINGS TO THE CIRCUMSTANCES

The principles of selective contact—using positive strokes adjusted to different people, purposes, and situations—can be illustrated by a look at how different touch meanings can be used. Here is a list for you to consider in expanding your repertoire of workplace touches.

The Basic Three: Motivating Task Accomplishment with Touch

1. Compliance.

Accompanying a stated or implied command ("I need this done by 5 o'clock") with contact is wasting a touch, especially if it's a routine type of task, and it may be insulting in the workplace. The best way to use the compliance touch is to make a request ("Could you finish this by 5 o'clock?"), sustaining a spot touch, usually to the shoulder, for the duration of the request. The touch itself says "It matters to me." If it's used selectively, only when it is an important request, the touch personalizes and emphasizes the message. Avoid the temptation to remove your hand before you complete the request (too timid) or to pat or caress (patronizing and manipulative). Use the compliance touch with your boss only if your relationship is one in which give and take in influence is accepted.

2. Appreciation.

The touch of thanks is a reward for carrying through in an exemplary way. One person told me he still remembers the day things were in chaos in the office, and he hustled around getting everything done. Just as he was leaving at night, his boss touched him on the shoulder and said, "Thanks for today, you were great." Like the compliance touch, this one should be reserved for special times; what Ken Blanchard calls "the verbal hug" (Oldenberg, 1985, p. B5) can be used for other, less meritorious favors or jobs well done. The appreciation touch is also more appropriately used with co-workers and subordinates than superiors. The boss may see it as presumptuous, depending on the relationship, and the verbal hug of thanks when he or she has done something special for you will do nicely.

3. Congratulations.

This one is a version of the "announcing-a-response" touch in which you emphasize what you are feeling at the moment, but it's a particular feeling: "I'm happy for you, nice going." This one you can use with your boss, although then the touch would usually be only a handshake. With co-workers or subordinates it could even be a hug.

Sometimes congratulations can be combined with appreciation if the toucher is the boss. One male executive I interviewed told me about a recent incident that occurred soon after he had announced a woman's surprise promotion in a meeting. She came just inside the door to his office to ask, "So what does it mean to be a director?" It was clear, however, that she just wanted to talk and express her feelings. Shortly, she said, "I love my job so much. I'm so happy to be here. I can't believe I found my way to this job." He crossed the room and embraced her. "At first," he reported, "I thought it was just a hug of congratulations. But now that I think about it, I realize it was also thanks, not just for her work but for the way her reaction made me feel." He added that the door was open and the hug was brief. "I wouldn't have hugged more affectionately or behind a closed door."

Encouragers: Helping People With Emotions

Touches of appreciation and congratulations are encouraging in the sense that they are rewards for work already accomplished. What I call "encouragers," however, have more to do with dealing with ongoing feelings. There is one type of touch for the downside of emotion, another for the upside.

1. The support touch.

This comforting or reassuring touch is always personal to some extent, but it can also influence how people respond to their work. Because of the vulnerable position of the person who is given support, this touch almost always occurs in private. One assistant manager told me of an incident in which he had overheard a new secretary, who was very open about her feelings, arguing with her estranged husband on the phone. Later, she came to his office and said, "Don't take this the wrong way, but I'm having a bad day. Would you hug me?" He said he was a little hesitant, but the fact that she asked and the way she put it made him feel comfortable about the hug. After the hug, she said, "Thanks, I'm O.K. now."

Support touches can also be offered with superiors in the right relationship. Another man described a situation in which his immediate superior, a Dean at a college, was in the middle of being evaluated, a process that recurred every three years. A positive evaluation was crucial to the Dean's contining in the position. The Dean had just come back from a meeting with his superior, the Provost, and he "came in perspiring, looking as if someone had just beaten him up." The subordinate walked over behind the other man and pressed his hands down firmly on his shoulders. The Dean visibly relaxed and said, "Oh, Bob, it was horrible." They then had a long conversation about how the Dean could deal with the situation. Obviously, these two men had a close working relationship; otherwise, such an intimate touch from a subordinate might not have been appreciated.

2. The enthusiasm stimulator.

Like the congratulatory touch, this one is a version of the announcing-a-response meaning, but the difference is that the emotion is excitement, and the other person is being asked to share in the feeling. It's gentler but has an effect similar to the slap of a teammate to a player who is going into a game. One person touches another and says, "That's a great idea!", "Listen, how about this?", or "Now we're getting somewhere!" Its function is to generate energy or creativity, and it works for the toucher as well as the person touched.

Building and Maintaining Relationships

Although all positive touches—including those which are mainly task-related—strengthen bonds between people, the ones listed below are focused specifically on developing one-to-one relationships on a daily basis. These touches meet individual needs, but they are also important in the long run in getting the job done. They are analogous to throwing the ball around the infield after a put-out in baseball. They keep the channels open so work-related information can flow freely at another time.

1. Simple greetings and departures.

These kinds of contact are brief. The greeting touch, usually a handshake, but sometimes a shoulder or elbow touch, is more common and essential than the departure touch. It reestablishes communication and can be used with anyone. The departure touch is used mainly by friends, and it's usually an arm, shoulder, or upper back touch. The closing handshake is reserved primarily for formal situations and for acquaintances you will not be seeing for some time.

2. Special greetings and departures.

These are the bonding touches I called "greetings-with-affection" and "departures-with-affection" in Chapter 4, and they are used predominantly in close relationships. However, special solidarity events such as retreats give more license for their use in other relationships. In the everyday workplace, the hugs, kisses, squeezes, or pats which characterize these touches are appropriate only after or in anticipation of a long absence. At these times, and depending on the formality of the organization, the superior/subordinate issue may not be an important consideration.

3. Playful touches.

These touches provide a way of getting around the problem of being overly personal in the workplace in contacts other than greetings and departures. One male vice president said he uses what I call the playful-aggression touch frequently with other men. For example, he was walking down the hall at a rapid pace and made eye contact and exchanged a smile with another man headed in the opposite direction. As he passed, he grabbed the other man on the arm with slight roughness and said, "No laughing!", continuing to walk forward "without missing a beat." His translation for the touch: "We're on the same team. I like you, we're busy, and we're powerful in what we do together."

The same executive described a playful-affection touch he often does with a close male friend in the workplace that is especially useful when others are present. It's a gesture that one of a mutual group of friends initiated at one time, and it caught on. The executive calls it "the silly handshake." It involves entwining or wiggling the fingers when a standard handshake is offered, a touch which he says is "sort of irritating in a fun way" and that undercuts the formality without being obviously affectionate.

The Minor Touches

These kinds of contacts generally do not meet the selective contact criteria of "making a difference," but they are generally safe and can be good for getting started in a touching relationship (see Chapter 3). They include: (a) the reference-to-appearance touch, such as complimenting a person on clothing while touching the fabric (watch out—it can be read as flirtation in opposite-sex relationships); (b) the incidental touch when handing someone an object; and (c) the instrumental or helping touch (guiding a person in a direction, assisting with putting on a coat, etc.). One other minor touch, the brief attention-getting touch which precedes a comment, can also be useful, and it has a dual advantage. It emphasizes the toucher's need for special attention to make a point and also to allow contact with seldom-touched acquaintances. However, the attention getter can be irritating if overused or used at times when the other person is busy.

THE UNPROFESSIONAL TOUCHES

In the previous chapter, I described 10 rules about touch which, when violated, are almost certain to bring a negative reaction from the person who is touched (whether or not this rejection is expressed overtly). In addition, however, there are certain touches that might be *accepted* by a recipient (or engaged in mutually by two people), but that are questionable professionally because they draw undue attention to the personal closeness of the relationship.

1. The togetherness touch.

Outside the workplace, this sustained touch is used almost exclusively by close friends and sexual intimates, primarily in opposite-sex pairs and occasionally between women friends. Yet, it is sometimes used inappropriately in organizational settings. On one occasion, I saw a male school superintendent walk down a hallway in an administration building with his arm around the shoulders of a male school principal, talking to him earnestly. Several persons who passed by gave them a wide berth, which explains why this touch is sometimes used in the workplace—it wards off intruders. However, it raises questions in onlookers about the nature of the relationship. Even opposite-sex intimates are best advised to wait at least until they reach the parking lot to hold hands or encircle one another with their arms.

2. Pure affection touches.

I saw one female clerk touch another on the waist as she passed by behind a counter—no hello, request, or comment of any kind. It did not seem to mean "watch out, don't step back, I'm coming through." It caught my attention even though it was fleeting because it is an odd touch to see in a place where people work. Generally, people interpret a touch, which has none of the other specific meanings I have described here and is not part of a greeting or departure, as a spontaneous expression of affection. It could be a spot touch, squeeze, caress, or hug.

Because the pure affection touch has no specific purpose other than to show liking, it is a special gesture between people who are close that is used primarily in private settings. Ordinarily, affectionate touches such as hugs are used in the workplace on special occasions—to give congratulations, to say good-bye, or to welcome someone back—and thus do not convey "pure" affection. Savvy professionals who have an intimate relationship and work in the same place do not display their affection for one another in the presence of colleagues, just as they avoid the togetherness touch.

Nevertheless, there are some exceptional situations—work settings in which the pure affection touch fits. Usually, these are organizations in which nurturing and affectionate touches are part of the professional work. One hospital employee explained such touching to me as an "overflow" among staff members of the kinds of touching they do with patients and family members. Children's museums and child-care facilities also often have this kind of special-permission touch climate.

3. Touches of sexual connotation.

Unwanted touches with sexual meaning are clearly taboo in the workplace, as I discussed in Chapter 10. However, sexual touches do not have to be unwanted to be inappropriate if others are present, and even among sexual intimates, touches of sexual connotation in the workplace suggest questionable judgment.

AVOIDING THE EXCESSES: YOUR CAST OF CHARACTERS

Some people can be identified as a "type" of toucher because they overuse a particular touch. At some time, they discovered a way of touching that felt comfortable to them and stuck with it. The touch itself may be positive, but if used unselectively, it loses its impact because others know exactly what is coming. The following are the most common types as identified by members of organizations.

The Shaker

This person is not a "mover and shaker," but a handshaker, and it's usually a man. Sometimes the shaker is uncomfortable with touch and personal relationships. He may use the handshake not only for greetings and departures, but also exclusively when expressing appreciation or giving congratulations. Another variation is the constant use of the handshake for greetings. In identifying this type, one person said, "If I see this man seventeen times in a day, he'll stop and shake my hand seventeen times, always with a little bow. It's phoney and insincere, as though he cared about me, but it's only a ritual." This style draws attention to itself as a sexist message, intended or not, when a man shakes only the hands of other males.

The Fleeting Toucher

This toucher makes quick, fleeting contacts with others, sometimes reaching out, but falling short of making contact at all. The examples described to me have usually been women. The behavior connotes caution or timidity, as though the individual were afraid of making a point or being involved with the other person. An authoritarian boss might be pleased by this submissive touch style on the part of a subordinate, but to others the fleeting toucher may seem to regard them as too foreboding to be touched.

The Glued Hand

The touch that lasts too long for the purpose is often puzzling, suggesting the desire to control, although it can be simply a matter of social awkwardness. One man described an incident in which another man at a convention stopped him with a handshake and continued to hold on, apparently as a way of getting him to listen to an idea. The person who uses this type of touching is sometimes labeled simply "the hand" when the touch is frequently flirtatious or sexually insinuating. For example, a man may leave his hand on a woman's shoulder after getting her attention and while continuing to talk to her, or a handshake may be transformed into an excuse for hand holding. The foil for the glued hand, incidentally, is to move out of the other person's shoulder grasp, or, in the case of a handshake, to squeeze momentarily and then withdraw the hand.

The Compliance-only Toucher

One person told me, "When my boss's hand lands on my shoulder, I know I'm in trouble. He's going to ask me to do something in a hurry or stay late." There is nothing wrong with a compliance touch, especially when a request is important, but it should be complemented by other touches at other times, including appreciation, or else the connotation of contact becomes negative.

The Kidder

This toucher pokes and jabs continuously while making teasing comments. It's friendly but irritating after a while. Since the only defense is to poke and jab back with banter, some people eventually learn to keep their distance from the Kidder.

The Constant-contact Toucher

This type always touches, regardless of the purpose, usually with subordi-nates. This pattern sometimes overlaps the "glued hand" approach, except that it is less objectionable because the touch is so consistently done in each interaction that people get used to it. One affectionate, middle-aged woman who supervised a group of younger men told me, "I'm not afraid of touching men." She came from a family of big football-playing brothers and was substantial in stature herself. "Usually, they [her subordinates] are at their desks," she said, "and I always place my hand on their shoulder while I'm talking to them." The style is friendly and can be relationship-building, but the disadvantage is that the touch has no special significance and does not emphasize anything. It often connotes a "motherly" or "fatherly" attitude.

Although the various types of excesses described above limit the options of the people who use them, the reverse excess of "the studious nontoucher" has more disadvantages. One woman described a boss she had when she was a secretary. "He kept his distance from all of the women in the office, apparently to avoid giving the wrong impression," she said. On one occasion, this woman and her boss were working late, and he had repeatedly brought back a document with revisions for retyp-ing. Finally, he said, "This is absolutely the last version." Then he touched her on the shoulder and said, "You're doing a really good job." In telling this incident, she commented, "On one hand, it was nice to receive the compliment, but he had never touched me before, so it lost some mean-ing. I couldn't help thinking he wouldn't have touched unless he was feel-ing guilty." Touches can lose their impact not only from being overdone, but also from being underutilized.

USING AND PASSING ON THE POWER OF TOUCH

When used with good intentions and some finesse, touching is a powerful tool in the workplace. It can significantly affect the impressions others form of the toucher. Before reading further, take a minute to do this simple exercise:

Think of a person from your work experience you would describe as a "nontoucher." Notice the image you generate. Get an impression of the person's character and personality. Now imagine the individual as "a toucher." How does it change your impression? (When you have completed both parts of the exercise, go on to the next paragraph.)

When people imagine a "nontoucher" as "a toucher," their impressions usually change in one or both of the following ways: (a) The person seems more "accessible," "human," or "warm" when seen as a toucher, or else the person's aggressive tendencies are seen as an acceptable "style," "quirk," or "idiosyncrasy," rather than an all-encompassing quality, and (b) he or she seems more "powerful," "self-assured," or "confident," or less "frantic," "flighty," or "desperate." The adjectives used to describe the person as a toucher characterize someone who has influence *with* people, but not *over* them. Appropriately used, touches are *em*powering moves.

One "charisma coach" recommends a technique she says makes for powerful touching in the workplace. She says, "Touching should be a business tool. It is a tool to control your effect on people." She also advises, "When you touch someone, make it a point to hold on for a second or two too long, even if the other person flinches, you should not remove your hand until a second or two after the other person would expect you to remove it."

The idea is to leave an impression, but following this recommendation may well mean leaving the wrong impression. It might possibly be good advice for the fleeting toucher, whose idea of how long others expect a touch to last may be wrong, but it comes very close to the "glued hand" approach. My advice is to use the touch code, not to abuse it. Touch is not a gimmick; it's a way of relating.

Touch can be used as a conscious strategy, but it's most effective when it is used to make a contribution to the other person's well-being, rather than as an attempt to manipulate purely for one's own ends. One man told me he sometimes touches his boss, an anxious nontoucher he cares about, "because I think he needs training." For example, when his boss shakes his hand, this man will sometimes reach out with his left hand to touch the boss's hand or shoulder. When I asked him how he learned to be a toucher, especially with other men, he said, "My dad was a big toucher. He used to carry me around and touch me a lot." In a sense, this man's father was his touch mentor, and he is now a touch mentor himself. When you have the gift of touch, you have something worth giving to others.

Section V
Special Applications

12

Reaching Across Cultural Boundaries: International and Interethnic Touch

O
N HIS maiden trip to the Middle East, a Midwestern public relations man stepped from the cool of an ultramodern conference
center into the dust and glare of an ancient roadway. Donkey
carts rustled up whirlwinds of stinging sand. The air rang with a
mullah's bullhorned call to prayer. Without a word, a Saudi
who had attended the same conference reached down and gently took his hand. The word exotic was taking on new meaning,
and the meaning set off a panic button in the visitor's brain.
"What does this Arab think. . .?" "What will all the *other* Arabs
think. . .?" (*Do's and taboos*, 1985, p. 40)

It is a common myth that nonverbal communication is an international language, understood in the same way around the world. When
people travel to another country where a language different from their
own is spoken, they expect to experience some difficulties in interpreting
what others are saying, even if they have had some training in the native

tongue or are accompanied by an expert translator. It is easy to forget that nonverbal behaviors are also a language. As the anthropologist Edward Hall pointed out in the first book on this subject, *The Silent Language* (1959), foreign visitors often "trip over invisible wires" in their dealings with members of other cultures.

It might seem as though touch would be an exception to this rule. After all, aren't touches such as the handshake found in nearly every culture? However, if we consider the different meanings this gesture has within the United States—as a ritual of introduction, a way of reaffirming a relationship, an expression of appreciation, or a means of congratulating or complimenting someone—it can be seen that even this commonplace touch is complex in meaning, and that the meanings may not be the same everywhere. Add to this the fact that each culture has its own rules about who shakes hands with whom when, and it becomes obvious that the handshake is not a symbol that is used in the same way everywhere.

The problems of understanding touch are not necessarily relieved when we move from international relations to contacts between people of different backgrounds within the same society. In the United States, there are not only cultural differences between the Anglo majority (whites), African Americans, Hispanics, and other minorities, but in addition, the history of relations among these groups may be a complicating factor. Also, in any country, there may be different customs in rural as opposed to urban settings and in different social class groups.

Fortunately, there are some guidelines and there have been some research studies on touching in intercultural relations as many others have been in situations in which you and I are likely to find ourselves as foreign travelers or interethnic emissaries. The information is not complete enough for me to be able to provide a blueprint for touching with all of the cultural groups you may encounter. However, even if such specific details were available, they would be difficult to remember and practice, and the information would often prove inaccurate as you deal with different subgroups within a society. On the other hand, it is extremely helpful to be aware of certain major variations in touching around the world and within the United States as you adjust to practices in different locales. In this chapter, I give a broad outline of the varied practices and some time-tested suggestions for learning how to touch in any culture, starting with international differences and then going on to cultural groups within the United States.

TOUCHING AROUND THE GLOBE

Edward Hall (1966) speaks of "contact" and "noncontact" cultures. This is not an absolute distinction because people in all societies touch, so the difference in the amounts of touching between one culture and another are a matter of degree, not of kind. However, there are some rather dramatic differences, and sometimes you need only go across a boundary line to encounter a whole new attitude towards touch and tactile stimulation. The Mexican-U.S. and French-German borders are both places where you can experience this rather dramatic shift, for example.

Touch Belts

Any sweeping statements about communication practices around the world must necessarily be inaccurate in some cases. Nevertheless, it is possible to divide up the world into certain kinds of "touch belts" according to the amount or type of touching which is common in each region. This can be helpful because it is possible to be in a completely new environment in a very short period of time by stepping on and off an airplane, so it's useful to figure out where you are.

The High-touch belt.

If you have a globe or a world map handy, take a look at it. Otherwise, use your imagination and memory. Picture an area in the Western Hemisphere that encompasses all the Latin American countries (Mexico, Central American, and South America). Then, move across the Atlantic into the Mediterranean region, starting with Morocco on the south and Spain and Portugal on the north, and making a slight side excursion up into France. Then go across the Mediterranean and its bordering countries, including Italy, Greece, and Egypt, and proceed into the Middle East, continuing eastward about as far as Afghanistan and Pakistan. Then dip south and east into the Indonesian islands and finally slightly north into the Philippines. This, roughly, is the high-touch belt. You can expect to see and perhaps to experience directly much more touching than you are accustomed to.

Obviously, the United States, Canada, Northern Europe, and Australia are excluded. There are some grey areas: in the Slavic nations, including Russia, the "bear hug" is common, but this gives outsiders the impression that these countries are more tactile than they are. The various nations of Africa are difficult to categorize because they are so diverse culturally. India might have been included, but is generally lower in contact than the countries included (see Watson, 1968, pp. 102-103). The high-touch belt definitely stops short of China and Japan, however, because touch in these countries, especially in public places, occurs even less frequently than in the United States (see Barnlund, 1975).

There is no simple explanation for the contact differences among societies. Climate has been suggested as one causal factor, and it is true that there is some tendency for people who live out of the tropical regions to be "colder" in other ways as well. However, this generalization cannot be pushed too far; it gets just as cold in parts of South America as it does in North America. Culture, including that of conquering nations, also has an effect. In former British protectorates in Africa, they shake hands a lot. In Spanish-speaking countries, as far west as Latin America and as far east as the Philippines, they hug more often.

The same-sex touch belt.

"High-touch" by no means suggests that everyone touches everyone. In this case culture plays an important role, especially in determining the amount of touching that occurs between the sexes. In many societies of the world, men touch men and women touch women, but men and women seldom have physical contact, especially in the presence of others. Thus, we may speak of a "same-sex" belt as well as a high-touch belt. It is roughly the same as the high-touch areas of the world. However, excluded from this belt are Israel (see Lomranz & Shapiro, 1974), France, and Brazil, which are relatively high in opposite-sex touching. In addition, the same-sex belt stretches much farther east—throughout Asia, including China and Japan. In some of these countries, women touch one another somewhat more than men—Japan, for example (see Elzinga, 1975). In others, especially the Arab nations of the Middle East, it is the men who touch one another more frequently, at least in public situations.

Here again, the exact reason for this pattern may vary according to the culture. Religious practices (in Moslem countries, especially) and the belief that opposite-sex touching encourages sexual promiscuity (in the Middle East and some Latin American countries) are two influential factors. In general, the more men and women are seen as being very different or having different roles, the more same-sex touching prevails. By way of contrast, the United States is primarily an opposite-sex touch culture.

You can expect some exceptions in particular societies, but in general, the distinctions between contact and noncontact and between same-sex and opposite-sex touch cultures will help orient you.

Kinds of Touch: Attuning Yourself to the Variations

What follows is a whirlwind tour of differences in the ways touch is used to communicate around the world. I have used a wide variety of sources, including research studies (when they are available), my own experiences as a traveler (especially as a faculty member on an around-the-world college program called Semester-at-Sea), and a particularly useful set of documents available from Brigham Young University titled Culturgrams (see

"Culturgrams" in References section). Specific references are not always cited, since the information often comes from a combination of sources.

The togetherness touch in public.

One of the first things you will notice, almost as soon as you step off the ship or airplane in certain countries, is how men and women touch on the streets. These togetherness touches, such as walking arm in arm, hand in hand, or with arms around waists, are considered to indicate an intimate and probably sexual relationship in the United States, so they are seen almost exclusively between men and women in public places in this country.

In the same-sex touch belt, however, this behavior has sexual connotations only for the opposite sexes, who rarely use it in public, and it is limited almost exclusively to male-male and female-female pairs. In Japan, I had not expected to see much touching at all, so I was surprised to see some women walking with linked arms, although I did not see this behavior among men. The togetherness touch between women is also practiced in some countries that are not in the same-sex belt—Germany, for example. I also saw a few young men and women with their arms around one another in Japan, but I learned that this is frowned upon by their elders and by many young Japanese as well. In the Middle East, I had expected to see men holding hands or walking arm in arm, and they did not disappoint me.

Dealing with the madding crowd.

In cities, it is almost impossible for Americans to escape some situations that they regard as "overcrowded" (including rush hours on the New York City subways). There are several variations on the ways people in different societies cope with close quarters and touching with strangers.

1. *Avoidance.* Americans, Northern Europeans, and Australians avoid brushing or pressing against strangers, if at all possible. Even though their culture tells them they should be on time, they will often wait for the next elevator or subway train, preferring to be late than to be jammed together in close quarters. When touch is unavoidable, they freeze uncomfortably, waiting for the first opportunity to escape to any open space.

2. *Passivity.* On the surface, the Japanese response to contact in places such as packed subway cars seems similar to that of Americans because the Japanese become immobile and adopt a passive expression on their face. However, the Japanese are better able to tolerate crowded situations than Americans (Hall, 1966, p. 61). They may even doze off while leaning against the next person (Morsbach, 1976, p. 256). Their

method of coping is to draw the sense of self inside, rather than "wearing it on the skin" as Americans tend to do. The message is, "I am not here."

3. *Jocular involvement.* In contrast to both the American and Japanese approaches, members of some other cultures actually seem to enjoy crowding and brushing, or at least regard it as no matter for concern. The Balinese, for example, take pleasure in crowded, involving activity, both in the art they appreciate, which is rich with detail and intertwining forms, and in the public settings where festivals take place. The French, Mexicans, and Italians are nonchalant and relaxed about unavoidable contact with strangers. For example, Ashley Montagu (1971) describes this behavior on the French Metro:

> Here the passengers will lean and press against others, if not with complete abandon, at least without feeling the necessity to either ignore or apologize to the other against whom they may be leaning or pressing. Often the leaning and lurching will give rise to good-natured laughter and joking, and there will be no attempt to avoid looking at the other passengers. (p. 264)

4. *Jockeying for position.* In Greece, I soon learned not to pass too closely to men heading in the opposite direction. While walking on a crowded sidewalk in Athens, I suddenly felt a sharp pain in my arm, as though an elbow had been thrust in my direction. Greek residents whom I asked about this behavior attributed it mainly to "street toughs," but I noticed a mannequin in the window of a men's clothing store dressed in an elegant suit, depicted throwing his elbows out to the side with a frowning facial expression and smiling, clenched teeth.

Edward Hall describes his experience while waiting in the lobby of a Washington, DC hotel:

> a stranger walked up to where I was sitting and stood close enough so that not only could I easily touch him but I could even hear him breathing. . . . I moved my body in such a way as to communicate annoyance. . . . Strangely enough, he moved even closer. . . . Fortunately, a group of people soon arrived whom my tormentor joined. Their mannerisms explained his behavior, for I knew from both speech and gesture that they were Arabs. (Hall, 1966, pp. 155-156)

Hall goes on to explain the insight he gained into this incident from a discussion with an Arab colleague:

> For the Arab, there is no such thing as an intrusion in public. Public

means public. . . . In Beirut only the hardy sit in the last row in a movie theatre because there are usually standees who want seats and who push and shove and make such a nuisance that most people give up and leave. Seen in this light, the Arab who intruded on my space in the hotel lobby had apparently selected it for the same reason I had: it was a good place to watch two doors and the elevator. My show of annoyance, instead of driving him away, had only encouraged him. He thought he was about to get me to move. (Hall, 1966, p. 156)

As frustrating as such experiences may be for Americans, it is important to remember that people in different cultures see public space and touching with strangers from different perspectives. This is true even in some "Western" societies where Americans feel relatively at home. I soon learned while traveling in Austria and in Italy that people did not necessarily form lines when waiting at counters or box offices. I found that I needed to maneuver myself with some pressing and squeezing forward until I reached the front where I could be served.

The handshake.

This formal gesture is used in most industrialized societies when people are being introduced and often when they see one another again on other occasions. However, there are many variations. In Colombia, for example, handshaking is done frequently, and males may shake the hand of every person in the room (Culturgram, Republic of Colombia, 1981). In addition, Columbians and some other Latin Americans may prolong the hand contact, causing Americans to wonder when the handshake is complete. There may also be other, especially friendly, touches combined with the handshake, including the left hand covering the joined hands or the gripping of the shoulder of the other person (Saitz & Cervenka, 1962, pp. 11-12, p. 14). Without being forewarned that these variations on the handshake are common in Latin America, North Americans are sometimes flustered or puzzled about the other person's motives.

When an Arab male talks with a male from another country, handshakes at the beginning of a conversation, again when both people are getting up to leave, and once more at the final departure will all be appreciated (Collett, 1971).

In France, India, and Japan, the hand grip may be much less firm than Americans are used to. In the United States, this handshake is regarded as effeminate, unfriendly, or—when offered by a man to a woman—patronizing, but it is entirely appropriate in these other cultures in which a stronger grip would seem aggressive.

Also, in the United States, outside the business community, men seldom offer a hand to a woman. In Kenya, Brazil, Chile, and many other countries, it is expected. In India, men will not ordinarily shake hands with a woman because it is regarded as an invasion of her privacy, but educated Indian women will often offer a hand to Westerners, knowing it is their custom (Culturgram, Republic of India, 1981).

Other greeting and departure gestures.

In many Asian societies, handshakes are accepted but are not preferred. The Japanese will readily shake hands in the United States, but in Japan they prefer to bow. The lower and more repeated the bow, the more respect conveyed. Sometimes, in an effort to adjust to American customs, the Japanese will bow and shake hands at the same time, but this should not be expected. As one writer puts it, this is a "procedure fraught with the danger of knocking heads together, apart from looking quite hilarious" (Morsbach, 1976, p. 248). In Thailand, only westernized people shake hands, and the *wai* is generally preferred, a gesture with the hands placed together in prayer fashion at the chest with a slight bow. The higher the hands, up to eye level, the greater the respect communicated (Culturgram, Kingdom of Thailand, 1984). In India, a similar gesture is used rather than shaking hands, especially with women who are dressed in traditional clothing.

The handshake is common throughout Mexico, Central America, South America, and Spain, especially for relationships in which are not close. The *abrazo*—a hug of hello or goodbye—is preferred for close relationships. The definition of "close," however, is rather broad compared to the United States and may include not only a relative or close friend, but also a member of a family you know and respect, or a not-so-close friend you have known for a long time but have not seen recently. The idea of "closeness by association" may be carried further. When I was introduced by a close American male friend to a Brazilian woman with whom he was romantically involved, she immediately hugged and gave me a kiss on the cheek.

There are also variations on touches in close relationships in these countries. The *abrazo* is used most commonly between men, but men and women use it in some countries, and then a kiss to the cheek may be added. Women more often simply kiss one another on the cheek, perhaps while grasping hands or touching on the arm. Children are often kissed by adults as a greeting or good-bye.

Touches with talk.

Except in intimate or very close relationships, Americans seldom touch after they start a conversation until they say good-bye, and they do not always touch even at these points. The exceptions when touch is sometimes used in the middle of the conversation include an occasional and brief attention-getting touch when the other person has become distracted, a touch that emphasizes the expression of a feeling, or a touch used to compliment the other person on clothing or jewelry. All of these touches are primarily directed by women to either a man or a woman (Jones & Yarbrough, 1985).

In contrast, among contact cultures like those of the Middle East, touch is often used as a running commentary on the discussion, and this happens between men as well as between women. Among Argentinians, Mexicans, and traditional European Jews alike, there is a touch used during conversation that has been termed "buttonholing" (see Efron, 1972). It involves fingering the lapel or clothing of the other person while talking. The message is, "You are my friend, and I want you to see the significance of the point I'm making." American men tend to read this gesture as flirtatious, so it is easy to predict the misinterpretations that could occur if they are unprepared.

Touch during conversation in contact cultures tends to facilitate more open, personal communication. When discussing intellectual topics, Latin Americans tend to stay farther apart than people from the United States (Forston & Larsen, 1968). At other times, when Latin Americans are trying to get to know the other person better, they will stand or sit closer than U.S. citizens, at a range where touching can occur (Hall, 1959, p. 164). One writer (Coulton, 1983, p. 266) points out, "After polite preliminaries, a Mexican businessman is apt to rise from his desk, take the visitor by the shoulder or arm and propel him toward the sofa, saying, 'Come, let's talk.'" In other words, "Let's get down to business and get to know each other." In Mexico, as in the Middle East, establishing a personal, trusting relationship comes before handling the details of a transaction, and touch is an expected part of the process.

Touching children.

In societies in which family ties are stressed, including those with an extended family of uncles, aunts, and cousins, there is also likely to be a great deal of touching with young children. This is not a coincidence. Early touching in families builds bonds. This pattern is especially evident in high-touch cultures like those of Mexico and the Middle East, but surprisingly, it is also found in many low-contact cultures of Asia, including Japan. Even though Japanese adults touch less than do Americans, infants are touched almost continuously by mothers, and family members may also bathe and sleep with children for a number of years after infancy (Morsbach, 1976, p. 254).

Another part of this pattern that does not seem coincidental is that it is ordinarily acceptable even for people who are not close to the family to touch young children. In Mexico, a stranger may touch when commenting on an especially adorable child, and some traditional Mexicans believe it is unlucky for the child not to be touched on such occasions. Commenting on Japan, one writer says, "It is not uncommon for maids in a *ryokan* (Japanese inn) to take a baby away without saying much to the parents and to play with it for long periods." This writer also adds that complete strangers may also touch small children in Japan (Morsbach, 1976, p. 255). Such practices obviously provide an opportunity for foreign visitors to these countries to build rapport with the parents.

Taboos of touch in specific cultures.

To my knowledge, there is no information about countries outside the United States that is equivalent to the "seven American taboos of touch" I discussed in Chapter 8. Certainly, there are numerous taboos in each society. The best rule of thumb is for a visitor to touch only in ways observed among the natives. Even so, the exact rules about who can touch whom at what times and in what ways are not always obvious. At the same time, it is reassuring to know that as a foreign visitor you are likely to be forgiven easily for any minor infractions of the touch code. Nevertheless, it is useful to be aware of the best-known and most important touch taboos.

Touching older persons. In many nations of the world, older persons are revered and are owed special respect. In the low-contact Asian societies, especially in China (Culturgram, People's Republic of China, 1984), but also in Korea and other countries, if there is a difference in age of some years between two adults, the older person should initiate touch or offer a handshake, if any touch occurs at all. In some countries, China included, a position of high authority carries a similar expectation of respect, although age is a more important factor.

Displays of affection. Affectionate touches such as an arm around the shoulder or a slap on the back are acceptable in the United States, even in not-so-close friendships, especially if they are done playfully. However, many Asians, notably Koreans (Culturgram, Republic of Korea (South) 1980) and citizens of Thailand (Culturgram, 1984), feel uncomfortable with such robust touches, unless the relationship is close.

A more important but related taboo, however, in cultures that emphasize same-sex touching, prohibits the display of affection between men and women in public. This rule applies in the Middle East, India, Pakistan, and in most of Asia. In these parts of the world, American romantic couples should avoid walking hand in hand or with arms around one another and particularly hugging or kissing if others are present. The naivete of Westerners about this rule sometimes works to their disadvantage in meetings with members of these cultures. Young American women on the Semester-at-Sea voyage, for example, reported that young men with whom they made quick friendships in Taiwan sometimes held their hands and put their arms around them, later attempting to kiss them. There may have been some problems of crossed signals in these incidents, the young men assuming that the acceptance of their touches was an invitation to intimate involvement, whereas the American women were trying to be accepting of what they assumed were customs in the country. In any case, this should not be taken as typical of Taiwanese behavior with foreign visitors. It points out, however, that taboos will sometimes be violated by members of the culture itself, especially some young people, just as is true in the United States.

Left-handed touches. In the Moslem societies of the Middle East and in many countries in Asia, the left hand is considered "unclean." Only the right hand is used for eating, passing objects, or touching. In some places, this practice had its origins in a lack of sanitation facilities, so the left hand was reserved for toilet functions. Even where this no longer applies, however, the custom persists, and left-handed contacts may be considered impolite or insulting. By way of contrast, in Korea (Culturgram, 1980) Zimbabwe (Culturgram, Republic of Zimbabwe 1984), and Malaysia (Culturgram, Malaysia, 1980), giving and receiving objects with both hands, especially for gifts, is a sign of respect.

Touching the head. Even in countries of Asia where children can be touched readily, the common American practice of patting children on the head or tousling their hair may nevertheless be taboo. In particular, in Thailand (Culturgram, 1984), the head is considered sacred, and such touches are regarded as demeaning. Elsewhere, in Taiwan and Korean, for example, this restriction applies mainly to adults. The one exception among adults, as a Korean citizen explained to me, would be if an older person has known someone since he or she was a child. As a joke, the senior person might pat the other on the head, saying, "My, haven't you grown up!"

Men touching women. Finally, beyond the taboo against affectionate displays in public, in some countries of the Middle East (Saudi Arabia as an example) and in some traditional Asian societies, males other than family members are not allowed to touch women. Even in modern societies such as Japan, where this is not strictly a taboo, American men should be cautious about initiating touches to females (Jensen & Jensen, 1983, p. 374).

Learning to Touch Overseas: Tips for Americans

Hopefully, all this information on cultural differences and taboos will not discourage you from touching people in other countries. The following are some principles you can use in learning about touch in a particular society.

1. Spend some time observing, especially when you first arrive.

Most people simply do not notice most touches among others, even in their own country. So the first step in learning about touch in another culture is to become more observant, even taking some notes. In particular, it's important to note how touch varies according to the closeness of the type of relationship, between men and women and in same-sex pairs, and in situations in which there is a status difference. Sometimes special occasions call for different kinds of touching as well. If you are with a friend or colleague some of the time, ask them about touches and other customs that puzzle you. They may not always have an immediate answer, but your question may stimulate them to examine what they know intuitively, and they can certainly tell you about formal gestures of touch (introductions, greetings, and departures).

2. Allow others to select the distance at which you will talk.

Cultures differ widely in how close people stand or sit for conversation, and this will largely determine whether touching is likely to occur. When you approach another person, stop and let them choose the distance. Japanese distances tend to be greater than those used by Americans (Engebretson & Fullmer, 1970), which, incidentally, allows room for bowing. After a handshake, a Japanese person may even step back. Even so, Americans tend to keep acquaintances and strangers "at arms length," a greater distance than that generally used by Latin Americans, Italians, and Middle Easterners. When a member of one of these contact cultures moves in, it is important to "stand your ground," not defiantly, but in a relaxed way. In anticipation of meeting members of these cultures, it is good to practice standing close to someone from your own culture, just to learn how to calm your nervous system.

3. Be receptive to touches from members of the host culture.

Especially at the start of your sojourn in another country, it is easiest to let others initiate touch. At that point, however, it is important that you accept the touch, assuming that you know the person or are being introduced. An exception would be a flirtatious touch, such as an arm around the shoulders, or, more obviously, a pinch or sexual touch. In the case of a touch such as a handshake or the Hispanic/Latino *abrazo*, each of which require mutual involvement, it is important to reciprocate appropriately. When I met a Mexican-American friend and colleague I had not seen for a long time at his office, he immediately hugged me. At the time, I noticed that I patted him on the back during the embrace—an unconscious gesture that signals "let's make this quick" for most people in the United States. Later, when talking about touch in his culture, I asked him if he had noticed my gesture and how he had reacted. He said, "I noticed you seemed uncomfortable, but I couldn't pinpoint the reason. It's simply that a back pat is not part of the *abrazo*."

4. Master greeting and departure gestures of the other culture.

These formal behaviors are the easiest ones to learn and practice, and they provide a good starting point for establishing a touching relationship in cultures in which greetings and departures involve contact. Once you have gained confidence in your ability to use these, you can move on to other kinds of touching you have observed or experienced in the culture.

CULTURAL DIFFERENCES IN TOUCH WITHIN THE UNITED STATES

When people share the same verbal language, and especially when they also live in the same country, there is a tendency to assume that their nonverbal messages mean the same things. This apparent common ground is deceptive and complicates problems of understanding between members of different cultural groups in the United States. In discussing ethnic differences in touch communication, I focus mainly on the three largest groups because there is little information available on other groups. I also use labels that refer to the cultural heritage of each group because this is what determines communication differences, rather than using labels that refer only to race: (a) African Americans (some blacks such as West Indians are very different in cultural background from others and are not included in this group); (b) Hispanics (which includes Mexican-Americans, Puerto Ricans, and other Spanish-speaking peoples); and (c) Anglos (white people who have been in this country for at least one generation and have assimilated into the majority culture).

In reading this section, you should keep in mind that not all of the information about African-American and Hispanic touch will hold true in all circumstances. One reason is that cultural practices in communication may change over time, and such changes tend to occur more rapidly in minority cultures as a way of maintaining the distinctive communication style of the group when Anglos have imitated minority behaviors. Another reason is that many minority group members are "biculturals." That is, they may adopt Anglo ways of communicating as a way of gaining acceptance when they are with Anglos, but retain minority behaviors for comfortable and familiar communication with members of their ethnic group. As a consequence, Anglos may find that the right touch with minorities varies according to what "territory" they are in—whether they are in an environment that is predominantly Anglo or minority.

Touch in the African-American Community

The primary meeting place for different racial and ethnic groups has been in the schools, rather than in the workplace. Social psychologist Frank Willis and his colleagues have used the school environment to study differences between African Americans and Anglos in touch and also to discover how being in school together affects touch between these two groups. In order to keep the setting constant, Willis observed students in cafeteria lines in the primary grades, junior high school, high school, and college. Here are the main findings of his studies (Willis & Hofmann, 1975; Willis & Reeves, 1976; Willis, Reeves, & Buchanan, 1976; Willis, Rinck, & Dean, 1978):

1. African Americans touched one another more frequently at all ages than did Anglos.
2. Students tended to segregate themselves by sex, boys with boys and girls with girls, and by race. So, there were few opportunities for touch between the two racial groups.
3. Cross-ethnic touch was rare. However, in the primary grades, African Americans touched Anglos more than vice versa; and, in fact, they touched Anglos more than Anglos touched each other. Yet, there was also a steady decline in cross-ethnic touch as the students grew older, suggesting that the African Americans had given up on touching Anglos by the time they had reached high school.
4. Willis primarily studied desegregated schools. There he found that the amount of touch decreased steadily during the primary grades for both African Americans and Anglos. In schools comprised of African-American children only, however, he found that touching did not decline during the primary grades. Both groups, however, sharply decreased in touching when they

entered junior high school (after puberty had begun), regardless of whether the school was integrated or not, with the African Americans still being the higher touchers.

Touch is a rather good indicator of attraction and affection between people. Willis's findings are therefore rather disappointing in terms of the effects of integration. African Americans and Anglos touched one another little at the beginning of school and even less when they left. In fact, the main effect of the two groups being together in integrated schools seemed to be that the younger African-American children became somewhat more inhibited about touch, later cutting off physical contact with the Anglos altogether. There are several possible explanations. It may be that the exposure of the two groups to one another in school alone was not enough to break down barriers. After being bused in, students return to their own segregated neighborhoods. It may also be that there is growing cynicism about the potential for interracial understanding as children grow older. However, there is another factor that is less obvious but which may explain more: The students understood one another's words, but used different nonverbal codes. They did not share the language of rapport. I explore this explanation in more detail in the section that follows.

Crossed signals.

Touch does not occur in isolation from other messages, and there are two kinds of nonverbal signals closely associated with touching that are used differently by many African Americans and Anglos.

Physical animation. Although there are individual exceptions within both groups, African Americans tend to be more physically expressive when they talk than are Anglos. A greater variety of gestures and facial expressions may be used, and movement from one spot to another may be more common and more energetic. These differences are especially apparent in children, but they apply to adults as well. Years ago, I was conducting a study of the conversational distances used by African Americans in comparison to Anglos (Jones, 1979). In my observations, it became clear that the differences in how close or far away members of each group stood were less important than the number of changes that occurred in spacing as people were talking. Among both children and adults, African Americans were more likely to use an "in and out" pattern. For example, a person might move in very close for a while, then walk away and come back again. On the "out" phase of movement, a person might even turn his or her back toward the other person, not as a sign of disagreement but the opposite, an acknowledgment that the other person had made a good point. Obviously, it was at the "in" phase that touch would occur, and frequently it was the person who had moved in who would initiate contact, sometimes holding on to emphasize a point, sometimes offering a hand for an approving slap.

It is easy to see how Anglos, who do not move much during conversation, might be confused by this pattern, not knowing when to touch or when a touch is coming. Paul and Happie Byers (1972) filmed scenes in a nursery school involving an Anglo female teacher, an Anglo girl, and an African-American girl. They described this puzzling series of exchanges: At one point, the Anglo child moved close to the teacher, who reached out and held the girl close to her for a while. At another time, the African-American girl also stood close to the teacher, but when the teacher reached out to touch the child, she wiggled away. Later, when the African-American girl had hurt her finger and had a sad look on her face, the teacher approached and comforted the girl, holding the child on her lap.

Here is my interpretation: When the Anglo child approached, the teacher accurately read this as a request for a touch. When the African-American child came close, she did not expect the teacher to initiate a touch to her, and may have been planning to touch the teacher, and so she resisted the contact. When the teacher approached the hurt child later, however, the signals were clear to both, and the touch was accepted. Whether or not this is exactly what happened in this incident, one thing is certain: There was some kind of misreading of messages in the first attempted touch.

Eye contact. Both Anglos and African Americans, especially males, like to kid others by using a fake-aggressive touch such as a light punch. African Americans also exchange palm touches or a hand slap to compliment the other person on a clever remark. These touches should be reasonably well understood by members of both groups. However, a conversation can get blocked at the beginning, before such good-natured touches can occur. A major problem of crossed signals is the difference in the way eye behavior is used.

Most African Americans are brought up with the belief that "staring," looking someone in the eye for an extended period of time, is impolite and possibly hostile. Anglo children, on the other hand, are taught "Look me in the eye when I talk to you," and lack of eye contact is believed to be a sign of disrespect or lack of interest. Complicating the problem of communication even more, according to research by Marianne LaFrance and Clara Mayo (1976), is this pattern: Anglos tend to look more when listening, less when talking. African Americans do the opposite, looking away more when they are listening and having more eye contact when speaking. So when the Anglo person is talking and looks to his African-American companion to see how his ideas are being received, it seems as though the other person, who is looking away, is not listening. When the African American is speaking, he wonders why the Anglo is looking so intensely rather than paying attention to what is being said. African-American college professor Charles Payne (1977) comments, "In my culture to show real interest in what someone was telling you, instead of looking the person straight in the eye you would find some object in the room to fix your eyes on and hold your head down slightly, but both the head and eyes are held very still" (p. 42).

Payne tells that he eventually learned in his work as a professor to maintain steady eye contact with Anglo students and faculty members when they were talking. It took considerable practice and concentration and even then he occasionally slipped back into familiar patterns, sometimes with amusing results. "On one occasion with one of the white faculty members," he comments, "I made intense eye contact and then let my eyes go toward the door. At that instant he jumped up as if someone had just given him an electrical shock" (p. 43). For Anglos, a person looking at the door is a sign that the conversation should come to a close, but a brief glance that happens to be in the direction of the door does not have the same meaning for African Americans.

Cultural differences in nonverbal behaviors such as physical animation and eye contact may account for the decrease in touching between African Americans and Anglos after elementary school. Children develop the ability to use the cultural code of their group throughout the grade school years; by the time they reach junior high school, some degree of mastery of these behaviors is essential to carrying on smooth, satisfying interactions (Burgoon, Buller, & Woodall, 1989, p. 40). If African Americans and Anglos are unable to have comfortable conversations by this age, it follows that touching, an inherently involving form of communication, will decline. The solution is to teach members of each group to read the other's signals accurately, although schools seldom take on this important task (see Hanna, 1984).

Distinctive African-American touches: Variations on the handshake

In the United States generally, the handshake is the traditional touch used mostly by men to signify acceptance of one another. In the African-American community, hand-to-hand contact serves a similar purpose for men, but it has also been elaborated on so that it can take on a number of subtle variations in meaning and act as an in-group gesture of cultural membership. Some examples of different types of handshakes are described below, although the reader should keep in mind that there may be variations in the behaviors from one city or region to another, and some details may have changed since the research reported here was conducted.

The black power handshake. This gesture in particular signifies more than "I accept you as an individual." It also says, "We are united in a common bond with others of our group." The handshake requires rapid-fire movements and coordination by the two men, a sort of hand-dance of togetherness. If you are not familiar with this handshake, practicing the gestures with another person will make the following description, as provided by Benjamin Cooke (1972, p. 61) in the book *Rappin' and Stylin' Out*, easier to visualize: (a) mutual encircling of the thumbs with palm and fingers clasping each other's hand (meaning "togetherness"); (b) grasping each other's fingers with bent fingers, so that they hook into one another (meaning "strength"); (c) mutual grasping of wrists with hands (signifying "solidarity"); (d) placing right hands on one another's left shoulders (interpreted as "comradeship"); and (e) stepping back and raising of the right arm, flexing the biceps while making a fist (summarizing all of the meanings, plus "Black power"). Cooke adds that "these five steps are often abbreviated by just using Step 1 for close-distance contacts and just Step 5 for greater distances" (p. 61).

"Getting and giving skin." One version of this touch gesture is familiar to all sports fans as the congratulatory or team-spirit hand slap, which originated among African Americans but has been widely adopted by athletes in general. Strictly speaking, it is not a hand*shake*, but it serves a similar purpose. It can be done with either the right or left hand and involves one person offering an open palm upward (to "get skin"), while the other lays a palm or the back of the hand on the palm ("giving skin"). Benjamin Cooke points out that the gesture has several meanings, depending on what is going on or what is being said, including greeting or saying good-bye, expressing agreement on a point, or complimenting the other person (1972, pp. 33-34).

Cooke also notes that there are numerous variations conveying nuances of meaning. For example, the hand slap, called "emphatic skin," expresses enthusiasm or puts special emphasis on an idea just presented. "Five on the sly" involves offering a palm inconspicuously, usually behind one's back, for the other person to touch. It is used to build special, private rapport between two men in reaction to some event in the environment. For example, the touch could be a compliment from one man to another in recognition that an attractive female nearby has shown interest in him. Or, if the two men were listening to a speech, it could be a comment on something the speaker said, showing that the two men are aware they are in strong agreement with the idea expressed.

The "dap." Chances are you will not see the dap, unless you spend time around a Vietnam veterans center. However, the history of this gesture, as traced by communication professor Robert Shuter (1979), has a lot to tell us about in-group minority gestures and the ways Anglos sometimes react to them. The dap was used by African-American servicemen overseas in the 1960s and 1970s, as a way of expressing solidarity, partly in reaction to racism in the armed forces. Like other African-American variations on the handshake, it required a speedy execution of a number of hand contacts, sometimes requiring up to 15 minutes to complete. The basic moves are as follows: (a) each man in turn bumped his clenched fist on top of the other's, symbolizing "I'm not on top of you, you're not on top of me;" (b) fists were then bumped on one side and then the other horizontally, meaning "We're side to side, we're together;" and (c) finally, some version of the black handshake was performed, sometimes the "hooked fingers" grasp followed by bumping the knuckles together, suggesting strength and determination.

Professor Shuter reaches the following conclusions: (a) Anglos were often intimidated by seeing African Americans dap, apparently misperceiving it as a black revolt in the offing, despite the fact that in some cases African Americans taught Anglos to perform the dap. There were attempts in some units to outlaw the use of the gesture, and men were often arrested for refusing to stop dapping. One man, for example, was court-martialed and sentenced to two months of hard labor. A Department of Defense investigation finally concluded that such reactions were out of proportion and mistaken and that the official punishments constituted intentional racial discrimination. (b) As efforts to repress use of the dap became greater, its importance among African Americans increased. Eventually, it was used as a test. Men who could dap with style and grace were more trusted by other African Americans.

Touching among African-American women.

Women touch more informally than men in the African-American community. They do not use the Black Power handshake, for example, except as a way of kidding. The humor comes in part from the fact that men need the handshake as a means of touching, something that African American and Anglo men seem to share. Some people have expressed concern that there is a trend for African-American men to become less affectionate, perhaps in imitation of Anglo men. In an article in *Ebony* magazine ("Touchin', Feelin'," 1982), clinical psychologist Ann Poussaint is quoted as saying that African Americans have always been touch-oriented, but that "as we become more assimilated, it may become an issue with us" (p. 41). In the same article, psychiatrist James Comer is quoted as saying, "Touching and feeling have always been a part of our culture," citing the African "rite of laying on of hands" and touching in church services as evidence.

Like Anglo women, African-American women are more expansive

in their touching than are men, and the hug is the nearest thing to a replacement for the handshake. The difference is that African-American women tend to hug and touch one another more frequently than do Anglo women. For example, one of my interviewees commented that she had hugged another woman when she saw her that day, even though she had just seen her on the weekend. She added, however, "There are individual differences. With one woman, I only hug as a hello or good-bye when I haven't seen her for a while."

Touching in Hispanic Communities

Most observers point out that there is more touching among Mexican-Americans, Puerto Ricans, and other Hispanics in the United States than among Anglos. I know of only one scientific study. Guthrie Ford and James Graves (1971) of Trinity University observed second- and eighth-grade Mexican-American and Anglo children in playgrounds at a school in Texas. They found that in the second-grade, Mexican-American children stood closer, although only the girls touched more than Anglos. By the eighth grade, these differences had disappeared. It may be that the public setting of the playground of a predominantly Anglo school does not reveal all of the cultural differences between these two groups, although it may also be that the Mexican-American children were assimilating toward Anglo ways of behaving.

More research is needed, but, in general, Hispanics qualify as a same-sex touching culture, like their Spanish-speaking counterparts in Mexico and Central and South America, with more permission being given for female-female touching. Especially in the family, the mother is likely to be a high toucher. As one Mexican-American explained to me, "The mother can touch anyone freely. The father is less likely to touch." The togetherness touch of "holding on to each other for a while," as another Mexican-American described it, is common between women, unlike the Anglo culture. However, opposite-sex couples who walk with arms around one another in public, according to my respondents, may be considered "Anglicized" (G. Rivera, A. Lucero, personal communications, April 1990). Men are less openly affectionate with one another than women, but there is an important exception which I discuss next.

The Abrazo: A distinctive Hispanic touch.

The *abrazo*, the hug for greetings and departures, is found among all Hispanic groups in the United States and is a part of their Spanish-speaking heritage. Although there are some variations in the way it is used among different groups, the specific version I will describe here is based on my interviews with Mexican-Americans. Like the handshake, the abrazo is a formal gesture, and there are rules for its use. It resembles the Anglo frontal embrace sometimes used for hellos or good-byes in close relationships, but it is quite different in the circumstances in which it is used:

1. It is used only between adults. Children are frequently hugged, but not as part of a formal greeting or departure. Children are generally greeted with a kiss by family members, especially women, or they may be offered a handshake.
2. The *abrazo* is used not only between men and women but also between men, the most distinctive difference from the Anglo hug. When used by a man and a woman, the woman may offer her cheek to the man for a kiss. Unlike the famous hugs of greeting between men in the French and Soviet Russian cultures, men do not kiss on the cheek. Women may also use the *abrazo* with one another, but grasping hands and kissing on the cheeks would be more common.
3. The *abrazo* is reserved primarily for long-term relationships (relatives or close friends), similar to Anglo hugging. However, it can also be used as a sign of respect for the parents of the person who is hugged, even though the two people are not close themselves. It can even be used by new acquaintances at a departure, especially if they will not see one another again for some time, as a sign that there is a potential for a close friendship. For example, a male Mexican-American told me that if he met another Hispanic at a conference, and they had a good conversation, he might do an *abrazo* as they were leaving. He also told me it could be an insult if they did not hug at the end of a second such meeting (G. Rivera, personal communication, April 1990).

Like the numerous versions of the African-American handshake, the *abrazo* is an in-group gesture. In fact, it is linked with the Spanish language. In English, we have only one word for "you." In Spanish, French, and some other languages, there is both an unfamiliar or formal "you," and, for a close relationship or at a time of particular closeness, a familiar "you." When Hispanics shift from using mostly the unfamiliar *usted* to the familiar *tu* with a person, it is also the time in the relationship when the *abrazo* should be used (G. Rivera, personal communication, April 1990).

In addition, like many Latin Americans, Hispanics in the United States make a relatively sharp distinction between "family"—meaning not only relatives, but others who are close—and everyone else. The use of the *abrazo* with a person who is not Hispanic is an unusual and special gesture. It says, "You are family," either because the relationship has lasted for a long time and is enduring, or because there is an especially strong friendship. In these circumstances, the *abrazo* might be used when the people are alone, but it would seldom be used in the presence of Anglos, either between two men or a man and a woman because the hug might be interpreted as suggesting romantic or sexual interest. On the other hand, in the presence of other Hispanics, using the *abrazo* with a non-Hispanic takes on particular significance. It says, "This person is not an outsider."

Touching People from Other Ethnic Groups: Some Guidelines

The "tips for Americans overseas" discussed earlier apply to learning about touch among different cultural groups within the United States as well to foreign travel. However, the special nature of interethnic relations brings up additional issues. My advice here is designed primarily for Anglos in their communication with minority group members, although the principles apply to touch between other ethnic groups as well.

The choice to concentrate on what Anglos need to know is based on my experiences during several years when I was co-teaching an undergraduate university course in interracial communication with a minority faculty member. The course enrolled a diverse ethnic population, and one of the exercises we asked students to perform involved role playing the part of a member of an ethnic group other than their own. Minorities found it easy and enjoyable to play Anglos, but Anglos had difficulty switching to minority behaviors. Although some Anglos may have been inhibited in their performances, knowing that minorities sometimes object to having their behaviors imitated, the main reason was simply that the Anglos knew less about how minorities act than vice versa. In general, when your group is in a low power position, it becomes necessary to learn the communication behaviors of the more powerful group, but it does not work the other way around. Similarly, we also found that women could play men more effectively than men could play women.

1. Learn to understand and accept in-group gestures of other ethnic groups.

As the history of the "dap" in the military demonstrates, Anglos are sometimes intimidated by displays of group identity among minority group members. I recently overheard a comment by a young Anglo woman during a discussion about recent fights between African-American football players and white students which had occurred in bars of the university town where I live. She said, "It's no wonder it happens. They [the football players] act like they're back in the ghetto." This remark reveals an insensitivity to two points: (a) many minority group members want to preserve ties with their own group, and the use of solidarity gestures such as the Black handshake is an important way of doing this; and (b) such gestures also provide a sense of security for members of the group when they are in strange—and sometimes hostile—environments. When the shoe is on the other foot, when Americans live overseas in societies that are very different from their own, they often seek out bars and other places for socializing that are frequented primarily by other Americans. There they can shake hands, slap backs playfully, touch members of the opposite sex, and generally act in a way that makes them feel comfortable.

2. Do not imitate in-group minority touches in the presence of members of the group and do not initiate these touches to them.

When you understand the principle behind the first guideline—the desire and need within minority groups for gestures of group unity—this second guideline also makes sense. Although it is usually true that "imitation is the most sincere form of flattery," minorities generally do not appreciate it when Anglos or members of other groups copy their gestures and mannerisms. This is especially true for distinctive gestures that draw attention to group membership and express solidarity. The Black handshake is an example. I have sometimes seen Anglo teenagers use it with one another. This would be annoying for many African Americans if they were to witness it. It is as though the persons were claiming membership without paying dues. The negative reaction would be still stronger if the Anglo were to initiate the in-group gesture with a member of the minority group. For example, although the *abrazo* looks like Anglo hugging, it is distinctive, especially when it is used by Hispanic males because men in other groups do not greet with a hug. A male from another group should not initiate the *abrazo* with a Hispanic male.

3. Recognize that the initiation of in-group touches by minorities to members of other groups is a compliment.

It is not that Anglos should never engage in in-group minority touches, but that they should wait for the minority person to initiate, especially the first time such a gesture is used. For example, African Americans sometimes teach Anglos and members of other cultural groups to do the Black handshake, a sign that the outsider is trusted. The initiation of the *abrazo* by a Hispanic to a non-Hispanic carries a similar message of acceptance.

Generally, when other members of the group see this kind of touch, they also develop a more positive and trusting attitude toward the outsider. The exception occurs when the minority group member is himself not accepted. As one African American explained to me, "If the guy who does the handshake with a white is recognized as a 'white identifier,' it won't create greater trust in the white person. It's considered 'Uncle Tomming,' to use an old-fashioned term. They're both out."

4. Avoid unconsciously segregating yourself.

In order for cross-ethnic relationships to get started and to progress to the point at which barriers can be reduced by touching, it is necessary that the two people spend time talking to one another on a number of occasions. Frank Willis's research shows that even at an early age—in the primary grades—children are already segregating themselves by race just by selecting who they stand next to, although they are not necessarily doing this consciously. Self-segregation is the first barrier to be overcome for a person interested in interethnic contact.

Although this principle is obvious, it often escapes notice. I learned it quite by accident a number of years ago when I was doing research in schools in African-American neighborhoods in New York City. I often rode the subway on the way home, and because I had just spent the day talking to and being around African Americans, it felt natural to sit down next to them in the first available seat, although I did this without thinking about it. I was surprised how often the person next to me initiated a friendly conversation. That is when I became aware that in the past I had usually unconsciously selected a seat next to another white person. Later, I was no longer surprised, but grew to expect that the conversations would often occur, and I began to initiate some myself. In addition, I became aware that it felt natural to look off into space during these talks because we would be seated side by side, and eventually it occurred to me that this was a comfortable situation for African Americans in terms of eye contact. Touching with the hands was rare in these conversations, but there were occasional brushes of the arms or shoulders, something which would be unusual for strangers or mere acquaintances among Anglos.

If you are a person who wants to establish relationships with persons from other ethnic groups, the lesson is this: When you enter a room of people in which more than one cultural/racial group is present, notice whether you tend to play it safe by gravitating toward those whose skin color is more like yours. If so, consider making some new choices.

5. Initiate touches characteristic of your ethnic background only when it would be appropriate within your own group.

This guideline also seems obvious, but it's not. In the book *Interracial Communication*, Andrea Rich draws attention to what she calls the "touch-don't touch" phenomenon. She says that it is

characteristically experienced by the white "liberal" who wishes to overcome the physical contact taboo in order to demonstrate overtly his lack of racism. Such a white liberal communicator frequently develops a "touch compulsion," in which he feels compelled to clasp eagerly the hand of a new black acquaintance or to take a bite casually from a black colleague's sandwich. This compulsion becomes evident when the "touching" moves are overdone, when the white is engaged in more hand clasping and embracing with nonwhites than he would normally engage in with whites. In a sense it might be advanced that the white communicator is "protesting too much," that his compulsion to touch is really an attempt on his part to overcome his own strong aversion to touching members of nonwhite racial groups. (Rich, 1974, pp. 170-171)

This does not mean that Anglos should avoid touching minority group members, but simply that they should be aware of their motives. In fact, the opposite pattern—avoiding contact with members of other racial groups—is more common. For example, one study has shown that Anglo teachers are more likely to touch Anglo students or African-American teachers to touch African-American students in integrated schools (Byalick & Bersoff, 1974). The tests for the authenticity of a touch with a member of another racial or ethnic group are simple and straightforward: How close do I feel to this person as an individual? Is he or she someone I have just met, an old acquaintance, a friend I get together with from time to time, or a very good friend? Given the level of our relationship, what touches would I use with this person if he or she were a member of my own racial group?

6. Be aware that helping roles give special permission for touches, regardless of the ethnicity of the other person.

When people place themselves "in the hands" of another person, when they have come for assistance or care, they are more likely to be open to touch. In fact, when the caregiver is a member of a different racial or cultural group, touch may be especially needed for reassurance that this is a caring relationship. Thus, doctors, counselors, and psychotherapists who feel comfortable using touch in their practices have ready access to overcoming the touch barrier in interethnic relations. Similarly, although teacher-student relationships are not ordinarily voluntary, young children are especially likely to be appreciative of touches from teachers, whether or not they are of the same race and ethnic background.

LESSONS FROM CROSS-CULTURAL STUDIES OF TOUCH

We can learn a great deal about human nature by studying behavior patterns and their outcomes in different cultures. This is especially true for touch because we are all members of the same "contact species," and there is only so much we can find out about human touch by studying other primates. The lessons I discuss here partly echo ideas presented earlier in the book, but the evidence from varied societies gives them special emphasis. In addition, they bring up issues about the American culture that deserve close consideration.

Touch and the Nature of Human Nature

1. Same-sex touching does not promote homosexuality.

Americans are especially concerned about the sexual implications of touching among members of the same sex. This is particularly true of American fathers, who tend to avoid affectionate touching with their sons for fear that this will create a preference for intimacy with other males. To the contrary, cross-cultural studies show that there is no relationship between same-sex touching and homosexuality. In fact, in those societies in which homosexuality is especially looked down on—the Middle East, Latin America, and most of Asia—same-sex touching is the norm. The point is not that touching either promotes or detracts from homosexual impulses, but that the the two phenomena are unrelated.

2. A high degree of contact and affectionate touching with children, especially in infancy, promotes attitudes of cooperation and strong family ties.

Americans like to think of themselves as being highly family-oriented. However, Ashley Montagu challenged this assumption in his influential book, Touching, published in 1971. He cited the work of numerous anthropologists who had studied so-called primitive societies, pointing out that in cultures in which infants are held or carried constantly, the children grow up to be cooperative, affectionate, and nonviolent. The generation gap does not exist in these societies (Montagu, 1971, pp. 225-240). More recent observations of tribal customs are reported by Jean Liedloff (1977) in her studies of Yequana Indians in the jungles of South America. Her book, *The Continuum Concept,* has attracted considerable attention among child development experts. In that society, infants are carried or held virtually 24 hours a day for at least the first six months of life, the "in-arms phase" that Liedloff believes is crucial to the healthy development of all children. She describes the behavior of these children at a later age:

> Toddlers played together all day without fighting or arguing, and they obeyed their elders instantly and willingly. . . . No child would have dreamed of inconveniencing, interrupting, or being waited on by an adult. And by the age of four, children were contributing more to the work force in their family than they were costing others. (Liedloff, 1989, p. 17)

The strong family ties that seem to result from a high degree of infant-parent contact can also be found in modern, industrialized societies. In Japan, Korea, and Mexico, infants are held and touched considerably more than in the United States, and family connections remain strong throughout life. Also, the transition phase from infancy to toddlerhood and beyond is eased in these cultures by such practices as prolonged breast-feeding and having children sleep with their parents or siblings. For example, when I asked an adult Korean male how long he slept with other members of his family, he laughed and said, "I slept with my brother until I was married."

3. A high degree of touch with infants and young children does not necessarily result in passivity.

Citing Korea and especially Japan as examples of high infant-touch cultures may suggest that a considerable degree of tactile involvement leads to what Americans would characterize as a passive, unassertive approach to life. This is a complex issue, however. First, it depends in part on how the infant is touched. Studies by Caudill and Schooler (1973) show that the ways Japanese mothers deal with their infants seem to promote dependency, a desirable trait from the point of view of the Japanese. For example, when the child is sleeping, the mother will stay nearby. If the baby should stir while sleeping, the mother is likely to adjust the covers, touch, or move the child in order to create greater comfort. Caudill and Schooler point out that this sets up a pattern in which children come to rely on the mother to take care of their needs, and this continues beyond infancy. However, this style of caretaking is not the only way in which a high degree of contact with infants can be maintained. For example, the approach used by the Yequana Indians studied by Liedloff is quite different. The child is carried, sometimes in a pack on the back, but not attended to constantly, and the children do not become highly dependent on their parents later on.

A second factor which determines the effect of a high degree of infant contact on the later development of children is the way infants are touched and socialized after the in-arms phase. In Middle Eastern cultures, in which high touch with children is extended through adolescence, the boys become highly assertive and verbal while the girls are brought up to be passive and submissive. The apparent reason for the difference is that the sexes are segregated at an early age. Increasingly, the bond between father and son is strengthened by touching between them, and the father takes the son out into the world, exposing him to varied experiences. The girls, on the other hand, touch mostly with the mother, and they also stay at home with her.

The American approach to touching children seems to be designed to develop independence. Caudill and Schooler studied infant touching among American as well as Japanese mothers for the purposes of comparison. They found that the American mothers were less likely than the Japanese to hold and cuddle infants and more likely to "prop them up" and talk to them, an apparent first step in getting them to talk early and be assertive.

However, does a low-contact style of parenting actually promote independence? Mary Ainsworth's studies of American mothers and their children, cited in Chapter 2, suggest that it does not, if practiced in the extreme (see Ainsworth, 1979; Bell & Ainsworth, 1972). She found that mothers who came closest to the in-arms approach during the first few months, often holding although not constantly carrying the infant, had children who were both more cooperative and more independent at age 1 than children who were touched less. These children were better able to play on their own, more responsive to corrections from the mother, and more comforted by touch when they were distressed. In fact, the children who were touched the least in their first months were more likely to reject or avoid touch from the mother at age 1. They were also more likely to act in a hostile way toward her (Bigger, 1984); that is, they were not "independent" but "counterdependent."

Implications for Americans

I have three recommendations for Americans which grow out of the ideas presented in this chapter. The first and most important is that infant childrearing practices that are more like those practiced in high-contact societies should be widely adopted in the United States. Specifically, babies should be carried or held by the mother as much as possible, to the degree that she can feel comfortable in so doing—for at least 6 to 8 months and ideally until the child signals a readiness for the transition phase. If the mother is gone part of the day, it is desirable that other caretakers share and feel comfortable with this philosophy. As we have learned in my family, if the mother travels, she can take the baby with her, and the La Leche League is a valuable source of contacts for part-time caretakers around the country. Once the in-arms phase is over, touch need not be as constant, but a good deal of affectionate contact and holding should be continued as a transition phase for the child.

My second recommendation is more controversial, but deserves serious consideration. Children who want to should be allowed to sleep with others: the parents during the transition phase, around 8 months to 1 1/2 years old, and thereafter with parents or siblings, until the child expresses a wish to sleep alone or until the approach of puberty.

These practices are common and taken for granted in many traditional societies and throughout most of the Far East. Westerners have trouble understanding this practice, but it makes sense if couched in psychological terms from a Westerner's perspective: At a rather primitive level, our self-concept is a product of the unconscious. We seldom consciously recall our earliest childhood experiences, but they are not forgotten. That is one reason why touch in infancy is so important. We are most aware of our hidden thoughts and feelings when we are asleep and dreaming. Anyone who can remember awakening from a nightmare as a child and running to their parents' room is aware that the presence of another person in bed is comforting at the deepest level of our being.

Most Americans feel uncomfortable with the idea of children sleeping with their parents. Co-sleeping among siblings is also looked down upon, and a separate room for each child is considered to be the ideal. In the present day, however, when family unity and communication between parents and children seem to be disintegrating, it may be time to reconsider an age-old concept. To be sure, there are issues to be considered, including the possible effects of family sleeping arrangements on the sex life of the parents. For an examination of such issues and a discussion of the various pros and cons, I recommend Tine Thevenin's (1976) book, *The Family Bed*.

Finally, I recommend touch as an important avenue for overcoming barriers in intercultural communication. Touching is virtually essential for establishing solid personal and professional relationships with members of high-contact cultures outside the United States. More time for familiarization with the culture may be required before touching members of other ethnic groups within the United States or persons in low-contact societies abroad. The reward for such patience, however, is a deeper understanding of the culture and greater rapport with its members. Edward Hall comments,

An old priest once explained, "To really know the Japanese you have to spend some cold winter evenings snuggled together around the *hibachi*. Everyone sits together. A common quilt covers not only the *hibachi* but everyone's lap as well. In this way the heat is held in. It's when you feel the warmth of their bodies and everyone feels together—that is when you get to know the Japanese. That is the real Japan." (Hall, 1966, p. 150)

13

Helping and Healing Touch: The Rediscovery of a Lost Potential

A N ADVERTISEMENT in a Columbus, OH newspaper shows a distinguished-looking doctor, dressed casually in a sweater, but clearly identified by his stethoscope and white smock. He looks straight out at the reader, and a quotation next to his face says, "I always touch the patient. It breaks down barriers." It's an ad for a medical care center. In the print at the bottom of the ad, it says that this doctor's sensitivity is characteristic of all members of the staff at this center, "physicians who reach beyond the clinical aspects of illness . . . to put their finger on the psychological implications."

At a time when hospital beds are often empty and some doctors are looking for patients to fill their appointment books, it may appear that economics has caused the medical profession to discover the appeal of touch. Actually, however, the use of touch for therapeutic purposes is a growing trend among professionals for the simple reason that it works, although this is not really a discovery but a rediscovery. Healing with touch is depicted in cave paintings and in carvings on the walls of Egyptian tombs. It's an ancient tradition practiced in many societies, not only by persons thought to have special powers, but also ordinary people in their everyday lives.

I begin this subject by discussing the potential role of touch in medicine and psychotherapy, going on to the helping professions such as teaching, and then the less orthodox "touch therapy" professions. Finally, I talk about the implications for everyone who is interested in helping and healing with touch.

DOCTORS

An occupational therapist, a healer with touch herself, reports on her experience as a patient:

> During my last hospitalization for surgery, I was able to compare the effect on my psyche by an intern who had not yet learned the caring touch, with the effect created by my primary physician who had learned it. I was distressed by the intern who invaded my intimate space with indifference. He appeared to be uncomfortable. When the surgeon came to see me the day after surgery, he approached the bed, put his hand on my knee, and asked how I was doing. I knew immediately that he cared about me as a human being. (Huss, 1977, p. 16)

Almost by the nature of their profession, practicing physicians must touch. Yet, unfortunately, many physicians fail to take advantage of the powerful, health-enhancing effects of simple caring touches and instead restrict themselves to the kinds of perfunctory contacts described in the example above.

Why don't more doctors use a caring touch? In some cases, lack of experience or confidence may be a factor, but there are also deeper, more pervasive influences. The rise of science and technology in the medical field means that diagnostic equipment and tests are often used whereas formerly the doctor relied more on touch and talk to evaluate a patient's illness. In addition, there is an increasing number of specialists who focus on only one aspect of the patient's problem and may be disinclined to develop a personal relationship. Responding to her hometown doctor's question about her experience of being diagnosed for an illness in a large city hospital, one woman said,

> To tell you the truth . . . I hated it. Oh, I'm sure the doctors did a good job, but the whole experience was frightening and distasteful. I must

have had a hundred tests and seen at least a dozen specialists. Each
was interested in a different part of my body. . . . It was as if I existed
as some curious object—a puzzle that had to be solved. The experience was all so cold; there wasn't anything personal about the care.
(Nolen, 1986, p. 37)

As desirable as scientific progress in diagnosis and treatment is, an
unfortunate side-effect of specialization has been to place doctors in the
position of unreachable authority figures, thus affecting their attitude
toward patients. In addition, the education of physicians sometimes
encourages this orientation. One doctor commented, "My medical training
drilled into me the need to be dignified, professionally distant, and emotionally reserved. Little was said about why, but I gleaned that it had to do
with showing respect and maintaining authority" (Alper, 1984, p. 39).

Doctors who are aware of these influences and see beyond them
cite a number of reasons why touch is significant in medical practice.
Patients like to think that their doctor cares about them personally, and
touch conveys this message quickly and effectively. This keeps patients
coming back, which is important to the doctor not only for financial reasons, but for continuity of treatment as well. Knowing that the doctor cares
also creates confidence that, in the long run, the treatment will be effective. As one M.D. put it, "My job is to reassure [the patient] that her problem is my problem. I want her to know that, if it's humanly possible,
together we can make her well" (Nolen, 1986, p. 38).

Used appropriately, touch decreases patients' anxiety and reserve.
It helps them to talk so that the problem can be diagnosed thoroughly, and
doubts about the proposed treatment can be resolved. In addition, the
right touch often facilitates the physical examination itself. One urologist,
who must routinely conduct rectal examinations, told me, "If the patient is
tense, I may not be able to conduct the examination at all. In any case,
being relaxed makes it easier on both of us."

Finally, a touch from the physician can be a reward for treatment
successfully sustained or completed by the patient, or it can provide support when continuing with treatment is difficult. One doctor illustrated
these uses of touch in the following examples:

a squeeze on the arm when Mrs. Jones succeeded in losing weight after
30 years of obesity; a kiss on the cheek when brave Mrs. Baker weath-
ered a potentially fatal illness and was ready to be discharged. . . . Even
when there's sorrow—say, when the biopsy proves positive—holding a
hand or stroking it gently seems to ease the pain. (Alper, 1984, p. 42)

How Should Doctors Touch?

In addition to concerns about professional decorum, the reasons that sometimes keep doctors from touching are often the same as those that inhibit people in other situations. A prominent reason is the fear that touching may be misinterpreted as a sexual overture. My interviews suggest that this is especially an issue for concern for male doctors in their dealings with younger female patients. Their concern is not surprising, as physicians must often touch body parts that are ordinarily reserved only for intimate relationships, and a lawsuit for molestation, however unlikely it is to happen, could be ruinous to a doctor's career.

Doctors have also suggested how to overcome this potential problem without becoming nontouchers. One method is to be especially aware of any flirtatious gestures on the part of the patient and then to proceed cautiously. One male doctor described to me a situation in which a female patient asked him to inspect something on her shoulder and then casually dropped her dressing gown over her shoulder in a coy way. I asked him, "What did you do?" He said, "I excused myself and returned with a nurse. She [the patient] got the message, and it didn't occur again."

Another problem can arise when a doctor is attracted to the patient. One doctor confided in me, "Maybe this is just my problem, but if the woman is very attractive, I would ordinarily avoid any but the most essential touches in the office so as not to communicate anything unintentionally. In the examination room, it's no problem. I just focus on my purpose."

Although either of these two factors would understandably increase caution, there is no reason for physicians to avoid touch altogether. Certain touches can be used with virtually anyone to add extra friendliness to an exchange:

1. Greeting touches can be used to break the ice—a handshake for someone the doctor does not know well, a touch on the shoulder or arm for an established relationship. One doctor told me, however, that if the patient seems obviously ill or upset, he would refrain from touching until he knew what was going on.
2. Departure touches, such as a pat on the arm as the doctor leaves the examination room, conveys not only the doctor's caring, but also the expectation that the relationship will continue.
3. At times when a patient is expressing concern, or just after surgery, almost any touch will be read as showing support and is likely to be welcomed. Doctors say that some caution has to be exercised with men because there are those who do not like to be comforted with a touch, but elderly patients, whether male or female, tend to be especially accepting of these support touches.

4. When congratulations are in order, more intimate touching—a squeeze or even a hug—is appropriate. This can be an extremely powerful message, especially when not only congratulations but also support are conveyed by the touch at a special time. Several hours after our second son's very difficult birth, the attending doctor, a woman, entered my wife's hospital room, asked how she was, and immediately hugged her. It was an emotional moment for both women, and it left no doubt about the caring attitude of the doctor.

Touch used in a physical examination of a patient for diagnostic purposes, sometimes called "medical touch," is very different from informal touch. It is impersonal, but this does not mean the touch should be mechanical or uncaring. Experienced and skillful physicians usually begin by preparing the patient, especially when the examination involves intimate body parts or potentially painful contact. For example, the doctor may discuss in advance with the patient what kinds of touches will occur. Later, the doctor may describe each step just before it happens. With children, some banter may precede any touch or perhaps time for the child to play with a stethoscope.

Transition touches may also be used to accustom the patient to contact. For example, the doctor may begin with a stethoscope examination, placing his or her free hand on the patient's shoulder. One urologist told me that he often places a hand on the hip of a male patient while talking about the rectal examination to follow. The doctor may also place a hand on a child before examination while talking to the parent.

Once the main part of the examination begins, a touch that is as gentle as possible is necessary. At this point the doctor must be especially sensitive to reactions such as an increase in body tension and be prepared to slow down and help the patient to relax. The urologist told me that humor often works with men during a rectal examination: "The guy may say, 'I don't like this,' and I'll say, 'Well, get out of here then!'"

Although a physician's facility with touch can enhance communication and assist in the patient's healing process, it is important to acknowledge that some physicians who may be uncomfortable with informal touch are nevertheless caring. In his article, "The Healing Touch," Dr. William Nolen (1986, p. 38) gives examples of alternative ways of "making contact": One doctor, toward the end of a medical interview, consistently asks, "Is there anything more I can do for you today?" Another "always sits down when he stops in a patient's room, even though he may only stay a minute." Others simply listen attentively while the patient is talking, without any mannerisms that suggest the need to be rushed.

It is best for most patients if the physician can touch in both senses, but communication of a personal interest in the individual being treated is essential. Dr. Nolen concludes, "patients deserve the best of both the science and the art of medicine. You shouldn't settle for less" (p. 39).

NURSES AND HOSPITALS

Although many doctors are now rediscovering the power of touch, nurses never really lost it. In part, this is because people who are attracted to nursing are also likely to feel at home with the caretaking role and the physical contact that goes with it. In part, the use of touch by nurses has been a simple matter of necessity. Especially in hospitals, they are responsible for administering the care prescribed by doctors and generally seeing to the patient's physical needs on an hour-to-hour basis. In addition, their availability in the hospital also places them in a position in which they can readily offer emotional support to the patient and family.

Touch and the Psychology of Hospitalization

Research has shown that the stress of a hospital stay has certain debilitating psychological effects on patients. As a result, special sensitivity on the part of the nurse in the use of touch is particularly helpful in minimizing or alleviating patients' discomfort related to the following consequences of hospitalization (Barnett, 1972; Huss, 1977):

Sensory deprivation.

Being confined to a bed and unable to engage in normal physical activities often creates a sense of disorientation, and medication may contribute to this effect. If a patient seems disconnected from what is happening, some nurses use an attention-getting touch to the shoulder when talking to the person in order to help reestablish alertness. More vigorous contacts such as a backrub can also serve to bring someone back to sensory awareness.

Anxiety about body disintegration.

When a person's body does not function normally, especially after surgery, a vague sense of fear may set in. It seems as though one's body is "falling apart." Touch can also help in this situation by making the patient aware that he or she can still enjoy contact even though mobility is temporarily lost.

Dependency.

Most people tend to regress to a more childlike state when they are ill. Individual patients differ, however, in how they deal with these feelings of dependency. Some respond very positively to a support touch accompanied by reassuring words, thus accepting their role as the child to be cared for. Others may respond by becoming defensive and rejecting attempts at comforting with touch.

Depersonalization.

When patients are shuffled around from place to place and han-dled by a variety of people, they may feel as though they are being treated as an object. That is why the nurse's use of "instrumental" touches—those that accomplish a task such as dressing or helping a person out of bed—should be done in a caring way. Talking to patients, using no more physi-cal pressure than is necessary, and showing concern for their reactions to these touches, rather than just moving or manipulating them, can help to accomplish this. Similarly, the use of other, more personal contacts—a touch when saying hello, for example—show that the person is being dealt with as an individual.

The Potential Therapeutic Effects of Touch in the Hospital

Most touches by nurses in a hospital bring positive responses from patients. This has been demonstrated in studies of seriously ill patients (McCorkle, 1974) and of women in labor (Stolte, 1976). In particular, one study by Sheryle Whitcher and Jeffrey Fisher (1979) showed just how dra-matic the impact of touch can be.

Prior to surgery, a nurse performed two simple touches with a ran-domly selected group of patients. First, she made brief contact with the patient's hand while introducing herself. Then, she touched the patient's arm for about a minute while talking about a brochure that explained sur-gical procedures. Other patients received the same talk from the nurse but were not touched.

In response to a questionnaire administered after the nurse had left the room, those who were touched reported less worry about the risk of surgical complications. They also described their hospital experience up to that point as being less unpleasant than did those who were not touched. Even more remarkably, routine tests given after surgery was over and the patients had been returned to their rooms showed that those who had received the nurse's touches had lower blood pressure than others. Obviously, their psychological state prior to surgery had been altered, and this influenced their later physical recovery.

There was only one negative effect of touch revealed in the Whitcher and Fisher study, and it applied only to men. Male patients reported becoming somewhat more anxious about the upcoming surgery as a result of being touched. Women, in contrast, were calmed by the touch. Apparently, the traditional male need for independence was threatened by the tactile message that suggested they required nurturing.

It may be that a congratulatory touch after a crisis is over will work best with men. In any case, this finding does not suggest that men who are hospitalized should not be touched at all, but it does underscore the importance of adapting to individual patient needs in the art of nursing.

PSYCHOTHERAPY AND COUNSELING

Even though it is obvious that the "healing" touch of doctors and nurses is helpful primarily because of the psychological support it provides, touch is nevertheless more controversial in psychotherapy than in professions that focus on physical healing. In fact, as one psychologist noted with regret, touching has long been considered a taboo practice for therapists (Older, 1977).

This cautiousness about physical contact with clients among psychotherapists has its origins in the psychiatric tradition established by Freud, who devised a method of therapy that relied solely on verbal communication. It should be remembered that Freud worked in the Victorian era of the late 19th and early 20th century. His "sexual theory" of human motivation was highly controversial at the time, and many considered his ideas to be perverted. Including touch in his therapy would have been considered all the more outlandish by Freud's peers because touch was widely believed to be sexual by its very nature.

The concern that touching by the psychotherapist will have sexual connotations carries over to a large extent in modern times, and it is one of the reasons for the taboo against touching in therapy. Among psychiatrists and psychoanalysts, who follow the Freudian tradition more closely than other therapists, there is an additional reason for avoiding touch. Their philosophy is that the client should work out problems verbally in order to gain intellectual insights, and touching or responding to touch in therapy would be considered acting out rather than interpreting. Yet, even in other approaches to psychotherapy in which the relationship with the client is more personalized and therapy is more likely to be short term, the taboo against touch persists to a surprising degree.

In rare cases in which either the therapist or client is seductive, or in which the client is inclined to misread touches as sexual, the concern is legitimate. In other situations, however, it would not seem to apply.

However, a more common reason given for concern about touching in therapy is based on the widely accepted principle that the therapist should meet the client's needs and not the other way around. This principle obviously includes issues about possible sexual relations between the therapist and the client, but it is broader. The value is sometimes interpreted as saying that touch is so personal as to make the therapist overly involved with the client.

"The problem with this philosophy, if carried to an extreme," says counselor and therapist Carmen Williams, "is that it ignores the importance of the relationship between the client and the psychotherapist" (personal communication, March 1989). Similarly, psychologist Jules Older (1977) observes that the restriction against touching is one of those taboos that may have contributed to the low success rate of therapy.

Research on Touch in Therapy

More therapists have become open to the idea of using touch, and as this has happened, an increasing number of studies have been conducted to explore the possible effects. In these experiments, some clients are touched and others are not, and the results are compared. Typically, there might be a handshake at greeting, a brief guiding touch in the direction of the counseling room, two more touches by the therapist at selected times during the session, and a closing handshake and another guiding touch at the end (cf. Hubble, Noble, & Robinson, 1981).

Most of these investigations have reported positive results. For example, the therapist or counselor may be rated by the client as more expert and more confident (Hubble et al., 1981), or the client may reveal more personal information during the session (Alagna, Whitcher, Fisher, & Wicas, 1979; Jourard & Friedman, 1970). Although virtually no negative effects have been found, one study failed to reveal any apparent effects of touch, and others showed only some of the expected positive influences (see Willison & Masson, 1986).

The finding in some studies that touch had limited or no impact is not surprising. The clients were meeting the therapist for the first time, and the touches themselves were contrived and artificial, done in the same way to each person each time. These conditions are necessary in a controlled experiment, but they do not apply to circumstances in which the therapist and client have had time to develop a relationship. That so many positive effects occurred even under contrived circumstances suggests that it would be wise for therapists to explore using touch in their practices.

When and How Should the Therapist Touch?

The right touch in psychotherapy is one that fits the client's needs at the time. As psychotherapist Don Johnson put it,

> There is a tendency to try to establish hard-and-fast rules like "touch" or "don't touch." Some people can be touched in therapy, others should not be. When touch is potentially appropriate for the individual, there are right times and wrong times to touch, right and wrong ways to touch. (Personal communication, March 1989)

Deciding whether or not a client should be touched depends on the therapist's evaluation of the individual and the diagnosis of his or her problem. For this reason, most therapists do not touch in the opening session, except possibly for a handshake. Certain kinds of clients are not good candidates for touching, even later on in the sessions. For example, a therapist might not initiate a touch with a client who has a history of being fondled inappropriately or sexually abused by a parent, especially if the therapist is the same sex as the parent because an affectionate touch could be misunderstood. Similarly, a client with strong fears of emotional abandonment by close persons and an insatiable desire to be held constantly will not be helped by supportive touches. As one therapist candidly stated to me, "It can be a bottomless pit. This patient needs to talk through these fears, not act on them" (R. Mazler, personal communication, January 1990).

However, therapists I have interviewed suggest that most clients can be touched at certain moments. Here are some examples of appropriate uses of touch.

"Personal corridor" touches.

In many offices, there is a corridor between a waiting room where the therapist or counselor greets the client and the room where the session takes place. This is a transition point where casual conversation often occurs and more personal, everyday touches can be used. The two people are not as yet situated in their roles. For example, in one incident, a client commented on something he had accomplished in the last week that had been difficult to do previously (related to issues discussed in therapy). The therapist touched him briefly on the shoulder, an exclamatory touch I call "announcing-a-response," as if to say "Good for you."

Emphasizing a significant revelation.

A male military officer who seemed very restricted emotionally—

literally "armored"—had agreed to go into couple therapy with his wife after she had threatened divorce. She was relating an incident, saying, "He just can't express his feelings," a theme she had brought up before but which he had ignored. The therapist reached out and touched the man's knee (the nearest available body part), a message which could be translated, "Now hear this. This is important." The therapist then went on to interpret the wife's remark: "I think she's saying it's terribly important to know what you're feeling so she can share it with you."

Expressing empathy.

One therapist said, "If someone is talking about a painful experience or feeling, I often touch briefly to show support and understanding. I don't hug, which might cut off the feelings, but I will touch a neutral area—even a foot works fine. I'd say something like 'I know you're feeling that deeply' or 'I know this hurts a lot'" (D. Johnson, personal communication, March 1989).

Giving affection.

Even a hug can be appropriate at times, especially with a client who is feeling isolated from others in relationships outside therapy. It says, "I think you are likeable or lovable," a message more convincingly conveyed by a touch than a verbal reassurance. In order to avoid overinvolvement or sexual connotations, the hug would ordinarily come at the conclusion of a meeting and the client would be involved in deciding whether to touch. In one incident, for example, an adolescent boy had been talking about feeling emotionally estranged from his family. The therapist said, "Sometimes I feel it's been helpful to hug at the end of a session. How do you feel about this?" The boy said, "I've been hoping someone would give me a hug." Another client, a man who always came dressed in a suit and tie, had expressed concerns about his inability to reach out emotionally to others. The therapist offered a hug at the end of one meeting, and the client said, "Oh, no, definitely not." Several sessions later, he said, "Could I have that hug now?"

Responding to client requests for touch.

One therapist said, "If the client asks for a hug or touches spontaneously, I would almost always accept it. However, I've had clients say, 'I really feel like a hug at the end of a session,' when I felt it was seductive or an escape from dealing with a problem. Usually, I'd say, 'That's good. That's what therapy is about—verbalizing feelings,' and then we'd talk about it." Sometimes, however, even a touch of questionable appropriateness, if initiated by the client, can lead to breakthroughs. At the close of one session, a female client spontaneously hugged her male therapist. At the next session, she talked about having guilt feelings about the touch. She then revealed, for the first time, that her father had instigated an incestuous relationship with her as a child. The therapist who told me this story commented, "We then began to deal with the underlying issue which had brought her to therapy."

Just as touching is not for all clients, it may not be for all therapists. In particular, a male therapist who finds that he touches only attractive female clients should consider whether his motives are sexual (see Alyn, 1988). On the other hand, I think therapists and counselors should also examine their motives for not touching. Reluctance may stem from worry about what conservative colleagues would say or from a hesitancy to deal with the client's needs for warmth. Touch is a powerful way for the therapist to use his or her most valuable resource, the human capacity for caring. As Jules Older (1977, p. 199) suggested, in psychotherapy, "Touch is not a technique. Not touching is a technique."

OTHER HELPING PROFESSIONS

Sometimes paraprofessionals or other persons in a helping role can more easily use touch to give psychological support than primary caretakers. The helper and the person in need may be less concerned about authority—the "proper" doctor-patient or therapist-client relationship—so the touch seems more personal. Many ministers do daily or weekly "rounds" in the hospital, touching and encouraging patients as they go. With liturgical reform in the Catholic Church, the "laying on of hands" by priests in the confessional, mass, and last rites of sacrament is now an accepted practice. Hospice volunteers, who visit dying persons, report that touch is especially comforting to most of their clients. Often, people stop touching someone they know is dying, so in addition to using touch themselves, volunteers encourage it in family members.

One nurse, who operates as a social worker to help families make decisions about care for elderly members, uses the need for touch in an indirect way. When she visits families in their homes, she passes around a large teddy bear called "Flo Nightengale." "Many of my clients need to hold and hug something cuddly," she says. "It's a soft, non-threatening way to get acquainted with people during an emotionally difficult time" (Barrett, 1986, p. 38).

Of all the professions, teaching has the most potential for significant, long-range impact from touch. Almost all of the 18 meanings of touch I have discussed in this book can be used effectively by teachers of young children, with the obvious exception of sexual touches. One teacher expressed it this way: "If you like teaching and you like kids, you're going to want to touch for many purposes. It's a full relationship." I once sat in on a first-grade classroom in a Waldorf school in which my son was enrolled. Creative individual work is emphasized in this kind of school. I was impressed with the amount of energy which was bursting forth from the children in all directions. The teacher frequently moved from child to child, touching and guiding them.

I have also attended classrooms in which young children were expected to sit quietly in rows. Deviations such as talking to a neighbor or touching another student were dealt with by verbal reprimands, threats of punishment, or sending the child from the room. The quiet ones often seemed listless. Their energies were being controlled, but not tapped for creative learning.

Especially in the early primary grades, children need touch, and they will get it, one way or another. Children who are physically aggressive with other children in school are sending out a message: "Touch me. Be involved with me."

Although there have been few studies specifically concerned with the effects of touch on learning, a number of broader investigations have looked at "warm" teacher behaviors—combinations of smiling, physical closeness, and touch. The research shows that these teacher acts increase student alertness (Ryans, 1960), verbal participation (Kleinfeld, 1973), academic achievement (McKeachie & Lin, 1969), and even performance on intelligence tests (Exner, 1966). Touch is by far the most attention commanding of these warm behaviors. It also has the advantage of being usable not only for conveying interest in the pupil, but also for exercising control and giving direction.

One study pinpointed the most common general categories of touch used by teachers (Heinig, 1975):

1. "Close work" is a type of togetherness touch in which the teacher helps or shares an activity with the child. A typical one would be placing an arm around the child's chair so slight contact is made while commenting on the child's work or giving instructions. This touch is used about twice as often with girls as with boys.
2. "Positive" touches are the most common of all and include a variety of meanings such as showing affection (a pat in passing or a hug), giving a compliment, showing appreciation for a task done for the teacher, playfully ruffling hair, or saying hello or good-bye. Surprisingly, boys received over three times more of these touches than girls.

3. "Guidance" touches involve efforts to control the child. Not surprisingly, they also are used about three times more often with
boys than girls. These compliance touches include holding or
maintaining contact for several seconds while telling the child
to be quiet, touching briefly with one hand while taking away
an object with the other, and more vigorous touching such as
grasping the child and placing him in his seat.

Effective use of the touches listed above relies on two principles.
The first is that guidance touches should not be done out of anger—not
easy when the teacher is frustrated, but important. Similarly, only the
degree of force necessary to bring compliance should be used. The message is, "I am here to help you calm down and control your impulses."
Children in the primary grades generally accept these touches when they
are done with this attitude.

The second principle is that close work and especially positive
touches, give permission for guidance touches at another time, particularly
if the positive ones are used more often than the controlling ones. This
probably accounts for why boys received more positive touches in
Heinig's study—they also required more guidance. A teacher cannot specialize in guidance touches without negative reactions. Conversely,
although a teacher could use the more positive touches exclusively, those
who touch a lot generally find it useful to employ both kinds. They might
as well capitalize on their advantage as a toucher.

What about teacher-student touching beyond the primary grades?
Teachers are, in effect, authority-figure substitutes for parents. It is not surprising that their touching drops off sharply with children who have
reached puberty, just as it does among parents, but the extent to which
this happens is unfortunate. Here again, the American preoccupation with
the mistaken notion that touch equals sex enters the picture. Opposite-sex
touching is especially low between teachers and adolescents because
many teachers are understandably concerned about potential misinterpretation. Actually, however, this pattern begins much earlier. Research
shows that even among preschoolers, male teachers touch boys more and
female teachers touch girls more (Perdue & Connor, 1978). Add to this the
fact that adolescents touch much less than they did when they were
younger, even with same-sex peers, and we emerge with the picture of the
virtually untouched adolescent student.

I think this is not only unfortunate but also unnecessary.
Overcoming the no-touch barrier requires that individual teachers have
clarity about their intentions (so that flirtatious messages are not communicated). Beyond that, the guidelines for appropriate touch with adolescents
are similar to those outlined for parents in Chapter 4: (a) The more physical

types of guidance touches can virtually be dropped from the teacher's repertoire. Teenagers will often react negatively to overtly controlling touches. (b) The sustained "close work" touches are taboo. They do have sexual connotations for persons who have entered puberty, regardless of the sex of the teacher and student. Hugging and extra-affectionate touches such as squeezes are near enough to having sexual connotations so that they also should be mostly eliminated. (c) The touches that can be used are those that the teacher might use with an adult friend, acquaintance, or co-worker, excluding touches reserved for close friendships. For example, congratulatory handshakes or pats on the back, brief touches of hello after an absence of some time, and attention-getting contacts are acceptable in most relationships. So are compliance touches, if they are accompanied by a request rather than a command, as they should be with any adult. These touches are not only safe with teenagers, they are often motivating as well.

THE TOUCH THERAPIES

In the established healing professions, touch is an adjunct to health care, a practice which rounds out the treatment. In certain less orthodox healing approaches, touch is the primary vehicle for treatment. The array of approaches is broad and includes chiropractory, rolfing, acupuncture, acupressure, Swedish massage, Chinese massage, Reichian massage, and numerous others. Although often characterized in the past as "crank" practices, or, more positively, "alternative medicine," some have gradually found acceptance among certain doctors and health care practitioners. Many lay people have believed in them for a long time.

The best known of the touch therapies are those that alleviate physical ailments or tensions. These include, for example, chiropractory and acupuncture, as well as the traditional "rub down in the spa"—the Swedish massage.

Less well known and more controversial are those approaches that may be used to deal with psychological problems. These treatments, which include rolfing and bioenergetics, are based on the notion that body and mind are so closely related that mentally repressed emotions result in the development of "emotional armor," chronic tension in certain parts of the body. The results of this variety of touch therapy are sometimes dramatic. For example, a practitioner of one of these approaches, called "body-centered therapy," described the following incidents from her work:

1. I was massaging a woman who was very relaxed until I came to her hand. I then became aware that it was mainly in her thumb. When I remarked on this, she said she remembered having her

thumb burned severely and being told not to cry—which she didn't—while being restrained and threatened. Then, the woman cried, much like a 3-year-old. I massaged her thumb for some time. It eventually relaxed and soon she stopped crying.

2. When I was massaging a woman on the back of her legs I noticed they were swollen. I told her I had the image of her having leggings on. At that point she cried and said her mother often beat her with a stick on her legs as punishment, and she began wearing leggings daily to protect herself. I massaged her legs with a downward stroke as though I were removing leggings. The swelling went down.

Until there is funding available for the study of the alternative methods of healing with touch that I have described here, it will not be possible to scientifically document the effectiveness of such approaches. For further anecdotal evidence of their impact, however, the reader may consult Sherry Suib Cohen's book, *The Magic of Touch* (1987).

WHY EVERYONE IS POTENTIALLY A HELPER AND HEALER WITH TOUCH

It may seem as though some people have a natural gift for touching others in need, something which cannot be acquired. In fact, however, those who have cuddled sick children to sleep or literally allowed others to cry on their shoulder have used helping and healing touch. As Delores Kreiger says in *The Therapeutic Touch* (1979), "there is little I have to teach you that you haven't done before at some time in your life" (p. 17). Those doctors, nurses, therapists, and teachers who employ touch skillfully in their professions are exceptional, mainly because they have had the initiative to acknowledge their natural impulses and to draw on their experiences to make it work.

Training in the use of touch can help, although it is seldom offered in medical schools or clinical psychology programs. Among the touch therapies, rolfing and Swedish massage are examples of methods that require the mastery of certain techniques under the guidance of an experienced teacher. However, basic skills in other touch therapies such as acupressure and the less complex forms of massage are often taught in short courses. My experience with such training suggests that a major element is the development of the awareness, motivation, and confidence to put healing hands to work.

Let's assume that you can do it at some level and that you are willing. What are some of the opportunities?

Touching the Elderly

I do not mean to stereotype in using the term "elderly" because many people who are well beyond the age of retirement are nevertheless quite vigorous. I use it to refer to those who have reached the stage in life in which impairment of physical or mental abilities has accelerated, especially those who are unable to move or travel about easily or who require special medical care.

There are two reasons why the elderly are especially likely to need touch: (a) they often have fewer family members or friends in their immediate environment to satisfy needs for intimacy and physical contact; and (b) with advancing age, there is a deterioration of the senses of sight and sound, but relatively little change in tactile responses, so touch becomes an especially important channel of communication (Rozema, 1986, p. 42).

You may or may not be in a position to see older persons regularly, but most nursing homes have volunteer programs in which members of the community are invited to come in to spend time with residents. In fact, the need for touch is so great in these situations that many institutions have made "pet days" a tradition, a time when cats and dogs from the ASPCA. are brought in as a form of substitution for human touch. Others have in-house domestic animals (Toufexis, 1987). Research in nursing homes shows that the touch of staff members is largely restricted to instrumental touches such as dressing or walking residents to meals (Watson, 1976).

Although caring, instrumental touches such as therapeutic touch or alcohol backrubs can have positive effects on the health and comfort of the elderly (Rozema, 1986, p. 42), what they especially need is the psychological boost of expressive, personal touching. These confirm the person's value as an individual. Doctors and nurses have told me that the elderly are often especially responsive to sustained contacts such as holding hands or placing an arm around the shoulder, touches that would seem overly intimate to younger people, except in romantic relationships.

There are individual differences among the elderly in reaction to touching. Among those who are severely impaired and who exhibit "agitated" behaviors (making odd "faces," picking at things, using repetitious mannerisms, uttering incomprehensible sounds, etc.), research in nursing homes shows that the majority were calmed by being touched, but some became more agitated and aggressive (Marx, Werner, & Cohen-Mansfield, 1989). For most elderly persons, however, the main precaution to be followed in the use of affectionate contact is to announce especially expansive touches in advance. You might say, "I'd like to give you a hug," which would allow the older person to say, "No, not right now" or "This shoulder is sore, be gentle" (Rozema, 1986, p. 43).

Touch and Illness in the Family

Some touches have mostly psychological impact, such as the kiss to an injured finger which gives a sense of completion to an episode and allows a child to stop crying. The fact that some physical illnesses are psychologically induced suggests that supportive touches may also be preventive. For example, a child who is upset about something which happened at school will usually be soothed by a touch which accompanies talking through feelings about the event. It may also prevent a stomach ache and a request to stay home from school the next morning. The attention of soothing backrubs to a spouse who is experiencing tension may also help to head off illnesses that are stress related.

Other touches in the family can be used to deal directly with physical ailments. I know of one couple who make an exception to the usual rule of maintaining privacy in their bedroom by allowing children who are sick to sleep in their bed. They believe it speeds up recovery. As a result of a workshop my wife and I took on healing touch, we gave "Reiki treatments" to our children for all kinds of aches and pains. It is a method that consists of simply placing a hand on the distressed area of the body for a period of several minutes. The physical (and psychological) warmth of the contact seems to be soothing. It does not always work, but it is surprising how often it takes away or reduces the symptoms.

One man, a victim of Parkinson's disease, told me that having his wife hold his hands helps tremors go away. He also has cramps in his stomach just after taking medicine for the disease, and at these times, his 7-year-old son often climbs into his lap and lies across his stomach. The warmth generated relieves the pain, and it is also a caring experience for both people.

Here again, the effect of touch on illness may be "merely" psychological, but in two senses—making the discomfort bearable and also inducing the relaxation which makes rest possible and the resulting recuperation go more quickly. It may also be that touch at times of illness operates on the basis of physical principles we do not yet understand.

Touch in Pregnancy and Labor

A special opportunity for touch in the family is provided during pregnancy. Soothing contact is especially likely to be wanted by the mother for a variety of reasons, including backaches, insomnia, and the need for loving reassurance.

Although she has the direct tactile experience of the child growing within her, the father and even the other children may feel left out. They also need tactile involvement. One approach is to have family members touch the mother's abdomen to feel the baby move and kick. Another is described in this account:

> "When I was pregnant, my husband sometimes said, 'I feel like you're just thinking of the baby,'" recalls Bridgette Dahdah. But through touch, her husband, Charbel, became part of the relationship. When Bridgette lay awake at night unable to get comfortable, she sometimes asked Charbel to massage her lower back and shoulders. That helped him realize how much she depended on him. (Henig, 1986, p. 16)

Touch is even more likely to be needed during the birthing process itself. There is an increasing trend for the father, a friend, or an experienced midwife to attend births, and many hospitals now permit such persons to be present in the birthing room. Professor of Pediatrics John Kennell of Case Western University says he has evidence that the presence of a companion can decrease the length of labor by half (Henig, 1986, p. 19). Except for a certified midwife, the usual requirement for such participation is attendance with the mother in a prenatal training class. There techniques for relaxation such as breathing exercises are taught, and the support person practices touch to discover what kinds of contact are particularly calming to the mother. (For details on the use of touch in labor, see Henig, 1986, p. 19.)

The right touch in labor may vary with the skill of the support person, and it may change from earlier practice sessions to the actual event. The father, for example, is usually inexperienced compared to a midwife. His touch may or may not relax the mother, but at the very least it provides psychological support for the efforts of labor. Research shows that touch from the husband, a relative, or a friend are especially recalled as positive by the mother after the birth is over (Stolte, 1976, pp. 102-104).

When I attended the birth of my second child, an unexpected physical problem emerged, and doctors stood poised to perform a caesarian operation, although it proved to be unnecessary. In the final moments before the baby came out, my touching was limited to wiping my wife's face and brow with wet cloths while a friend held her hand tightly and gave verbal encouragement. These were the only touches she could accept at that point, but she said it helped to give her the courage to get through a rapid and traumatic delivery.

Other Opportunities for the Layperson

The use of caring touch is not limited to the elderly, family members, and emergency situations. However, many people do have inhibitions about giving or receiving sustained touches to areas of the body other than arms and shoulders, except in the most intimate of relationships. These barriers can often be overcome by the simple device of offering a special service that the helper is in some way qualified to give, a redefinition of the usual connotations of such touches. If a person is in pain or under stress, it is much easier to say, "I've just taken a course in massage—would you like to try it?" than to say "Let me touch you to make you feel better."

LESSONS FROM THE EXPERIENCE
OF PROFESSIONAL PRACTITIONERS

You may have noticed that certain themes appear again and again throughout this chapter. They are principles that generalize across the many ways touch is used to help and heal, even though each profession may emphasize certain ones. The concepts described below can be read as a checklist of ideas for professionals to consider in reviewing their own touch practices or as guidelines for learning by nonprofessionals.

Make a decision about whether you are willing to be involved.

People who use touch in a therapeutic, caring way will find that others will open up to them. The doctor and the teacher will receive more questions and more volunteered personal information. A sensitive masseuse will have clients who talk about their feelings and problems. Sometimes this is time-consuming, and it always involves the expenditure of mental energy. Some people will decide this is not for them at all, and others will have to choose which persons they are willing to be involved with in this way.

Keep the other person's needs in the forefront.

The kind of involvement I am talking about means caring, but not ego involvement in the sense of proving something about one's self or satisfying primarily personal ends. The teacher who touches mostly in order to be popular with students, the doctor who touches only to keep patients coming back, and the therapist who touches out of physical attraction to the client have crossed a line. They are often likely to touch at the wrong time or in the wrong way from the point of view of the other person's needs. For example, a guidance touch by a teacher or parent should be used to help the child control impulses. If it is done out of anger, a frustrated response to what is seen as a challenge to one's authority, it will create a cycle of further challenge and frustration.

Clarify and focus on your intention.

Many of the concerns that professionals have about the risks of sexual connotations from touch can be dismissed if the person touching is clear about his or her own motivations. For instance, even a sustained touch or one directed to a vulnerable body part such as a knee, which often has sexual connotations in everyday circumstances, will seldom convey a sexual message if the doctor's intention is solely to convey support. The reason is that the other signals which often accompany and betray a sexually motivated touch—extra, unnecessary caresses, a look of intense interest in the eyes rather than concern, and so on—will be absent.

Provide transitions to touch for the other person.

Requesting permission to touch helps to avoid rejection. So does explaining the reason for a touch in advance. Similarly, touches prior to more intrusive contacts serve to prepare the other person. The doctor who makes contact before going fully into the medical examination is giving the patient time to adjust. Similarly, the teacher who uses casual or affectionate touches frequently can more easily use controlling touches at other times.

Become sensitive to nuances of reaction to your touch.

Reading feedback and adapting your touch are essential in helping and healing. At the most basic level, this means noticing the response you get to an expressive touch such as the one used in saying hello or offering comfort—is it acceptance or rejection? For more extensive instrumental touches such as giving a backrub or inspecting an injury, the principle means interpreting subtle reactions from moment to moment, often using your tactile as well as visual senses. If the helpee has to say "That hurts!" you may not have been reading closely.

Concentrate on being present.

The capstone principle is to stay in the here and now. Practitioners of therapeutic touch or massage prepare for this by "centering," entering a meditative or mentally calm state (L. Jemsek, personal communication, May 1988). For any purpose, being present at least requires temporarily blocking out thoughts or concerns unrelated to the condition of the person being touched. Even for the teacher who has a room full of pupils to manage, it means being completely with that child for the moment. Following this principle is what allows the toucher to focus on intention, make skillful transitions, and respond appropriately to feedback.

One central insight emerges from the experience of caretaking practitioners of touch: The attitude with which a touch is done produces subtle variations in the quality of the touch itself. This adds a dimension to the symbolic meanings of touch discussed in this book. Consider, for example, a touch given at the moment when another person is obviously needy. It will consistently communicate the message of giving support. However, the way the contact is made—rough or vigorous or gentle, abrupt or cautious or gradual—determines the degree or kind of caring which is conveyed.

Here we are talking about perfecting the art of touch, and the principle applies beyond the uses of touch discussed in this particular chapter. Regardless of the context, the sincerity and sensitivity of the toucher at the moment always influences the effect of any kind of touch. It is just that the significance of attitude becomes even more obvious and pronounced when the purpose is helping or healing.

14

Learning to Touch

I F THE number and diversity of magazine articles which treat a subject is an indication of general interest, there are many different people who want to know how to use touch more effectively. In the past few years, articles have appeared in such varied publications as *Seventeen*, *Glamour*, *Parents*, *Woman's Day*, *McCall's*, *Working Woman*, *Omni*, *Psychology Today*, *Today's Health*, *Medical Economics*, and *Nursing Homes*, to name only a few.

The approaches that have been used to encourage people to touch are also varied. For example, in the belief that everyone should touch more, a group of high school students in England initiated Touch for Health Month. Using posters, buttons, and press releases, they urged others to join in what *Psychology Today* called a "physical chain letter." Each person was supposed to touch three males and three females he or she would not ordinarily have touched and to ask them to do the same to an additional six people. The students received letters from others praising the effects of trying out their idea, and they documented an increased amount of touching in their own school cafeteria as a result of their campaign ("A Touching Story," 1983).

One writer objects to promotional campaigns, advice on how to touch, and suggestions that one should touch on the grounds that they create self-consciousness. She poses the question, somewhat tongue-in-cheek:

Have you seen that bumper sticker that asks, "Have you hugged your
child today?" which, depending on your answer, plunges you into the
depths of guilt or produces a smug smile of righteous satisfaction. If
this is the morning you ran out of the house too fast to do your duty as
a parent, hug goes down on your mental to-do list along with clean
oven and have *tires rotated.* (Welch, 1979, p. 70)

Like the British students referred to above, Welch believes touch
is important, and her approach is only slightly different. She proposes a
private evolution in which individuals take note of how much or little they
touch and then respond "naturally": "Just becoming aware of how you feel
about touch will open you up to a delicious pleasure you may have been
denying yourself for too long" (p. 72).

Unfortunately, the "Just do it" or "Doing what comes naturally"
approaches usually do not work. I have yet to hear that touching has
swept across Great Britain. Although all mammals have a need to touch,
knowing how to touch is not instinctual or natural for humans. Like most
communication behaviors, the ability to touch effectively is either learned
or not learned at some point in life, sometimes unlearned as inhibitions set
in, and available for new learning or relearning at any time. The self-consciousness which often accompanies behavior changes is an uncomfortable, but only temporary, part of the process of becoming more effective.

"Communication skills training" is a method that has been tested
and proven effective for learning out-of-awareness behaviors such as
touch. It is used by educators, psychologists, and human relations specialists, although it can be used by anyone. In this chapter, I suggest a number
of ways to utilize this method. The only prerequisite for the learner is a
desire to improve. The basics of the approach are simple: (a) *Find out what
you usually do so you can discover what to change.* In touch, this means
discovering not only how much you touch, but also who you touch, in
what ways, and with what meanings. (b) *Know the behaviors associated
with effective performance of the skills that interest you.* (c) *Practice the
skillful behaviors, at first in "safe" learning situations and later in circumstances that seem more risky.*

HOW DO YOU TOUCH NOW?

You can start by assessing your overall attitude toward touch. Table 1 is a
questionnaire developed by communication professors Peter Andersen and
Kenneth Leibowitz (1978) to measure your outlook on touch. It is called
"The Touch Avoidance Scale," although it could just as well have been
named "The Enjoyment of Touch Scale." It has been scientifically tested

Table 1. The Touch Avoidance Scale

DIRECTIONS: This instrument is composed of 18 statements concerning feelings about touching other people and being touched. Please indicate the degree to which each statement applies to you by circling whether you (1) Strongly Disagree, (2) Disagree, (3) Are Undecided, (4) Agree, or (5) Strongly Agree with each statement. While some of these statements may seem repetitious, take your time and try to be as honest as possible.

1. A hug from a same-sex friend is a true sign of friendship.	1	2	3	4	5
2. Opposite-sex friends enjoy it when I touch them.	1	2	3	4	5
3. I often put my arm around friends of the same sex.	1	2	3	4	5
4. When I see two people of the same sex hugging, it revolts me.	1	2	3	4	5
5. I like it when members of the opposite sex touch me.	1	2	3	4	5
6. People shouldn't be so uptight about touching persons of the same sex.	1	2	3	4	5
7. I think it is vulgar when members of the opposite sex touch me.	1	2	3	4	5
8. When a member of the opposite sex touches me, I find it unpleasant.	1	2	3	4	5
9. I wish I were free to show emotions by touching members of the same sex.	1	2	3	4	5
10. I'd enjoy giving a massage to an opposite-sex friend.	1	2	3	4	5
11. I enjoy kissing persons of the same sex.	1	2	3	4	5
12. I like to touch friends that are the same sex as I am.	1	2	3	4	5
13. Touching a friend of the same sex does not make me uncomfortable.	1	2	3	4	5
14. I find it enjoyable when a close opposite-sex friend and I embrace.	1	2	3	4	5
15. I enjoy getting a back rub from a member of the opposite sex.	1	2	3	4	5
16. I dislike kissing relatives of the same sex.	1	2	3	4	5
17. Intimate touching with members of the opposite sex is pleasurable.	1	2	3	4	5
18. I find it difficult to be touched by a member of my own sex.	1	2	3	4	5

Table 1. The Touch Avoidance Scale (cont.)

DIRECTIONS FOR SCORING:

(1) Add up the circled numbers for items 1, 2,
   3, 5, 6, 9, 10, 11, 12, 13, 14, 15, and 17:   _____
(2) Score items 4, 7, 8, 16, and 18 in reverse,
   so a circled 1 is scored as 5, 2 as 4,
   3 as 3, 4 as 2, and 5 as 1, and add them up: _____
(3) Add up columns (1) and (2) to get your score: _____

Note: Item 15 from the original scale (Andersen & Leibowitz, 1978) has been altered from "when my date and I embrace" to "when a close opposite-sex friend and I embrace." Also, the scoring has been reversed from the original, so that a higher score indicates a more positive attitude toward touch.

Table reprinted from *Environmental Psychology and Nonverbal Behavior, 3.* Permission granted by Human Sciences Press, Inc.

with a large number of people, so it will give you a good idea of where you stand. You might take it now and score it according to the instructions at the bottom of the table before reading the explanation below.

Your score will tell you more about how you feel about touch at this time than how you actually touch, but it's helpful in assessing your motivation. The following norms are based on data gathered with a diverse population of people (Berryhill, 1982): A score of 70 or higher indicates a very strong motivation to touch. Less than 14% (about one-seventh) of the population scores this high. If your score is right around 60, your motivation is about average, but still generally positive, since the midpoint between positive and negative on the scale is 54. A score of 50 or lower would place you approximately in the lower 14% in terms of motivation for touch.

You should keep in mind that your attitude is a product of your past experiences with touch, positive or negative. With this in mind, you might go back to check and score your answers again, this time in terms of how you would ideally like to feel or respond. This can be read as your wish for having satisfying experiences with touch. If your original score or your "wish score" is around or above the cutoff point between negative and positive (54), chances are good that the rest of the exercises I suggest in this chapter will help you to improve your touch skills.

Recording Your Touches

This exercise is much more time- and energy-consuming than the one above, but it will pay off in two ways: (a) it will make you much more aware of touch; and (b) it will help you to assess how you actually touch on an every-day basis so that you can make choices about how you want to change.

The idea is to write down information on all of your touches, given or received, for at least one full day (2-3 days is even better). Record your touches as soon as you you can after each occurs so that you do not forget details. Pick typical days when you will be around a variety of people, or, depending on your interests, decide on specific situations for recording—at work, at home, with certain people who are important to you, and so on. You may be able to disguise your recording as part of your work, or, if asked about what you are doing, say, "I'm supposed to keep track of certain behaviors for something I'm studying."

Ideally, you would record information on each of the following (Table 2, the Recording Form, could be photocopied and used for rapid recording), although you may find you need to limit yourself to certain items (1, 2, and 4 are especially important):

1. Who initiated the touch (you or the other person), or was it mutual (like a handshake)?
2. What kind of touch was it (frontal hug, side hug, spot touch to arm or shoulder, etc.)?
3. What is the relationship of the other person to you (romantic partner, friend, acquaintance, co-worker, etc.)? Also record name or initials of the other person if not a stranger.
4. What was the meaning of the touch (see Table 3 at the end of this chapter for a list of meanings)? You could write down your translation of the touch, as though it were stated in a few words rather than with a touch, figuring out the meaning type later.
5. Was the touch accepted or rejected?
6. Was there anything about the situation which influenced the touch (hadn't seen the person for a long time, etc.)?

When you have completed the recordings, inspect them to answer at least some of these questions: (a) Were you more often a toucher or touchee? How many touches did you experience per day (the average is about 12 for females, 9 for males)? (b) What kinds of touches (hugs, spot touches, etc.) did you use? What kinds would you like to use more? (c) How many touches did you have in each kind of relationship? Who would you like to touch more? (d) What meanings did you convey? What meanings would you like to incorporate into your repertoire? (e) Were there any rejections? Was it because a taboo was violated (see Chapters 8 and 10)?

Table 2. Recording Form for Touches

DIRECTIONS: Circle the appropriate response or responses under each numbered category. Write out answers in the designated spaces.

Incident #_____ Date:_____ Time: _____ Circle: AM or PM.

(1) *Initiator:*

a. Me   b. Other   c. Mutual

(2) *Type of Touch*: (Main body parts involved: _____ to_____.)

a. Frontal hug b. Side hug c. Hold d. Caress e. Press against f. Spot touch

g. Handshake h. Pinch i. Punch j. Pat k. Squeeze l. Other:_____.

(3) *Relationship of Other to You*: (Initials/name of other:_____)

a. Romantic intimate b. Close friend c. Friend (not close)

d. Acquaintance e. Stranger f. Relative (specify:_____)

g. Co-worker h. Superior i. Subordinate.

(4) *Meaning of the Touch:*_____.

(5) Response to the Touch:

a. Accepted by me b. Accepted by other c. Rejected by me

d. Rejected by other. If rejected, tell why (taboo violation?):

_____

(6) *Circumstances influencing the touch or reaction (explain):*_____

_____.

The Quick-change Method

After you have assessed how you touch and know how you would like your touch behavior to change, you may be able to use a "just do it" approach that has been successful for some people. This quick-change method involves recording touches again for one or more days, but with a specific purpose in mind—to increase your total initiated touches or to use certain kinds of touches more. Obviously, you have to wait for the right circumstance for each touch, but the idea is to act on your impulse to touch when the opportunity presents itself. It is useful to have a "model" for imitation in mind, one or more persons you have observed who are especially effective in using touch. It also helps to set quotas—for example, doubling your usual number of touches per day.

I have worked with people who report remarkable results with this method: going from being a "low toucher" to a "high toucher," learning to express affection with close persons, acquiring the ability to influence their children in facilitative ways, and so forth.

WORKSHOPS IN TOUCH

The training activities described here are designed primarily for groups working under the guidance of a leader, but most exercises can also be done by two people. There are also some ideas for how individuals can work independently in developing skills. The format for the workshops is suggestive and can be varied to suit your particular purposes.

Workshop A: Rediscovering the Pleasures of Touch

The objectives of this sequence of exercises are to motivate people by creating appreciation for the values and pleasures of touch and to serve as a warm-up for Workshop B, in which more focused practice on communicating different meanings of touch is treated. The experiences in Workshop A are drawn from the human relations, encounter/sensitivity-training tradition, and are not recommended for use by themselves. The skills will not transfer readily to everyday situations without the Workshop B activities.

The more risky, psychotherapeutic kinds of exercises are not included. Even so, Workshop A may not be appropriate for all groups because of the intensity of involvement the exercises bring. I have found that this approach works especially well with such participants as nurses, students, other young adults, and singles. The leader should be someone experienced in facilitating group activities.

At the beginning of the workshop, the leader would ordinarily explain the objectives, perhaps talking about the importance of touch. A good icebreaker is the "First Names" exercise, which helps to make a transition to touching. Participants should be told that the purpose of this activity is for everyone to learn the first names of all group members. Sitting on the floor or on chairs in a circle, each person in turn tells his or her first name and provides a little personal information, such as why he or she is interested in the workshop. Each person repeats the names of all the participants who have gone before in advance of telling his or her own name. At the end, the person who began the exercise may be asked to scan the circle visually while telling as many names as possible, and others may be invited to do the same.

Exercise 1: Feeling Space (20-30 minutes).

Sitting close together on the floor and with eyes closed, participants are asked to begin silently feeling the space all around them with their hands, exploring their "personal space bubble," and contacting others. They may also be told that they can get up and move about after the beginning of the exercise. Some people will touch cautiously or withdraw, whereas others will initiate and reciprocate touches readily. Some may even get up to walk around and contact others.

After about five minutes of activity, group members are encouraged to talk about their personal reactions—although discussion will usually erupt without urging. Feelings about "invading" or "being invaded," enjoying touch, waiting for others to initiate before responding, wanting to touch more, and so on, will come out.

Exercise 2: Blind Walk (1 hour).

Participants choose a partner for this exercise. In order to facilitate interaction throughout the entire group, they can be asked to pick someone they do not know. One way to do this is have people mill around silently until another person is chosen.

One person is blindfolded and led around by the other. The "blind" partner is told where to walk and what is coming up, can be asked to touch certain objects to discover what they are, to report sensations and reactions, and so forth. After 20 minutes, the roles are reversed, and the procedure is repeated.

Group discussion at the end is likely to center around issues about feeling dependent on another person and how the partner's guiding touches felt. Some individuals, often men, may report feeling uncomfortable about relying totally on another person, whereas others will find the experience pleasurable. Related topics can be introduced when they are appropriate to the group: reactions to being touched and cared for in illness, the centrality of tactile experiences in the learning of infants, the need for supportive and affectionate touching with young children, and the relative tactile deprivation of adults.

Exercise 3: Hand Communication (20-30 minutes).

Group members are asked to pick a new person for an exercise. If they are still sitting next to their blind-walk partner, this can be accomplished by having them simply turn in the other direction. This may result in the selection of some same-sex as well as opposite-sex partners, which will be useful for the purposes of the exercise. They are then asked to close their eyes and communicate with their partner, discovering as much information as they can, using one or both hands to make contact with one or both hands of the other person. Suggest the possibility of exploring tactile sensations (using light or more firm contact, becoming aware of different textures and contours) as well as conveying messages (shaking hands, patting, etc.).

Watch the participants closely to decide when to stop and call for discussion, but about 5 minutes may be sufficient. The hands are surprisingly intimate vehicles for communication, especially when contact is sustained. There is also an element of safety here, however, because people are used to shaking hands or making brief incidental hand-to-hand contacts in passing objects or asking for attention. You may observe that male-male combinations start off with a handshake and are unsure where to go from there, whereas women feel more comfortable holding or caressing hands with one another.

Feelings of eroticism, surprise at how much information can be gleaned from the hands, and ideas about the mutuality of tactile communication may emerge. Issues about same-sex vs. opposite-sex touching by men and women, the importance of the hands in touch as a body part that has many nerve endings (exceeded only by the head and face), and the significance of subtle nuances of the quality of hand touches may be discussed if reactions from participants evoke these topics.

Exercise 4: Tactile Exploration (40 minutes).

This exercise is more involving than the previous one because it asks participants to experiment with different qualities of touch and utilizes more parts of the body. New partners may be selected simply to allow contact with still another person, although this is not essential. Of the two body areas used in this exercise, the shoulders are slightly less and the back slightly more intimate areas than the hands, so this activity provides a good transition to further tactile exploration.

The exercise is the same as the one described in Chapter 9 for parents of abused children, but it is appropriate for any group (Older, 1981, p. 488). One member of each pair gives touch while the other receives and then roles are reversed. The following progressive steps are involved, each taking about 2 minutes: (a) light rapid tapping on the shoulder; (b) more vigorous tapping with all fingers of both hands in the same area; (c) gliding touch across the shoulder and back with heels of hands; (d) slapping lightly with slightly cupped hands across both areas; and (e) deeper massage with circling thumbs or tips of the fingers held firm. At the end of the sequence, the recipient is asked which type of contact is preferred or whether he or she would like a different kind of touch, and the person is given another round of touch.

Discussion at the end may be brief, but participants may want to talk about their reactions of comfort or discomfort with certain kinds of touch. Comments can be made on the importance of being sensitive to individual preferences for different qualities of touch.

The next two exercises are more emotionally involving and the touching may be more personal in nature. Therefore, the leader should decide whether they are appropriate for the persons involved. In particular, Exercise 7, Expressions of Affection, works best in situations in which the people have known each other for some time, and the exploration of personal relationships is fitting. With other groups, it might make more sense to end Workshop A at this point and proceed to Workshop B.

Exercise 5: Relaxation Touches.

There are two variations here, and one or both can be used.

"Back lift." For this activity, persons of roughly comparable height and weight are paired. The leader may demonstrate with a volunteer. About 30 minutes should be allowed for completion. Here is a description of the procedure from William Schutz's book *Joy* (1967):

> Two persons stand back-to-back with their arms stretched high over the head, hands together. The stretcher grabs the hands firmly and dips slightly to ensure the stretchee's buttocks are next to the small of his back. The stretcher now slowly bends forward until his back is approximately parallel to the ground. The stretchee relaxes and breathes heavily through the mouth, sucking in and blowing out. When this rhythm is established, the stretcher dips toward the ground during the inhale and rises slightly during the exhale, thus facilitating the deep breathing. (p. 38)

Partners then switch roles. Participants should be told that there may be slight pain in the chest for the stretchee, and persons with severe back problems, especially with disc problems, should not attempt the exercise (Schutz, 1967, p. 39).

Most people report feelings of greater relaxation and energy afterwards. The commonness of chronic chest and back tensions and the potential use of touch for reducing stress can be discussed. This exercise also helps prepare participants to fully enjoy the next relaxation activity.

"Rock and Roll." This activity involves all participants together and is designed to promote further relaxation as well as a particularly pleasurable touch experience (Schutz, 1967, p. 181). The time requirement depends on the number of people in the group. Allow about 5 minutes for each person for the activity itself. In addition, some people may want to

discuss reactions immediately after their turn, and some time for discussion at the end should be allowed.

One person at a time lies on the floor in the center of the group circle, eyes closed, with hands and arms crossed and resting on the midsection and stomach, feet close to one another. The entire group silently surrounds and carefully picks up the person, making sure that the neck is supported lightly with two fingers of one person's hand, the head tilting back slightly. The person is then swayed gently back and forth. After 1-2 minutes, at a nonverbal signal from the leader, the person is slowly lowered to the floor, with the swaying motion continued.

Discussion at the end, when everyone has been swayed, may focus on feelings of trust and the pleasure of being taken care of by others. Some may comment that they cannot remember having such an experience before, or that it was similar to being held and rocked as a child. Along these lines, it may be appropriate for the leader to comment that intimate body contact can be sensual without being sexual and that the intent of the toucher influences the meaning of touch.

Exercise 7: Expressions of Affection.

There are several options here, and a combination can be used. The most powerful activity involves having one person at a time stand in the center of the group with eyes closed, while others approach individually to express positive feelings via touch toward the person. Having the entire group provide support in this way often creates strong feelings. Some reactions may be tearful, as people recognize their needs for affectionate touching that they may not be receiving in other situations.

An alternative activity is somewhat less intense. Participants are asked to mill around with eyes open but without talking, expressing any positive reaction they wish with touch to each person. Discussion at the end may not be necessary, but should be allowed by the leader. The point may be made by the leader that not only hugging but also other touches such as pats and caresses convey affectionate messages.

Exercise 8: Group Touch.

A final concluding activity, which may be done in combination with either of those described above or by itself, involves simply asking group members to form a circle and place their arms around the people on each side. Participants might introduce some variations spontaneously at this point, like swaying from side to side or requesting a "group hug." The leader would ordinarily make some kind of a concluding statement, perhaps suggesting that Workshop B provides an opportunity for participants to learn skills for putting the warm feelings generated by Workshop A into practice in daily life.

Workshop B: Practice in Conveying Everyday Touch Messages

Workshop A is more evocative than instructive. It helps people to discover or recall how powerful and pleasant touch can be. The kinds of touching practiced, with some adaptation, are applicable primarily to very close relationships outside the group, even though other possible uses may be suggested in discussions. Workshop B, on the other hand, is designed to enhance the participants' repertoire of touches for everyday situations.

If Workshop A precedes B and there has been an intervening period of at least a day, the leader should begin by asking participants to talk about what has happened since the first workshop. Accounts may range from experiences of being able to touch more affectionately to incidents in which the participants' touches surprised others or brought rejections. Whether or not Workshop A came first, the leader should briefly explain the purpose of Workshop B. The 18 basic meanings of touch should be discussed, but without going into detail on how each can be communicated. Participants may be given a handout to follow during this discussion (see Table 3 at the end of this chapter), which can be given out prior to this session.

Directions.

The activity of this workshop can be presented as an imaginary "acting tryout," in which the purpose is to see how quickly people can assume a role. Or, it can be simply described as "role playing." Each person may be asked to pick a partner, or the leader may assign partners if advance planning about who will be assigned what roles is possible. One person in each pair becomes "A" and the other "B". Pairs are numbered off. "A" persons line up on one side of the room in the order of their pair numbers, "B" persons in the same order on the other side.

Participants are told that as their pair number comes up, A and B will be assigned roles in which one or both will initiate touch. They then meet at "center stage" to perform their brief skit. Onlookers are assigned to observe closely, translate what they believe the touch means into words, and comment on how effectively the meaning is conveyed. They should share their observations on the way the touch is done, accompanying behaviors, and how the touch is received. After feedback is given, each pair may or may not be asked to repeat their enactment of the scene, depending on whether possibilities for different approaches have been discussed.

Enactment situations.

The leader (or "director") picks a scene that fits the sex composition of each pair as they come up and assigns roles, telling which person will initiate the touch or whether the touch will be mutual. When necessary, the leader can describe the environment and occasion for the scene, place chairs in appropriate positions, and specify furnishings or props to be imagined and pantomimed. Instructions on roles can be given orally in front of the group. Generally, however, giving private instructions to the "actors" by whispering in their ears or giving them written directions increases the challenge for the observers to figure out the touch meaning in each scene. This approach also makes feedback more revealing when a different meaning from the one intended is conveyed.

Box 1 describes examples of scenes for role playing. Others could be invented by the leader. The incidents are listed in random order so that you can test your own "TQ" (Touch Quotient) without knowing the suggested touch meanings in advance. To respond to the items as a test, first select the probable meaning of the touch in each item from the list of 18 provided in Table 3. Then describe briefly how the touch would most likely be done (hug, spot touch, caress, etc. and roughly the body parts contacted for toucher and touchee)—"a spot touch to the hand or arm," "a hand hold to the shoulder," etc.

Box 2 gives the "answers," the most probable meaning or combination of meanings which would be conveyed in each scene. When the situations are used for role-playing, the leader should be prepared for the possibility that participants may come up with some creative solutions as to how to touch in each scene, even if they are not the most probable responses.

You might take the test now by going to Box 1. Then score your answers by referring to Box 2.

Box 1
Examples of Role-Playing Scenes
(and Touch Quotient Test Items)

Scene and Roles	Touch Meaning	Type of Touch
1. A married couple, A (female) and B (male), are sitting on a couch at home watching a sports event on TV. A wants to make contact to show her pleasure at being with B without drawing attention away from the game.	_____	_____ _____
2. A brother, Person A, approaches Person B, and hugs her, but with a light tickle to in her ribs, saying "Are you still ticklish?"	_____	__(specified __in scene)

                                        Touch Meaning   Type of Touch

3. Person B approaches A, a co-worker, to
   touch and ask if A could answer B's phone
   for a brief period of time. B's touch should   _____   _____
   be sustained through the request. (Either per-
   son could be of either sex in this incident.)

4. Person A (male) has a brief conversation   _____   _____
   with B (male), a friend but not a close one,
   and touches just before leaving.

5. Person A (female) comments on the attrac-   _____   _____
   tiveness of an item of clothing on Person B   (primary)
   (male, a friend but not a close one).
   (Decide on both the primary meaning and   _____   _____
   a secondary, implied one.)   (secondary)

6. Person A (male) wants to say hello to Person
   B, an acquaintance. B has his back turned   _____   _____
   and does not initially see A, who initiates.

7. A daughter, Person A, is shown to her car   _____   _____
   by both of her parents, persons B-1 (moth-
   er) and B-2 (father). The daughter, who is   (meaning)
   leaving for a trip, initiates (who touched the _____   _____
   touch to each. (Decide who is likely to be   (who touched
   touched first, who last.)   last?)

8. Person A (female) acknowledges Person B   _____   _____
   (female) on the street with a friendly touch.
   They are acquaintances who run across
   one another regularly.   _____   _____

9. Person A (female) initiates a touch to a   _____   _____
   friend, B (male or female), to say she is
   excited about what they are going to do
   together that day.   _____   _____

10. A male, Person A, is home with his parents
    for a vacation from college. A period of time
    after the initial hellos, the father, Person B,
    passes by the son, who is seated at the din-   _____   _____
    ner table, on his way to his chair at the
    table. The father wants to show he is glad to
    have the son home and initiates a touch.
    (Rate as father-son, although the situation
    could just as well involve mother-son, moth-
    er-daughter, or father-daughter touch.)

11. Person A (male) introduces Peson B   _____   _____
    (female), his romantic partner, to another
    couple, his close friends. A wants to convey
    his close feelings for B and touches her.   _____   _____

	Touch Meaning	Type of Touch
12. Person A (female) has just been denied a promotion and tells Person B (female), a co-worker and acquaintance. A is obviously dejected. Location is in the office; others are nearby, but not involved in the exchange. B initiates touch.	_____	_____ _____
13. Person A (male) has just given an unexpected gift to Person B (female), a friend. B initiates.	_____	_____
14. Person A (male) comes to the hospital to be with a close male friend (B) whose father has just suffered a heart attack. Knowing that the father is in stable condition and resting at the time, A approaches B in the corridor outside the room and initiates a touch.	_____ _____	_____ _____ _____
15. Two unattached people who are acquaintances, A (male) and B (female), have met again at a party and are seated together at a close distance, with others nearby but not involved in the conversation. The man is attracted to the woman, and she seems to reciprocate his feelings. A touches to let his interest be known without being obvious.	_____	_____ _____
16. Two business associates, Person A, a man, and Person B, a woman, meet in A's office to discuss a possible contract between their two companies. (Decide on the meaning and type of touch and who should initiate.)	_____ (meaning) _____ (initiator)	_____ _____
17. Person A (female) meets B (female), a close friend, at the arrival gate of an airport. The touch is mutually initiated.	_____	_____ _____
18. Person A, a male auto salesman, is showing a car to Person B, also male. A wants to touch to show friendliness and interest without being intrusive. (Decide on at least one option for touch, eliminating an opening or closing handshake from consideration.)	_____	_____ _____
19. Person A, a male, approaches a male friend, Person B, saying "Are you still a tough guy?" and initiates a friendly touch.	_____	_____ _____
20. Person A (female subordinate) has stayed late at work to help out Person B (male boss). Professional relationship only. The work is nearly complete. B initiates touch.	_____	_____ _____

Box 2
Answers to Items in Box 1

Scoring Your Touch Quotient: Give yourself 2 points for a correct choice of meaning on each item. Give yourself 1 point for correctly identifying the type of touch or other responses asked for in the item. Allow yourself a certain amount of latitude in scoring when information in the item may be ambiguous and allow credit when your answer is listed as a second or third choice.

1. Togetherness (sustained touch). A could place arm around B, but limited touch such as a hand on his thigh or simply making contact knee to knee or side to side is more likely. Second choice: Affection touch such as kiss or pat, but only one limited in duration and degree of involvement.

2. Playful—probably playful affection, although it borders on playful aggression. (Either answer is acceptable. Type of touch is specified in the item, so give yourself 3 points if you identified the meaning correctly.)

3. Compliance. Spot touch or possibly a gentle hold, probably to the shoulder. Could also be a combination of attention-getting and compliance (second choice), but an attention-getting-only touch would be more brief and would precede the request rather than being sustained through it. (No credit for attention-getting unless compliance is also listed.)

4. Departure (simple leave taking, not departure/affection). Could be a handshake (second choice), but a spot touch to the shoulder would be more friendly.

5. Reference-to-appearance touch. The item of clothing itself is touched, pointing out literally, "This is what I'm talking about." The secondary message is strong, however, and could be either "I like you" (affection) or "I'm attracted to you" (flirtation). (Give yourself 1 point for identifying the primary meaning, 1 point for the secondary meaning.)

6. Attention-getting or combination of attention-getting and greeting (2 points for either single or double-meaning answer; 1 point for greeting only). Brief touch of hand to arm or shoulder (possibly to hand).

7. Departure/affection hybrid touch. Hugs, kisses, or both are the most likely touches for both people, with father receiving the first touch, since the honor of the final touch is reserved for mother. (2 points for the hybrid meaning, but not departure or affection alone. 1 point for naming mother as the receiver of the last touch, although if you assumed her relationship was closer with the father, either answer could receive credit.)

8. Greeting (simple greeting, not greeting/affection). Spot touch or pat with a hand to a nonvulnerable body part, probably an arm or shoulder.

9. Announcing-a-response. Implicitly, the toucher is asking the other person to be excited or involved. A brief touch—pat, squeeze, or spot contact—is most likely.

10. Affection. The touch is likely to be a brief pat, caress, or spot touch, done without accompanying words. (Although the father could say, "Good to have you home," the words are unnecessary.) A side hug to the shoulders is possible (second choice on type of touch), but this is more likely in a mother-daughter or father-daughter touch.

11. Togetherness. A places arm around B and leaves it there. Holding hands possible (second choice on type of touch), but less likely.

12. Support. Spot touch to shoulder, arm or possibly hand is mostly likely.

13. Appreciation. Could also be "announcing-a-response" if B expresses surprise or excitement rather than thanks. Kiss to cheek or hug likely; however, could be another touch such as a spot touch, caress, and so on.

14. Support. Support/greeting hybrid meaning could also be correct, although the greeting purpose is clearly secondary. Spot touch, squeeze, or caress to the shoulder most likely; hug less probable, but possible.

15. Sexual—but flirtation only. A subtle touch such as leaving his knee in contact with hers or if seated side by side possibly resting a hand on her shoulder is most probable. Technically, it looks like a togetherness touch, but it's ambiguous (and flirtatious), since they are not yet "a pair." (2 points for "togetherness" answer, as well, however.)

16. Greetings with a handshake. Person A, the man, should initiate because it is his office, although the touch is also mutual in the sense that after the first split second, both reach out. His decision to shake hands should not be dependent on the woman offering her hand first. If he failed to offer his hand, she should initiate. Score your answer according to whatever assumption you made about the man's motives. Neither person should offer a limp hand. (1 point for greeting touch, 1 point for handshake, 1 point for identifying the initiator.)

17. Greeting/affection hybrid meaning. Hug and/or kiss to cheek most likely.

18. There are several possible touches the salesman could use: (a) instrumental (brief guiding touch in pointing out a direction); (b) attention-getting (brief touch to call attention to some car feature); (c) incidental touch (brief hand contact while handing an object such as keys to the other person). The touch would be limited to a hand contact to a hand (passing an object), arm, or shoulder. Announcing-a-response—for example, reacting to a joke made by the other person—is possible, but unlikely between two men (1 point). A compliance touch with words such as "I want to see you drive away in this car," while sometimes used by salespeople, would be highly inappropriate and likely to backfire.

19. Playful aggression. Touch might be a pulled punch, a half-nelson, and so on. The touch should not be too aggressive, and the words spoken by the initiator should not come after the touch.

20. Appreciation. Spot touch to shoulder or arm.

Total your score (60 points possible):
50-60 points: Excellent
40-49 points: Good
30-39 points: Fair

Handling the Role-playing Activity.

There are several options for ways in which the leader can handle the role-playing exercise to encourage participants to experiment with touch. The role assignments should be geared to the sex composition of each pair, calling for a male- or female-initiated touch in opposite-sex pairings depending on which would be most common in everyday situations. If the leader does not plan pairings and assignments in advance, role-playing incidents such as those described in Box 1 can be reorganized into the categories presented in Table 3, designating appropriate sex compositions for each scene. Then the leader can quickly decide on a scene as each pair comes up.

As the participants become more relaxed and comfortable with the role playing, the usual sex roles for certain touches can be varied, often with results that are both amusing and instructive. For example, in one workshop, a male volunteered the information that he had "no problem" initiating affectionate touches to other males. I asked him to role play a scene in which he was to greet his best friend at the airport, and a male friend from the group was chosen for the other part. When they met at center stage, they performed a frontal hug, but their heads were pointed out over one another's shoulders in a kind of modified side hug, so that body contact was minimal. The observers picked up on this, and in the process of the discussion we talked about how males could negotiate being more affectionate with one another.

In another situation, a female was instructed to approach another female (a "friend" in the role assignment) with a playfully kidding touch. In the scene, she said "Hi, how ya' doin'?" and poked the other woman twice on the front of the shoulder. Observers and the other woman were confused about the meaning of the touch—was it an attention-getting touch, indicating she had to tell the other woman something, or was it just an awkward greeting touch? We talked about the fact that women are not used to performing playful touches, especially with one another.

Another variation on the role-playing procedure is to have participants redo the scene after feedback, using a different kind of touch or different accompanying behaviors. People are surprised to discover, for example, that a support touch elicits further expressions of feelings from the person touched, and an affection touch is more powerful when no words are spoken by the touchers. After the airport greeting scene described above, the men decided to retry the touch, this time achieving a regular frontal hug, to the applause of the rest of the group. One woman said, "It was beautiful to see two men hug in an unself-conscious way."

Other group members may also demonstrate how they would do a certain touch. After the attempt at playful touching in the scene between the women, two men from the group demonstrated a playful aggression mock wrestle. In the replay, the women were instructed to imagine they were members of the same sports team. During the touch, both women broke into laughter as they wrestled lightly with one another. The woman assigned to initiate the touch said, "It felt strange, but it was fun."

Workshop C: Touch in Special Situations

An alternative or adjunct to Workshop B is to design activities for circumstances of particular interest to a certain group. The participants might consist of salespeople, teachers, or hospital nurses, for example. Role-playing scenes can be devised in advance to represent typical or problematic situations in which touch might be used, or examples of recent actual events could be elicited from the group and made into role-playing scenarios.

The following skills training procedure can be used for each scene, with each phase lasting around 5-7 minutes.

First enactments.

The setting is suggested with chairs or other furnishings and appropriate props. The scene is enacted apart from the observers, who remain in the background. It is understood that one or both role players are to look for opportunities to use touch.

Feedback.

Next, observers comment on what they saw. One person, the "primary toucher" in the scene, usually receives the most feedback. Observers should avoid giving advice at first and simply describe specific verbal and nonverbal behaviors and perhaps describe the impression made by each act. Later, alternative possible ways of handling the situation, including different kinds of touches, can be suggested.

Replay.

Ordinarily, the role players would then redo the scene, experimenting with any changes in behavior that occur to them. A "coach," the leader or a member of the group, can be assigned at the beginning of the replay to stand behind the role player who is the central focus of attention. When the coach wants to make a suggestion, he or she touches the participant, a signal that the role-players should freeze momentarily. The coach talks in the first person as though expressing the role player's possible inner thoughts. For example: "I need to move closer to the person so I can touch easily" or "I realize I could have touched on the shoulder at that point to show support." The role player then "backs up" slightly in the scene, trying the suggested behavior if it makes sense, a kind of "instant re-play."

Final feedback.

The observers comment briefly on the re-play, especially whether the communication and touching was more effective this time. (Almost inevitably, it is.)

My experience in using these techniques with business people, students, and others shows the method works. Behavior can literally be changed. It is interesting to have at least a brief follow-up session several days later when participants can report their experiences in actual situations that approximated the role-playing situations.

The situation-specific workshop is even more powerful when used with intact groups such as families or couples. This approach capitalizes on the "systems approach" principle that when all members of a group have agreed to changes and practiced the needed skills, long-range impact is enhanced. The touch workshop can often be incorporated as a central part of a broader workshop on family or couple communication, in which it often makes sense as the very first activity.

As an example, here is a brief outline for a workshop in touch for couples:

1. Some of the sensitivity exercises from Workshop A can be utilized, along with others that allow more intimacy of touch and one-on-one caring.

    a. The "blind walk" can be surprisingly revealing with couples for bringing out issues of trust, mutual dependency, and playfulness.

    b. "Hand communication" can also be useful for introducing a new experience of tactile sensitivity into the relationship, and it can be extended by having couples go on to "mutual hand-to-face exploration." The face is both a more sensual area of the body than the hands and also one that is clearly identified by the individual with "the self." So, this exercise may bring out feelings of attraction, the desire to give and receive gentleness, and a discussion of the wish for being accepted as one is. After this exercise, one woman said, "I have never really felt pretty enough, but I liked the way you [the husband] touched every part as though you were discovering it." The husband replied, "I was aware of how much I like your face and how often I see it when I'm thinking of you."

    c. "Giving and receiving" exercises involve trading roles,

one person at a time being cared for by the other's touch. A simple but effective exercise of this type involves one person lying prone on their back while the partner gently lifts the head from behind and rotates it gradually from one side to the other, finally slowly placing it back on the floor. Others involve various kinds of massages to the back, neck, legs, and arms with the receiving partner commenting on which kinds of touch are more relaxing and pleasurable.

2. Although the sensitivity activities can be used by couples when the workshop is over, other exercises can be employed which are similar to those of Workshop B. They allow practice in everyday kinds of touches. This type of practice is more likely to transfer to "back home" situations. The suggestion should be made that couples try out or increase their use of certain kinds of touches during breaks or at other times when they are away from the group, returning to the workshop to discuss their reactions. These kinds of touches include:

a. the togetherness touch (walking or sitting with arms around one another, etc.);

b. solicited or spontaneous hugs;

c. more casual and brief touches of affection without prior announcement;

d. prolonged kisses or hugs with caresses but without further sexual touches (see Chapter 5 for the rationale).

The idea of the couple workshop in touch is to provide a kind of "cushion of support and affection" to carry the couple through other times when the inevitable conflicts of any intimate relationship must be dealt with. If communication techniques are practiced to help couples to talk out problems during another part of a couple communication workshop, the appropriate times for touching or avoiding touch can also be discussed (see Chapter 5).

WHY "TOUCH" NOW?

Why have so many newspapers and popular magazines carried articles on touch in recent years? Why would people be interested in learning to touch? In the book *Megatrends,* author John Naisbitt (1984) described the findings of his research team, a group that monitored and analyzed large masses of data from publicly available sources. Their purpose was to discover the directions American society was taking.

One of the identified major trends of the past three decades is what Naisbitt calls "high tech/high touch." The idea is that as technology has expanded, there has been a counterbalancing human response, a new emphasis on personal values and relationships—"high touch." We are now in "the age of information," which began with the growth of the popularity of network television and is now extended into the cable system. With even more far-reaching implications, computers have become firmly established as a necessity in the workplace and increasingly in homes.

One effect of all of this information technology can be to alienate people from one another unless they take action to correct the imbalance. There is now a growing cottage industry in which people work at home and communicate with fellow workers by means of computers. As a result, many of these workers have become dissatisfied with their separation and feel "out of touch." In the family, as Naisbitt points out, "You may have to drag your children away from the computer or video games" in order to spend time with them (p. 50).

In this context, the reaffirmation of the importance of touch is an emerging lifestyle—a way of life—for Americans. Naisbitt says "trends are bottom-up, fads are top-down." Touch is not a fad like a new clothing style, engineered by the fashion industry or the media, but a genuine trend, a long-range direction in response to the imbalance created by our high-tech society.

I do not mean "touch" in a strictly literal sense, and neither does Naisbitt, but rather as a metaphor, as in all those expressions we use such as "making contact" and "staying in touch." At the same time, however, communication by means of physical contact is a basic and essential part of this lifestyle. It is also one of the most effective ways of bringing about the personal involvement that is the key to this change of consciousness.

Beyond being a reaction to technological overload, I believe the current interest in touch also reflects a growing awareness by many Americans that there is something missing in the path they have been following in the pursuit of happiness. Following the turmoil and sometimes-euphoria of the 1960s, the 1970s and the 1980s were times when people became more concerned with finding a job, securing their financial future, and, in general, being "a success." Economic problems in the early 1990s have accelerated this trend.

As Paul Wachtel (1989) points out in his best-selling book, *The Poverty of Affluence*, this has not brought the happiness people sought. Despite the fact that the standard of living is significantly higher today than it was 15 years ago, most people believe it has declined. As Wachtel demonstrates, the pursuit of success as a way to happiness is a neverending and disappointing cycle. As soon as the pursuer gets to the next level, happiness wiggles out of reach again, there are more things "needed," and dissatisfaction with the new status quo sets in. What is more, we have arrived at a place where this game has become increasingly frustrating to play. We are already confronted with the Japanese economic challenge. In the near future, we will have to face the cutbacks in industrialization and private luxuries that will be necessary to counteract the greenhouse effect, pollution, and the poisoning of our waterways.

A ray of hope is suggested by Naisbitt (1984) in *Megatrends*: "I have noticed an important shift in public perception . . . *the end of denial*" (p. xxi), the recognition that our industrial base has been eroding for some time. The next step is to recognize that something else is needed, something more satisfying in the long run than just climbing the ladder and acquiring more things.

In a presentation on "The Truth About Success," consultant and counselor Susan Baile (1991) presents a view of what this "something else" would be like. There is nothing wrong with making money, gaining status, and obtaining the material benefits which go with these accomplishments, she says. However, in themselves, these will not satisfy the more basic wishes that motivate their pursuit. What we really need and are hoping to experience in our search for external success is the internal sense of success that arises from (a) high self-esteem—liking and respecting ourselves, (b) the comfort and pleasure of supporting and loving relationships, and (c) a sense of contributing to the world, of making a difference. Seeing that these three goals are interrelated and acting on this insight gives a person a feeling of wholeness, a unity of purpose. Building relationships is central in several ways. First, being liked and loved is a major element in a positive self-concept. Second, relationships also facilitate acts which lead to a sense of making a difference. Although a few people can make a contribution by working alone, most do it in large part by facilitating and encouraging others. Finally, caring for others by creating a loving environment for children, encouraging students, mentoring colleagues, or helping clients to deal with personal problems in itself makes a contribution to the future.

Realizing the three wishes for success means translating them into everyday behaviors. This is when learning to touch in the literal sense becomes especially important. Tactile communication can convey or strengthen almost any positive personal message. It is not the only way to create involvement, but in interpersonal relationships, as in other areas of one's life, mastery is often a matter of having the right touch.

Table 3
A Blueprint for Touching: The 18 Meanings

INSTRUCTIONS FOR READING THE TABLE: The 18 meanings of touch are grouped into 8 broad categories: emotionally positive, sexual, playful, controlling, ritualistic, hybrid (combined meaning), task-related, and accidental touches. In the left-hand column of the table are the names of each type, with a definition of the meaning. In the next column, on the right, is a description of the "key features" of the meaning, the way the touch is done or elements of the context that must ordinarily be present for the meaning to come across clearly. In the far-right column are examples of each kind of touch. If you imagine what the touch would look (and feel) like, or act out the touches with someone else, the way each meaning is communicated becomes clearer. The abbreviation "NVBP" stands for "nonvulnerable body parts" (hand, arm, shoulder, and upper back). "VBP" means "vulnerable body parts" (all other body regions). "Close relationships" refers to romantic intimates, close friends, and immediate family members. The table is adapted from Jones and Yarbrough (1985, pp. 29-35) and Jones (1990, pp. 239-243).

Meaning Type	Key Features	Typical Examples
A. POSITIVE TOUCHES:		
1. *Support*: serves to nurture, reassure, or promise protection.	(1) Situation calls for comfort or reassurance. (2) Hand, sometimes arm, directed to 1-2 body parts. (3) Initiated by person giving support.	(1) Knowing from a conversation the night before that a roommate is worried about a test, the toucher pats him on the shoulder when he sees him in the morning and says, "You'll do O.K." (2) After a friend expresses sadness, the toucher silently reaches out and squeezes her arm. (3) Cuddling a crying child who is injured. (Hugs are rare events, reserved for a person who expresses strong feelings, except with a child.)

Meaning Type	Key Features	Typical Examples
2. *Appreciation*: expresses gratitude.	(1) Situation: receiver has performed a service for toucher. (2) Toucher verbalizes appreciation.	(1) A boss touches a subordinate on the shoulder at the end of a day's work and says, "Thanks for the way you handled things." (2) A woman kisses a close male friend on the cheek after a meal he has prepared and says, "Thanks a lot."
3. *Togetherness*: draws attention to act of being together; suggests psychological closeness.	(1) Sustained touch. (2) Close relationships, mainly romantic; rarely adult family members except spouses.	(1) A couple walks down the street holding hands or with arms around one another. (2) A couple sits on a couch watching TV with one person leaning against the other. (3) A couple talk in a restaurant with knees touching. (4) Parent with arm around a child while reading a bedtime story.
4. *Affection*: expresses liking or loving.	(1) Close relationships. (2) Absence of a more specific positive meaning suggests affection.	(1) (Highly intense form) Spontaneous hugging of romantic partner or close friend with words of endearment. (2) (Less intense but more common type) Patting or caressing a close person when passing by him or her in the room. (3) Many different kinds of touches—kisses, squeezes, and so on; "Out of blue" quality signifies affection.

Meaning Type	Key Features	Typical Examples
B. SEXUAL TOUCHES: 1. (One main type): expresses physical attraction or sexual interest.	(1) Holding, caressing, and/or prolonged kissing. (2) Includes sexual body parts (breast, pelvis, buttocks, thighs).	(1) *Type #1*: Embracing with hand movement on body, usually with kissing (caressing or long kiss distinguishes it from hug of affection.) (2) *Type #2*: A simple hand touch to a sexual body part (for example, reaching over and casually touching the buttock). (3) Variations include flirtation and seduction which appear to be affection touches, but are overly affectionate for the relationship.
C. PLAYFUL TOUCHES: 1. *Playful affection*: lightens interaction by qualification of affection.	(1) Affectionate or sexual message with play signal.	(1) A male saying "How's about a kiss?" (I'm just kidding around) to a female friend or romantic partner, followed by a quick kiss. (2) With others present, a male puts his arm around his male roommate, who is doing the dishes and says, "You'd make a good wife" (I am teasing about being affectionate).
2. *Playful aggression*: lightens interaction by qualification of aggression.	(1) Aggressive message with play signal.	(1) *Type #1*: Aggressive contact with a comment that clarifies the intent as play ("Let's wrestle"). (2) *Type #2*: Aggressive comment with a touch play signal. (Customer to waitress: "No, we don't want the check—tear it up," followed by smile and spot touch to her arm.)

Meaning Type	Key Features	Typical Examples
D. CONTROL TOUCHES:		
1. *Compliance*: attempts to direct behavior.	(1) Initiated by person who attempts influence. (2) Toucher usually states or implies wanted action in words.	(1) A boss touches an employee on the shoulder and says, "Could you get this done by 5 o'clock?" (2) Grabbing a friend by the arm and saying, "Let's go."
2. *Attention-getting*: directs other's perceptual focus.	(1) Initiated by person who requests attention. (2) Initiator clarifies purpose verbally after touch. (3) Brief touch (usually just spot or pat) to one body part.	(1) A woman touches her male companion's arm to say, "Look at that." (2) A woman touches a female acquaintance's hand to ask a question. (3) A man touches another man's shoulder to ask, "Excuse me, do you have the time?" (75%, however, are female-initiated touches.)
3. *Announcing-a-response*: emphasizes a feeling of initiator; often implicitly requests similar response from the other.	(1) Initiated by person who announces the response. (2) Words along with the touch state or imply the feeling.	(1) A woman touches a male companion's knee while saying, "This should be a lot of fun today!" (2) A woman holds a female friend's arm briefly to say, "Guess what I heard?" (Translation: "Be interested too.") (3) (Men initiate this one also, but most are female-initiated.)

Meaning Type	Key Features	Typical Examples
E. RITUAL TOUCHES:		
1. *Simple Greeting*: part of act of acknowledging another at the opening of an encounter.	(1) Situation is first time two people see one another on an occasion. (2) Standard greeting phrase(s) before or with touch. (3) Hand to one body part. (4) Minimal form of contact (handshake, spot touch, pat, or squeeze).	(1) *Type #1*: (Formal) handshake greeting (mainly used between males). (2) *Type #2*: (Slightly less formal) hand to body part, usually only to shoulder or arm (mainly female-female or female-male).
2. *Simple Departure*: part of act of closing an encounter.	(1) Situation is end of an encounter. (2) Standard good-bye phrase(s) before or with touch. (3) Hand to one body part (not always minimal touch—some caresses or holds), but mainly spot touch or pat.	(1) Male pats male friend on shoulder when leaving (even among men, handshake as good-bye is rare, except in formal situations). (2) Female touches lower back of female friend when saying good-bye. (3) (Mainly used among friends, not romantic partners or family.)
F. HYBIRD TOUCHES (combination of meanings—2 most common below):		
1. *Greeting-with-affection*: expresses affection at the initiation of an encounter.	(1) Situation is beginning of interaction. (2) With greeting verbalization. (3) Close relationships. (4) VBP touches (face or torso often involved; could be caress, squeeze or pat).	(1) Hug and/or brief kiss between male and female (friends, intimates, family members). (2) Hug between close female friends at airport on arrival. (3) (Most common after a period of absence—most of a day or longer; rare among men.)

Meaning Type	Key Features	Typical Examples
2. *Departure-with-affection*: expresses affection at end of encounter.	(1) Situation is end of interaction. (2) Good-bye phrases (usually just after touch). (3) Close relationships. (4) VBP touches, mainly hugs and/or kisses.	(1) Opposite-sex prolonged hug and/or kiss (at the airport, for example); close relationships. (2) Hug between female friends when one is leaving. (3) (More common and more extensive the longer the expected separation; rare between men.)

G. TASK-RELATED TOUCHES:

1. *Reference-to-appearance*: a touch that points out or inspects a body part or artifact referred to in comment about another's appearance.	(1) Words go with and justify touch. (2) Spot touch by a hand to a VBP. (3) Usually close relationships, but could communicate flirtation or desire for closer relationship when used with others.	(1) A woman inspects a female friend's necklace and says, "This is pretty." (2) A woman brushes a male friend's hair with her hand and says, "I like your haircut." (3) Males rarely use it, but they could (saying, "Nice suit," while feeling the material at lapel, for example).
2. *Incidental*: a touch that occurs as an unnecessary part of the accomplishment of a task.	(1) Mainly hand-to-hand contacts. (2) Part of performing a task that does not require touch (secondary message of interest or friendliness is implied).	(1) Most common is handing an object to someone and allowing hand-to-hand contact (a clerk returning change, etc.).
3. *Instrumental*: touch that accomplishes a task in itself.	(1) meaning is clear from the touch itself, but secondary positive meaning may be implied.	(1) Assisting a person in putting on a coat. (2) Placing a hand on a person's forehead to check for a fever (implies support). (3) Putting suntan lotion on person's back (may imply flirtation or affection).

Meaning Type	*Key Features*	*Typical Examples*

H. ACCIDENTAL TOUCHES:

1. (One type only): touches that are usually perceived as unintentional.	(1) Touches consist of single, momentary contacts, mainly brushes. (2) Touches seem to be mistakes, although a secondary message such as attention-getting or flirtation may be implied.	(1) Brushing a person when passing by, getting up to go, etc. (2) (Bumps or brushes between strangers are usually rejected and brief apology is offered by one or both persons.)

References

Aguilera, D. (1967). Relationship between physical contact and verbal interaction between nurses and patients. *Journal of Psychiatric Nursing, 5*, 5-21.

Ainsworth, M.D.S. (1972). Attachment and dependency: A comparison. In J. L. Gewirtz (Ed.), *Attachment and dependency* (pp. 97-138). New York: Wiley.

Ainsworth, M.D.S. (1979). Attachment as related to mother-infant interaction. In J.S. Rosenblatt, R.A. Hinde, C. Beer, & M.C. Busnel (Eds.), *Advances in the study of behavior,* (Vol. 9, pp. 1-51). New York: Academic Press.

Ainsworth, M.D.S., & Bell, S.M. (1969). Some contemporary patterns of mother-infant interaction in the feeding situation. In A. Ambrose (Ed.), *Stimulation in early infancy* (pp. 133- 163). London: Academic Press.

Alagna, F.J., Whitcher, S.J., Fisher, J.D., & Wicas, E.A. (1979). Evaluative reaction to interpersonal touch in a counseling interview. *Journal of Counseling Psychology, 26,* 465-472.

Alper, P.R. (1984, August 20). "Getting physical" is good medicine. *Medical Economics,* pp. 39, 42, 45.

Altman, L.K. (1989, June 5). Optimism shown at aids meeting: Largest conference on disease starting with some hopes and harsh predictions. *New York Times,* p. A15.

Alyn, J.H. (1988). The politics of touch in therapy: A response to Willison and Masson. *Journal of Counseling and Development, 66,* 432-433.

Andersen, J.F., Andersen, P.A., & Lustig, M.W. (1987). Opposite sex touch avoidance: A national replication and extension. *Journal of Nonverbal Behavior, 11,* 89-109.

Andersen, P.A., & Leibowitz, K. (1978). The development and nature of the construct touch avoidance. *Environmental Psychology and Nonverbal Behavior, 3,* 89-106.

Andersen, P.A., & Sull, K.K. (1985). Out of touch, out of reach: Tactile predispositions as predictors of interpersonal distance. *Western Journal of Speech Communication, 49,* 57-72.

Anderson, E.S. (1987). *Communication of significant touch.* Unpublished doctoral dissertation, University of Denver.

Argyle, M. (1967). *The psychology of interpersonal behavior.* Harmondsworth, England: Penguin Books.

Argyle, M. (1969). *Social interaction.* Chicago: Aldine.

Baile, S.M. (1991, May). *The truth about success.* CareerTrack, Inc. seminar presentation, Columbus, OH.

Bardeen, J. P. (1971, April). *Interpersonal perception through the tactile, verbal, and visual modes.* Paper presented at the convention of the International Communication Association, Phoenix.

Barnett, K. (1972). A theoretical construct of the concepts of touch as they relate to nursing. *Nursing Research, 21,* 102- 110.

Barnlund, D.C. (1975). Communication styles in two cultures: Japan and the United States. In A. Kendon, R.M. Harris, & M.R. Key (Eds.), *Organization of behavior in face-to-face interaction* (pp. 427-456). The Hague: Mouton.

Barrett, M. (1986, January 8). Denver nurse gives respite to families who need care. *Rocky Mountain News,* Denver, p. 38.

Bartusiak, M. (1983). Feeling a profit. *Omni, 5,* 41.

Beier, E.G., & Sternberg, D.P. (1977). Subtle cues between newlyweds. *Journal of Communication, 27,* 92-97.

Bell, S.M., & Ainsworth, M.D.S. (1972). Infant crying and maternal responsiveness. *Child Development, 43,* 1171-1190.

Berne, E. (1964). *Games people play.* New York: Grove Press.

Berryhill, N.B. (1982). *The influence of age, sex, family size, and community size on attitude toward tactile communication.* Unpublished Master's thesis, Texas Tech University.

Bigger, M.L. (1984). Maternal aversion to mother-infant contact. In C.C. Brown (Ed.), *The many facets of touch* (pp. 66-72). Johnson & Johnson Baby Products Company.

Birdwhistell, R.L. (1970). *Kinesics and context.* Philadelphia: University of Pennsylvania Press.

Bly, R. (1992). *Iron John: A book about men.* New York: Vintage Books.

Borden, R., & Homleid, G. (1976). Paper presented at the Midwestern Psychological Association meeting in Chicago. (Cited in J. Horn, The Dominating Touch: Kojak Does it Too, *Psychology Today,* December, 1976, p. 28.)

Borkin, J., & Frank, L. (1986). Sexual abuse prevention for preschoolers: A pilot program. *Child Welfare, LXV,* 75-81.

Brassard, M.R., Tyler, A.H., & Kehle, T.J. (1983). School programs to prevent intrafamilial child sexual abuse. *Child Abuse and Neglect, 7,* 241-245.

Breton, M., & Welbourn, A. (1981). A nurturing and problem-solving approach for abuse-prone mothers. *Child Abuse and Neglect, 5,* 475-480.

Brockner, J., Pressman, B., Cabitt, J. & Moran, P. (1982). Nonverbal intimacy, sex, and compliance: A field study. *Journal of Nonverbal Behavior, 6,* 253-258.

Brown, R.A., & Field, J.B. (1988). *Treatment of sexual problems in individual and couples therapy.* New York: PMA Publishing Corporation.

Brown, R., & Kulik, J. (1977). Flashbulb memories. *Cognition, 5,* 73-99.

Bully [16 mm film]. Available from the Agency for Instructional Television, Box A, Bloomington, IN 47402, (812) 339-2203.

Burgoon, J.K., Buller, D.B., & Woodall, W.G. (1989). *Nonverbal communication: The unspoken dialogue.* New York: Harper & Row.

Burgoon, J.K., & Walther, J.B. (1990). Nonverbal expectations and the evaluative consequences of violations. *Human Communication Research, 17,* 232-265.

Byalick, R., & Bersoff, D. (1974). Reinforcement practices of Black and white teachers in integrated classrooms. *Journal of Educational Psychology, 66,* 473-480.

Byers, P., & Byers, H. (1972). Nonverbal communication and the education of children. In C. B. Cazden, V. P. John, & D. Hymes (Eds.), *Functions of language in the classroom* (pp. 3-31). New York: Teachers College Press.

Cates, J. (1985, July). Sexual harassment: What every woman and man should know. *Library Journal,* pp. 23-28.

Caudill, W.A., & Schooler, C. (1973). Maternal care and infant behavior in Japan and the U.S.: An interim report. *Journal of Nervous and Mental Diseases, 157,* 323-338.

Chapin, S. (1989, April 30). Date rape. *Boulder Sunday Camera,* pp. C1, C3.

Child Sexual Abuse: The Untold Story. [16 mm film]. Available from University of Calgary, 2500 University Drive, N.W., Calgary, Alberta, Canada T2N 1N4.

Clark, L., & Lewis, D. (1977). *Rape: The price of coercive sexuality.* Toronto: The Women's Press.

Clark, R.D., III, & Hatfield, E. (1981). *Gender differences in receptivity to sexual offers.* Unpublished manuscript. (Available from Dr. Elaine Hatfield, Psychology Department, 2430 Campus Road, Honolulu, HI.)

Clay, V.S. (1966). *The effect of culture on mother-child tactile communication.* Unpublished doctoral dissertation, Teachers College, Columbia University. (Article by the same author and title is in The Family Coordinator, July 1968, pp. 204-210.)

Coates, D., & Winston, T. (1983). Counteracting the deviance of depression: Peer support groups for victims. *Journal of Social Issues, 39,* 169-194.

Cofer, C.N., & Appley, M.H. (1964). *Motivation: Theory and research.* New York: Wiley.

308 References

Cohen, S.S. (1987). *The magic of touch: Revolutionary ways to use your most powerful sense.* New York: Harper & Row.

Cohn, A.H., & Daro, D. (1987). Is treatment too late: What ten years of evaluative research tell us. *Child Abuse and Neglect, 11,* 433-442.

Collett, P. (1971). Training Englishmen in the non-verbal behavior of Arabs: An experiment on intercultural communication. *International Journal of Psychology, 6,* 209-215.

Comfort, A. (1972). *The joy of sex: A gourmet guide to love making.* New York: Simon & Schuster.

Comstock, C.H. (1982). Preventative processes in self-help groups: Parents Anonymous. *Prevention in Human Services, 1,* 47-53.

Conte, J.R., & Berliner, L. (1981). Sexual abuse of children: Implications for practice. *Social Casework, 62,* 601-606.

Conte, J.R., Rosen, C., Saperstein, L., & Shermack, R. (1985). An evaluation of a program to prevent the sexual victimization of young children. *Child Abuse and Neglect, 9,* 320-321.

Cooke, B.G. (1972). Nonverbal communication among Afro-Americans: An initial classification. In T. Kochman (Ed.), *Rappin' and stylin' out: Communication in urban Black America* (pp. 57-74). Urbana: University of Illinois Press.

Cooper, C.L., & Bowles, D. (1973). Physical encounter and self-disclosure. *Psychological Reports, 33,* 451-454.

Coulton, H. (1983). *Touch Therapy.* New York: Zebra Books/Kensington.

Crusco, A.H. & Wetzel, C.G. (1984). The Midas touch: The effects of interpersonal touch on restaurant tipping. *Personality and Social Psychology Bulletin, 10,* 512-517.

Culturgram, Kingdom of Thailand. (1984). Provost: Brigham Young University.

Culturgram, People's Republic of China. (1984). Provost: Brigham Young University.

Culturgram, Republic of Columbia. (1981). Provost: Brigham Young University.

Culturgram, Republic of India. (1981). Provost: Brigham Young University.

Culturgram, Republic of Korea (South). (1980). Provost: Brigham Young University.

Culturgram, Malaysia. (1980). Provost: Brigham Young University.

Culturgram, Republic of Zimbabwe. (1984). Provost: Brigham Young University.

Culturgrams. Available from Brigham Young University Center for International and Area Studies, Publications Service, Box 61 FOB, Provost, UT 84602, (801) 378-6528.

DeAnglis, B. (1987). *How to make love all the time.* New York: Dell.

Davidowitz, E. (1986). The healing power of touch. *Redbook, 167,* 126.

Deaton, F.A., & Sandlin, D.L. (1980). Sexual victimization within the home: A treatment approach. *Victimology: An International Journal, 5,* 311-327.

Deethardt, J.F., & Hines, D. (1983). Tactile communication and personality differences. *Journal of Nonverbal Behavior, 8,* 143-156.

Deley, W. W. (1988). Physical punishment of children: Sweden and the U.S.A. *Journal of Comparative Family Studies, 19,* 419- 431.

Do's and taboos around the world. (1985). Compiled by the Parker Pen Company. Elmsford, NY: The Benjamin Company, Inc.

Dychtwald, K. (1977). *Body/Mind.* New York: Jove Publications.

Dykema, J. (1986). *A pilot study on touch communication between intimates.* Unpublished manuscript, University of Colorado.

Efron, D. (1972). *Gesture, race, and culture.* The Hague: Mouton.

Egeland, B., & Jacobvitz, D. (1984). *Intergenerational continuity of parental abuse: Causes and consequences.* Paper presented at Conference on Biosocial Perspectives in Abuse and Neglect, York, ME.

Elkind, D. (1984). *All grown up and no place to go: Teenagers in crisis.* New York: Addison-Wesley.

Ellis, E.M. (1983). A review of empirical rape research: Victim reactions and response to treatment. *Clinical Psychology Review, 3,* 473-490.

Elzinga, R.H. (1975). Nonverbal communication: Body accessibility among Japanese. *Psychologia, 18,* 205-211.

Engebretson, D., & Fullmer, D. (1970). Cross-cultural differences in territoriality: Interaction distances of native Japanese, Hawaii Japanese, and American caucasians. *Journal of Cross-cultural Psychology, 1,* 261-269.

Exner, J.E. (1966). Variations in WISC performance as influenced by differences in pretest rapport. *Journal of General Psychology, 74,* 229-306.

Faley, R.H. (1982). Sexual harassment: Critical review of legal cases with general principles and preventive measures. *Personnel Psychology, 35,* 583-600.

Finkelhor, D. (1980). Sex among siblings: A survey on prevalence, variety, and effects. *Archives of Sexual Behavior, 9,* 171-194.

Field, T. (1990). *Infancy.* Cambridge, MA.

Field, T., Scanberg, S.M., Scafidi, F., Bauer, C.R., Vega-Lahr, N., Garcia, R., Nystrom, J., & Kohn, C. (1986). Tactile/kinesthetic stimulation effects on preterm neonates. *Pediatrics, 77,* 654-658.

Fisher, J.D., Rytting, M., & Heslin, R. (1976). Hands touching hands: Affective and evaluative effects of an interpersonal touch. *Sociometry, 39,* 416-421.

Flanagan, J.C. (1954). The critical incident technique. *Psychological Bulletin, 51,* 327-358.

Floyd, N.M. (1985). "Pick on someone your own size!": Controlling victimization. *The Pointer, 29,* 9-17.

Ford, J.G., & Graves, J.R. (1971). Differences between Mexican-American and white children in interpersonal distance and social touching. *Perceptual and Motor Skills, 45,* 779- 785.

Forston, R.F., & Larsen, C.U. (1968). The dynamics of space: An experimental study in promexic behavior among Latin Americans and North Americans. *Journal of Communication, 18,* 109-116.

Frank, L.K. (1957). Tactile communication. Genetic *Psychological Monographs, 56,* 209-255.

Freize, K.L. (1988). *A pilot study on touch communications between parents and their children.* Unpublished paper, University of Colorado.

Fromme, D.K., Jaynes, W.E., Taylor, D.K., Hanold, E.G., Daniell, J., Rountree, J.R., & Fromme, M.L. (1989). Nonverbal behavior and attitudes toward touch. *Journal of Nonverbal Behavior, 13,* 3-14.

Furman, E. (1986). The abused child in the nursery school. In E. Furman (Ed.), *What nursery school teachers ask us about: Psychoanalytic consultations in preschools* (pp. 197-206). Madison, CT: International University Press.

Gallehugh, D.S. (1982). *The relationship between touch behavior and marital satisfaction in stable marriages.* Unpublished doctoral dissertation, University of North Texas.

Gartner, D., & Schultz, N.M. (1990). Establishing the first stages of early reciprocal interaction between mothers and their autistic children. *Women and Therapy, 10,* 159-167.

Gelardo, M.S., & Sanford, E.E. (1987). Child abuse and Neglect: A review of the literature. *School Psychology Review, 16,* 137-155.

Gilmartin, B.G. (1987). Peer group antecedents of severe love-shyness in males. *Journal of Personality, 55,* 467-489.

Gladney, K., & Barker, L. (1979). The effects of tactile history on attitudes toward and frequency of touching behavior. *Sign Language Studies, 24,* 231-2ɔ2.

Glenn, H.S., & Nelsen, J. (1989). *Raising self-reliant children in a self-indulgent world.* Rocklin, CA: Prima Publishing & Communications.

Goffman, E. (1963). *Behavior in public places.* New York: Free Press.

Goffman, E. (1967). *Interaction ritual.* Garden City, NY: Doubleday.

Goldberg, S., & Lewis, M. (1969). Play behavior in the year-old infant: Early sex differences. *Child Development, 40,* 21-31.

Goldstein, A.G., & Jeffords, J. (1981). Status and touching behavior. *Bulletin of the Psychonomic Society, 17,* 79-81.

Gondolf, E.W., & McFerron, J.R. (1989). Handling battering men: Police action in wife abuse cases. *Criminal Justice and Behavior, 16,* 429-439.

Greenbaum, P.E., & Rosenfeld, H.M. (1980). Varieties of touching in greetings: Sequential structure and sex-related differences. *Journal of Nonverbal Behavior, 5,* 13-25.

Gutek, B.A., & Nakamura, C.Y. (1983). Gender roles and sexuality in the world of work. In E.R. Allegeier & N.B. McCormick (Eds.), *Changing boundaries: Gender roles and sexual behavior* (pp. 182-201). Palo Alto, CA: Mayfield Publishing Company.

Hall, E.T. (1959). *The silent language*. Greenwich, CT: Fawcett Publications.

Hall, E.T. (1966). *The hidden dimension*. Garden City, NY: Anchor Books/Doubleday.

Hall, E.T. (1981). *Beyond culture*. Garden City, NJ: Anchor Books/Doubleday.

Hall, J.A., & Veccia, E.M. (1990). More "touching" observations: New insights on men, women, and interpersonal touch. *Journal of Personality and Social Psychology, 59*, 1155-1162.

Handshake turned tide of summit. (1985, November 23). *Denver Post*, pp. 1-A, 8-A.

Hanna, J.L. (1984). Black/white nonverbal differences, dance, and dissonance: Implications for desegregation. In A. Wolfgang (Ed.), *Nonverbal behavior: Perspectives, applications, intercultural insights* (pp. 373-409). Lewiston, NY: C. J. Hogrefe.

Hardison, J. (1980). *Let's touch: How and why to do it*. Englewood Cliffs, NJ: Prentice-Hall.

Harlow, H. F. (1958). The nature of love. *American Psychologist, 13l*, 673-685.

Heinig, R. B. (1975). *A descriptive study of teacher-pupil tactile communication in grades four through six*. Unpublished doctoral dissertation, University of Pittsburgh.

Henig, R. M. (1986). Please touch. *Pre-parent Advisor*. Johnson & Johnson Baby Products Company, pp. 14-19.

Henley, N. M. (1973). Status and sex: Some touching observations. *Bulletin of Psychonomic Sociology, 2*, 91-93.

Henley, N. M. (1977). *Body politics: Power, sex, and nonverbal communication*. Englewood Cliffs, NJ: Prentice-Hall.

Hickson, M., III, Grierson, R.D., & Linder, B.C. (1991). A communication perspective on sexual harassment: Affiliative nonverbal behaviors in asynchronous relationships. *Communication Quarterly, 39*, 111-118.

Hollender, M. H. (1970). The need or wish to be held. *Archives of General Psychiatry, 22*, 445-453.

Hollender, M. H. (1976). Wish to be held and wish to hold in men and women. *Archives of General Psychiatry, 33*, 49-51.

Howard, J. (1970). *Please touch*. New York: McGraw-Hill.

Hubble, M. A., Noble, F. C., & Robinson, S. E. (1981). The effect of counselor touch in an initial counseling session. *Journal of Counseling Psychology, 28*, 433-534.

Hunt, M. M. (1974). *Sexual behavior in the 1970's*. Chicago: Playboy Press.

Huss, A. J. (1977). Touch with care or a caring touch? *The American Journal of Occupational Therapy, 31,* 1-18.

Incest: The Hidden Crime. [16mm./color/16 minutes]. Available from The Media Guild, c/o Association Film, 7838 San Fernando Road, Sun Valley, California 91352, cost for 16 mm. is $275; videocassette, $229. (For commentary, see Deitrich, G. (1981). Audiovisual materials with critique. In P. B. Mrazek & C. H. Kempe (Eds.), *Sexually abused children and their families* (p. 258). Oxford: Pergamon Press.)

Jaschik, M. L., & Fretz, B. R. (1991). Women's perceptions and labeling of sexual harassment. *Sex Roles, 25,* 19-23.

Jensen, I.K.K., & Jensen, J.V. (1983). Cross cultural encounters: The newly arrived Asian student. *College Student Journal, 17,* 371-377.

Jocks. (1988, November). *People Magazine,* pp. 72, 74, 77.

Johnson, K.L., & Edwards, R. (1991). The effects of gender and type of romantic touch on perceptions of relational commitment. *Journal of Nonverbal Behavior, 15,* 43-55.

Jones, S.E. (1979). Integrating etic and emic approaches in the study of intercultural communication. In M.K. Asante, E. Newmark, & C.A. Blake (Eds.), *Handbook of intercultural communication* (pp. 57-74). Beverly Hills, CA: Sage Publications.

Jones, S.E. (1986). Sex differences in touch communication. *Western Journal of Speech Communication, 50,* 227-241.

Jones, S.E. (1990). Communicating with touch. In J.A. DeVito & M.L. Hecht (Eds.), *The nonverbal communication reader* (pp. 233- 244). Prospect Heights, IL: Waveland Press.

Jones, S.E. (1991). Problems of validity in questionnaire studies of nonverbal behavior: Jourard's tactile body-accessibility scale. *The Southern Communication Journal, 56,* 83-95.

Jones, S.E., & Yarbrough, A.E. (1984, February). *Taboos of touch: An analysis of prohibitive rules of tactile communication.* Paper presented at the annual meeting of the Western Speech Communication Association, Seattle.

Jones, S.E., & Yarbrough, A.E. (1985). A naturalistic study of the meanings of touch. *Communication Monographs, 52,* 19-56.

Jourard, S.M. (1966). An exploratory study of body-accessibility. *British Journal of Social & Clinical Psychology, 5,* 221- 231.

Jourard, S.M., & Friedman, R. (1970). Experimenter-subject distance and self disclosure. *Journal of Personality and Social Psychology, 15,* 278-282.

Jourard, S.M., & Secord, P.F. (1955). Body-cathexis and personality. *British Journal of Psychology, 46,* 130-138.

Kagan, J., & Lewis, M. (1965). Studies of attention in the human infant. *Merrill-Palmer Quarterly, 11,* 95-127.

Kaitz, M., Lapidot, P., Bronner, R., & Eidelman, A.I. (1992). Parturient women can recognize their infants by touch. *Developmental Psychology, 28,* 35-39.

Karger, R.H. (1979). Synchronization in mother-infant interactions. *Child Development, 50,* 882-885.

Kaufman, B.N. (1976). *Son-rise.* New York: Harper & Row.

Kaufman, J. & Zigler, E. (1987). Do abused children become abusive parents? *American Journal of Orthopsychiatry, 57,* 186-192.

Keen, S. (1991). *Fire in the belly.* New York: Bantam.

Kempe, C.H., Silverman, F.N., Steele, F.N., & Droggemueller, B.B. (1962). The battered child syndrome. *Journal of the American Medical Association, 18,* 17-24.

Kennedy, A.P., & Dean, S. (1986). *Touching for pleasure: A guide to sensual fulfillment.* Chatsworth, CA: Chatsworth Press.

Khartoum, S.U. (1977, Autumn). Who is the bully? *Home and School,* pp. 3-4.

Kilpatrick, D.G., & People Against Rape. (1983). Rape victims: Detection, assessment and treatment. *The Clinical Psychologist, 36,* 92-95.

Klaus, M.H., & Kennell, J.H. (1976). *Maternal-infant bonding.* St. Louis: C. V. Mosby.

Klaus, M.H., & Kennell, J.H. (1982). *Parent-infant bonding.* St. Louis: C. V. Mosby.

Kleinfeld, J. (1973). *Using nonverbal warmth to increase learning: A cross-cultural experiment.* Eric document, ED 081 568, RC 007 280.

Kleinke, C.L. (1977). Compliance to requests made by gazing and touching experimenters in field settings. *Journal of Experimental Social Psychology, 13,* 218-223.

Kleinke, C.L., & Meeker, F.B. (1974). Effects of gaze, touch, and use of name on evaluation of "engaged couples." *Journal of Research in Personality, 7,* 368-373.

Korner, A.F. (1990). The many faces of touch. In K.E. Barnard & T.B. Brazelton (Eds.), *Touch: The foundation of experience* (pp. 269-298). Madison, CT: International Universities Press, Inc.

Koss, M. P. (1983). The scope of rape: Implications for the clinical treatment of victims. *The Clinical Psychologist, 36,* 88-91.

Koss, M. P. (1992). Rape on campus: Facts and measures. *Planning for Higher Education, 20,* 21-28.

Koss, M. P., Gidycz, C. A., & Wisniewski, N. (1987). The scope of rape: Incidence and prevalence of sexual aggression and victimization in a national sample of higher education students. *Journal of Consulting and Clinical Psychology, 55,* 162-170.

Koss, M. P., Leonard, K. E., Beezley, D. A., & Oros, C. J. (1985). Nonstranger sexual aggression: A discriminate analysis of the psychological characteristics of undetected offenders. *Sex Roles, 12,* 981-992.

Krieger, D. (1973). *The relationship of touch with intent to help or heal to subjects' in-vivo hemoglobin values: A study in personalized interaction*. Paper presented at the American Nurses Association Ninth Nursing Research Conference, San Antonio, TX.

Krieger, D. (1975). Therapeutic touch: The imprimatur of nursing. *Journal of Nursing, 16,* 784-787.

Krieger, D. (1979). *The therapeutic touch: How to use your hands to help or to heal.* Englewood Cliffs, NJ: Prentice- Hall.

Krols-Riedler, B., & Krols-Riedler, K. (1979). *Redirecting children's misbehavior: A guide for cooperation between children and adults.* Austin, TX: R.D.I.C. Publications.

Kuykendall, G.B., Jr. (1981). *An experimental tactile affective communication training program for husbands.* Unpublished doctoral dissertation, University of Kansas.

LaFrance, M., & Mayo, C. (1976). Racial differences in gaze behavior during conversation. *Journal of Personality and Social Psychology, 33,* 547-552.

Lamb, M.E. (1977). Father-infant and mother-infant interaction in the first year of life. *Child Development, 48,* 167-181.

LaPlante, M.N., McCormick, N.B., & Brannigan, G.G. (1980). Living the sexual script: College students' views of influence in sexual encounters. *The Journal of Sex Research, 16,* 338- 355.

Larzelere, R.E. (1986). Moderate spanking: Model or deterrent of children's aggression in the family? *Journal of Family Violence, 1,* 27-36.

Larzelere, R.E., Klein, M., Schumm, W.R., & Alibrando, S.A., Jr. (1989). Relations of spanking and other parenting characteristics to self-esteem and perceived fairness of parental discipline. *Psychological Reports, 64,* 1140-1142.

Leap, T.L., & Gray, E.R. (1980). Corporate responsibility in cases of sexual harassment. *Business Horizons, 23,* 58-65.

Lenox, M. C. & Gannon, L. R. (1983). Psychological consequences of rape and variables influencing recovery: A review. *Women & Therapy, 2,* 37-49.

LeShan, E. (1981, November 3). Hugging. *Women's Day,* p. 42.

Lewis, M. (1972). State as an infant-environment interaction: An analysis of mother-infant interaction as a function of sex. *Merrill-Palmer Quarterly, 18,* 93-121.

Lewis, R. A. (1978). Emotional intimacy among men. *Journal of Social Issues, 34,* 108-121.

Lewis, T. (1982, November). How doctors have lost touch. *McCall's,* p. 210.

Liedloff, J. (1977). *The continuum concept: Allowing human nature to work successfully.* Reading, MA: Addison-Wesley.

Liedloff, J. (1989, Winter). The importance of the in-arms phase. *Mothering,* No. 50, 17-19.

Livingston, R. B. (1967a). Brain circuitry relating to complex behavior. In

G. C. Quarton, T. Melnechuck, & F. O. Schmitt (Eds.), *The neurosciences: A study program* (pp. 499-514). New York: Rockefeller University Press.

Livingston, R. B. (1967b). Reinforcement. In G. C. Quarton, T. Melnechuck, & F. O. Schmitt (Eds.), *The neurosciences: A study program* (pp. 586-576). New York: Rockefeller University Press.

Lomranz, J., & Shapiro, A. (1974). Communicative patterns of self-disclosure and touching behavior. *The Journal of Psychology, 88*, 223-227.

Longacre, B. (1987). *The significance of touch and its relation to status and sex.* Unpublished paper, University of Colorado.

Lorenz, K. (1966). *On aggression.* New York: Bantam Books.

Lynch, J. J. (1977). *The broken heart: The medical consequences of loneliness.* New York: Basic Books.

Major, B. (1981). Gender patterns in touching behavior. In C. Mayo & N. M. Henley (Eds.), *Gender and nonverbal behavior* (pp. 15-37). New York: Springer-Verlag.

Major, B., Schmidlin, A.M., & Williams, L. (1990). Gender patterns in social touch: The impact of setting and age. *Journal of Personality and Social Psychology, 58*, 634-643.

Malamuth, N. M. (1981). Rape fantasies as a function of exposure to violent sexual stimuli. *Archives of Sexual Behavior, 10*, 33-47.

Malamuth, N.M., & Check, J.V.P. (1981a). Penile tumescence and perceptual responses to rape as a function of victim's perceived reactions. *Journal of Applied Social Psychology, 10*, 528-547.

Malamuth, N.M., & Check, J.V.P. (1981b). The effects of mass media exposure on acceptance of violence against women: A field experiment. *Journal of Research in Personality, 15*, 436- 446.

Malamuth, N. M., Haber, S., & Feshback, S. (1980). Testing hypotheses regarding rape: Exposure to sexual violence, sex differences, and the "normality" of rapists. *Journal of Research in Personality, 14*, 121-137.

Mann, C. A., Hecht, M. L., & Valentine, K. B. (1988). Performance in a social context: Date rape versus date right. *Central States Speech Journal, 39*, 269-280.

Marx, M. S., Werner, P., & Cohen-Mansfield, J. (1989). Agitation and touch in the nursing home. *Psychological Reports, 64*, 1019-1026.

Masters, W. H., & Johnson, V. E. (1966). *Human sexual response.* Boston: Little, Brown & Company.

Masters, W. H., & Johnson, V. E. (1970). *The pleasure bond: A new look at sexuality and commitment.* Boston: Little, Brown and Co.

McAnarney, E. R. (1990). Adolescents and touch. In K.E. Barnard & T.B. Brazelton (Eds.), *Touch: The foundations of experience* (pp. 497-516). Madison, CT: International Universities Press.

McCorkle, R. (1974). Effects of touch on seriously ill patients. *Nursing*

Research, 23, 125-132.

McCormick, N.B., & Jesser, C.J. (1983). The courtship game: Power in the sexual encounter. In E.R. Allgeier & N.B. McCormick (Eds.), *Changing boundaries* (pp. 64-86). Palo Alto: Mayfield.

McCormick, N.B., & Jones, A.J. (1989). Gender differences in nonverbal flirtation. *Journal of Sex Education and Therapy, 15,* 271-282.

McKeachie, W.J., & Lin, Y. (1969). Achievement standards, debilitating anxiety, intelligence, and college women's achievement. *Psychological Record, 19,* 457-459.

McMurty, S.L. (1985). Secondary prevention of child maltreatment: A review. *Social Work, 30,* 42-48.

McNeely, R.L., & Robinson-Simpson, G. (1987). The truth about domestic violence: A falsely framed issue. *Social Work, 32,* 485-490.

McNeely, R.L., & Robinson-Simpson, G. (1988). The truth about domestic violence revisited: Reply to Saunders. *Social Work, 33,* 184-188.

Montagu, A. (1971). *Touching: The human significance of the skin.* New York: Columbia University Press.

Moore, M.M. (1985). Nonverbal courtship patterns in women: Context and consequences. *Ethology and Sociobiology, 6,* 237- 247.

Moore, M.M., & Butler, D.L. (1989). Predictive aspects of nonverbal courtship behavior in women. *Semiotica, 76,* 205- 215.

Morris, D. (1971). *Intimate behavior.* New York: Random House.

Morsbach, H. (1976). Aspects of nonverbal communication in Japan. In L. A. Samovar & R. E. Porter (Eds.), *Intercultural communication: A reader* (2nd ed., pp. 240-259). Belmont, CA: Wadsworth Press.

Mosby, K.D. (1978). *An analysis of actual and ideal touching behavior as reported on a modified version of the body accessibility questionnaire.* Unpublished doctoral dissertation, Virginia Commonwealth University.

Muehlenhard, C.L., & Linton, M.A. (1987). Date rape and sexual aggression in dating situations: Incidence and risk factors. *Journal of Counseling Psychology, 34,* 186-196.

Naisbitt, J. (1984). *Megatrends* (updated ed.). New York: Warner Books.

Nash, B. (1978, July). Keeping in touch. *American Baby,* pp. 57, 36-37.

National Center on Child Abuse and Neglect. (1978). *Child sexual abuse: Incest, assault, and sexual exploitation* (Special Report; U.S. DHEW Publications No. 79-30166). Washington, DC: Author.

National Center on Child Abuse and Neglect. (1983a). *National study of the incidence of child abuse and neglect.* Washington, DC: U.S. Department of Health and Human Services.

National Center on Child Abuse and Neglect. (1983b). *Understanding child sexual abuse.* Annual Report. Washington, DC: U.S. Department of Health and Human Services.

Nolen, W.A. (1986, March). The healing touch. *50 Plus,* pp. 37-39.

Noller, P. (1978). Sex differences in the socialization of affectionate expression. *Developmental Psychology, 14,* 317-319.

Oldenburg, D. (1985, February 11). The touchy topic of hugging. *The Washington Post,* p. B5.

Older, J. (1977). Four taboos that may limit the success of psychotherapy. *Psychiatry, 40,* 197-204.

Older, J. (1981). A restoring touch for abusing families. *Child Abuse and Neglect, 5,* 487-489.

Olweus, D. (1978). *Aggression in the schools: Bullies and whipping boys.* Washington, DC: Hemisphere.

Ouchi, W.G. (1981). *Theory Z: How American business can meet the Japanese challenge.* New York: Avon Books, Addison-Wesley.

Pagelow, M.D. (1992). Adult victims of domestic violence. *Journal of Interpersonal Violence, 7,* 87-120.

Patterson, M.L. (1976). An arousal model of interpersonal intimacy. *Psychological Review, 83,* 235-245.

Patterson, M.L., Powell, J.L., & Lenihan, M.G. (1986). Touch, compliance, and interpersonal affect. *Journal of Nonverbal Behavior, 10,* 41-50.

Payne, C. (1977). Cultural differences and their implications for teachers. *Integrated Education, 15,* 42-45.

Perdue, V.P., & Connor, J.M. (1978). Patterns of touching between preschool children and male and female teachers. *Child Development, 49,* 1258-1262.

Perper, T. (1981). *Sex signals; The biology of love.* Philadelphia: ISI Press.

Peters, T.J., & Waterman, R.H., Jr. (1982). *In search of excellence: Lessons from America's best-run companies.* New York: Harper & Row.

Pierce, R. (1986, December 26). Longmont police chaplains offer compassion in crises. *Boulder Daily Camera,* pp. 1B, 2B.

Pizzey, E. (1977). *Scream quietly or the neighbors will hear.* Hillside, NJ: Enslow Publishers.

Post, E. (1940). *Etiquette: The blue book of social usage.* New York: Funk & Wagnall.

Powell, G.N. (1983). Sexual harassment: Confronting the issue of definition. *Business Horizons, 26,* 24-28.

Prescott, J.W. (1975, April). Body pleasure and the origins of violence. *The Futurist,* pp. 64-74.

Quinsey, V.L., Chaplin, T.C., & Upfold, D. (1984). Sexual arousal to non-sexual violence and sadomasochistic themes among rapists and non-sex offenders. *Journal of Consulting and Clinical Psychology, 52,* 651-657.

Rabinowtiz, F. E. (1991). The male-to-male embrace: Breaking the touch taboo in a men's therapy group. *Journal of Counseling & Development, 69,* 574-576.

Radecki, C., & Jennings, J. (1980). Sex as a status variable in work settings:

Female and male reports of dominance behavior. *Journal of Applied Social Psychology, 10,* 71-85.

Reite, M.L. (1984). Touch, attachment, and health—Is there a relationship? In C.C. Brown (Ed.), *The many facets of touch* (pp. 58-65). Johnson & Johnson Baby Products Company.

Remland, M.S., & Jones, T.S. (1985). Sex differences, communication consistency, and judgments of sexual harassment in a performance appraisal interview. *The Southern Speech Communication Journal, 50,* 156-176.

Resnick, P.A. (1983). The rape reaction: Research findings and implications for intervention. *The Behavior Therapist, 6,* 129-132.

Rich, A. (1974). *Interracial communication.* New York: Harper & Row.

Rivera, G.F., Jr., & Regoli, R.M. (1987). Sexual victimization experiences of sorority women. *Sociology and Social Research, 72,* 30-42.

Rosenfeld, A., Bailey, R., Siegel, B., & Bailey, G. (1986). Determining incestuous contact between parent and child: Frequency of children touching parents' genitals in a nonclinical population. *Journal of the American Academy of Child Psychiatry, 25,* 481-484.

Rosenfeld, L.B., Kartus, S., & Ray, C. (1976). Body accessibility revisited. *Journal of Communication, 26,* 27-30.

Rozema, H.J. (1986). Touch needs of the elderly. *Nursing Homes, 35,* 42-43.

Ryans, D.G. (1960). *Characteristics of teachers.* Washington, DC: American Council on Education.

Saitz, R.L., & Cervenka, E.J. (1962). *Columbian and North American gestures: A contrastive inventory.* Bogota, Colombia: Centro Columbo Americano.

Sartre, J. (1956). *Being and nothingness.* London: Methuen.

Saslawsky, D.A., & Wurtele, S.K. (1986). Educating children about sexual abuse: Implications for pediatric intervention and possible prevention. *Journal of Pediatric Psychology, 11,* 235-245.

Saunders, D.G. (1988). Other "truths" about domestic violence: A reply to McNeeley and Robinson-Simpson. *Social Work, 33,* 179-183.

Schaffer, H.R., & Emerson, P.I. (1964). Patterns of response to physical contact in early human development. *Journal of Psychological Psychiatry, 5,* 1-13.

Scheflen, A.E. (1965). Quasi-courtship behavior in psychotherapy. *Psychiatry, 28,* 245-257.

Schiffrin, D. (1981). Handwork as ceremony: The case of the handshake. In A. Kendon (Ed.), *Nonverbal communication, interaction, and gesture* (pp. 237-250). The Hague, Netherlands: Mouton.

Schnarch, D.M. (1991). *Constructing the sexual crucible: An integration of sexual and marital therapy.* New York: Norton.

Schutz, W.C. (1967). *Joy.* New York: Grove Press.

Shuter, R. (1979). The Dap in the military: Hand-to-hand communication.

Journal of Communication, 29, 136-142.

Shatter the Silence. [16 mm film]. Available from S-L Film Productions, P.O. Box 41108, Los Angeles, CA 90041.

Silverman, A.F., Pressman, M.E., & Bartel, H.W. (1973). Self- esteem and tactile communication. *Journal of Humanistic Psychology, 13,* 73-77.

Smith, P.K. (1991). The silent nightmare: Bullying and victimisation in school peer groups. *The Psychologist: Bulletin of the British Psychological Society, 4,* 243-248.

Sorensen, G., & Beatty, M.J. (1988). The interactive effects of touch and touch avoidance on interpersonal evaluations. *Communication Research Reports, 5,* 84-90.

Spitz, R. A. (1946). Anaclitic depression. *Psychoanalytic Study of the Child, 2,* 313-342.

Stacey, W., & Shupe, A. (1983). *The family secret: Domestic violence in America.* Boston: Beacon Press.

Steele, B., & Alexander, H. (1981). Long term effects of sexual abuse in childhood. In P.B. Mrazek & C.H. Kempe (Eds), *Sexually abused children and their families* (pp. 223-234). New York: Pergamon Press.

Steinmetz, S. K. (1977). Wifebeating, husbandbeating—A comparison of the use of physical violence between spouses to resolve marital fights. In M. Roy (Ed.), *Battered women: A psychosociological study of domestic violence* (pp. 63-71). New York: Van Nostrand Reinhold.

Steinmetz, S.K., & Straus, M.A. (Eds.). (1974). *Violence in the family.* New York: Dodd, Mead.

Stembridge, D.A. (1973). *An exploratory study of tactual behavior.* Unpublished doctoral dissertation, University of Houston.

Stier, D.S., & Hall, J.A. (1984). Gender differences in touch: An empirical and theoretical review. *Journal of Personality and Social Psychology, 47,* 440-459.

Stolte, K.M. (1976). *An exploratory study of patients' perceptions of the touch they received during labor.* Unpublished doctoral dissertation, University of Kansas.

Straus, M. & Gelles, R. (1986). Societal change and change in family violence from 1975 to 1985 as revealed in two national surveys. *Journal of Marriage and the Family, 48,* 465-479.

Stroufe, L.A., & Waters, E. (1977). Attachment as an organizational construct. *Child Development, 48,* 1184-1199.

Summerhayes, D.L., & Suchner, R.W. (1978). Power implications of touch in male-female relationships. *Sex Roles, 4,* 103-110.

Swan, H.L., Press, A.N., & Briggs, S.L. (1985). Child sexual abuse prevention: Does it work? *Child Welfare, LXIV,* 395-405.

Touch [16 mm film and videotape] (1984). Available from Illusion Theater Company & Media Ventures, Inc., Deerfield, IL, MTI Teleprograms.

Touchin', Feelin'. (1982, August). *Ebony Magazine*, pp. 39-42.

A touching story. (1983, September). *Psychology Today*. p. 71.

Thevenin, T. (1976). *The family bed: An age old concept in child rearing.* Available from Tine Thevenin, P.O. Box 16004, Minneapolis, MN 55416.

Toufexis, A. (1987, March 30). Furry and feathery therapists. *Time*, p. 74.

Tweeton, L. (1986, March). The politics of touch: Hands-on/hands-off rules. *Glamour*, pp. 310, 347.

Vecsey, G. (1992, July 6). Andre and Goran grow up in public on center court. *New York Times*, pp. B5, B9.

Vizard, E., Bertovin, A., & Tranter, M. (1987). Interviewing sexually abused children. *Adoption and Fostering, 11,* 20-25.

Wachtel, P.L. (1989). *The poverty of affluence: A psychological portrait of the American way of life* (2nd ed.). Philadelphia: New Society Publishers.

Walker, D.N. (1970). *Openness to touching: A study of strangers in non-verbal interaction.* Unpublished doctoral dissertation, University of Connecticut.

Watkins, H.D., & Bradbard, M.R. (1982). Child maltreatment: An overview with suggestions for intervention and research. *Family Relations, 31,* 323-333.

Watson, O.M. (1968). *Proxemic behavior: A cross-cultural study.* Unpublished doctoral dissertation, University of Colorado.

Watson, W.H. (1976). The meanings of touch: Geriatric nursing. *Journal of Communication, 25,* 104-112.

Webb, J.R. (1989). Recent developments in the law of sexual harassment. *The Colorado Lawyer, 18,* 263-266.

Weiss, S.J. (1975). *Familial tactile correlates of body image in children.* Unpublished doctoral dissertation, University of California, San Francisco.

Weiss, S.J. (1978). The language of touch: A resource to body image. *Issues in Mental Health Nursing, 1,* 17-29.

Welch, M. S. (1979). Touching. *Glamour, 77,* No. 7, 70-72.

Whitcher, S., & Fisher, J.D. (1979). Multidimensional reaction to therapeutic touch in a hospital setting. *Journal of Personality and Social Psychology, 37,* 87-96.

White, B.L., & Castle, P.W. (1964). Visual exploratory behavior following postnatal handling of human infants. *Perceptual and Motor Skills, 18,* 497-502.

Wilbarger, P. (1984). Planning an adequate "sensory diet"—Application of sensory processing theory during the first year of life. *Zero to Three, 5,* 7-12.

Willis, F.N., & Hamm, H.K. (1980). The use of interpersonal touch in securing compliance. *Journal of Nonverbal Behavior, 5,* 49-55.

Willis, F.N., & Hofmann, G.E. (1975). Development of tactile patterns in relation to age, sex, and race. *Developmental Psychology, 11,* 866.

Willis, F.N., & Reeves, D.L. (1976). Touch interaction in junior high school students in relation to sex and race. *Developmental Psychology, 12,* 91-92.

Willis, F.N., Reeves, D.L., & Buchanan, D.R. (1976). Interpersonal touch in high school relative to sex and race. *Perceptual and Motor Skills, 43,* 843-847.

Willis, F.N., & Rinck, C.M. (1983). A personal log method for investigating interpersonal touch. *The Journal of Psychology, 113,* 119-122.

Willis, F.N., Rinck, C.M., & Dean, L.M. (1978). Interpersonal touch among adults in cafeteria lines. *Perceptual and Motor Skills, 47,* 1147-1152.

Willison, B.G., & Masson, R.L. (1986). The role of touch in therapy: An adjunct to communication. *Journal of Counseling and Development, 64,* 497-500.

Winnicott, D.W. (1984). *Playing and reality.* London: Tavistock Publications.

Winnicott, D.W. (1987). *The child, the family, and the outside world.* Reading, MA: Addison-Wesley.

Woodrum, R.L. (1981). Sexual Harassment: New concern about an old problem. *Advanced Management Journal, 46,* 20-26.

World Health Organization. (1991). *The AIDS epidemic and its demographic consequences.* New York & Geneva: United Nations and World Health Organization.

Yates, A. (1982). Children eroticized by incest. *American Journal of Psychiatry, 139,* 482-485.

Zales, J. (1988, September 4). Juvenile detective: It's better to ask questions. *Boulder Sunday Camera,* pp. D1, D3.

Zellman, G.L., & Goodchilds, J.D. (1983). Becoming sexual in adolescence. In E. R. Allgeier & N. B. McCormick (Eds.), *Changing boundaries* (pp. 49-63). Palo Alto: Mayfield.

Zilbergeld, B. (1978). *Male sexuality.* Toronto: Bantam Books.

Zillman, D., & Bryant, J. (1982). Pornography, sexual callousness, and the trivialization of rape. *Journal of Communication, 32,* 10-21.

Author Index

Subject Index